GOLD

advanced

with 2015 exam specifications

coursebook

Sally Burgess
Amanda Thomas

CONTENTS

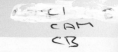

196 879   *EFL ZONE*

Exam information

The Cambridge Certificate in Advanced English (CAE) is an examination at level C1 of the Common European Framework of Reference for Languages (CEFR). There are four papers, each testing a different skill in English. There are five grades: *A*, *B* and *C* are pass grades; *D* and *E* are fail grades.

Reading and Use of English (I hour 30 minutes)

The Reading and Use of English test is divided into eight parts. Parts 1–4 test use of English and parts 5–8 test reading comprehension. You shouldn't spend too long on the use of English section as this represents 36 marks and the reading section carries 42 marks. There is one mark given for each correct answer in Parts 1–3 and in Part 8, up to two marks for each correct answer in Part 4 and two marks for each correct answer in Parts 5–7.

Part 1 Multiple-choice cloze	Focus	Vocabulary/Lexico-grammatical
	Task	You read a text with eight gaps and choose the best word for each gap from a choice of four options (A, B, C or D).
Part 2 Open cloze	Focus	Grammar/Lexico-grammatical
	Task	You read a text with eight gaps and think of an appropriate word to fit in each gap.
Part 3 Word formation	Focus	Vocabulary
	Task	You read a text with eight gaps. You are given the stems of the missing words in capitals at the end of the lines with the gaps. You have to change the form of each word to fit the context.
Part4 Key word transformations	Focus	Grammar and vocabulary
	Task	There are six sentences. You are given a sentence and a 'key word'. You have to complete a second gapped sentence using the key word. The second sentence has a different grammatical structure but must have a similar meaning to the original.
Part 5 Multiple choice	Focus	Detail, opinion, attitude, main idea, text organisation, purpose
	Task	There are six four-option multiple-choice questions. You read a long text and choose the correct option (A, B, C or D) based on the information in the text.
Part 6 Cross-text multiple matching	Focus	Attitude, opinion, comparing and contrasting points of view across texts
	Task	You read four short texts on a related topic. You have to decide which text expresses a similar/different opinion to the text mentioned in each question.
Part 7 Gapped text	Focus	Text structure, cohesion and coherence
	Task	You read a long text from which six paragraphs have been removed and put before the text. You have to decide where in the text each paragraph (A–G) should go. There is one paragraph you do not need to use.
Part 8 Multiple matching	Focus	Specific information, detail, attitude, opinion
	Task	You read ten questions or statements about four to six short texts, or a text which has been divided into sections. You have to decide which section or text contains the information relating to each question or statement.

Writing (I hour 30 minutes)

The Writing test is divided into two parts. You have to complete one task from each part. Each part carries equal marks, so you should not spend longer on one than another.

Part 1	Focus	Content, communicative achievement , organisation, language
	Task	Part 1 is compulsory and there is no choice of questions. You have to write an essay of 220–260 words on a given topic using the notes provided.
Part 2	Focus	Content, communicative achievement, organisation, language
	Task	Part 2 has three tasks to choose from: an email/letter, a report/proposal or a review. You have to write 220–260 words using the prompts provided.

Listening (approximately 40 minutes)

There are four parts in the Listening test, with a total of thirty questions. You write your answers on the question paper and then you have five minutes at the end of the exam to transfer them to an answer sheet. In each part, you will hear the text(s) twice. The texts may be monologues or exchanges between interacting speakers. There will be a variety of accents.

Part 1 Multiple choice	Focus	Attitude, agreement, opinion, gist, detail
	Task	You hear three short conversations. You have to answer six multiple-choice questions – two questions for each conversation – by choosing the correct option (A, B or C).
Part 2 Sentence completion	Focus	Specific information, opinion
	Task	You hear a monologue. You complete eight sentences using words from the listening text.
Part 3 Multiple choice	Focus	Attitude, opinion
	Task	You hear a conversation. You answer six multiple-choice questions by choosing the correct option (A, B, C or D).
Part 4 Multiple matching	Focus	Gist, attitude, main point
	Task	You hear five short monologues on a related topic. You have to match six statements (A–F) in Task 1 and Task 2 to each speaker. There is one statement in each task you do not need to use.

Speaking (approximately 15 minutes)

You take the Speaking test with one or two other candidates. There are two examiners. One is the 'interlocutor' who speaks to you and the other is the 'assessor' who just listens.

Part 1 Interview	Focus	General interaction and social language skills
	Task	The interlocutor asks each of you questions about yourself.
Part 2 Individual long turn	Focus	Comparing, contrasting, speculating
	Task	The interlocutor gives you three pictures and asks you to answer the questions on the task card by discussing two of the pictures. You have to speak for one minute. Then you answer a question briefly about the other candidate's pictures.
Part 3 Collaborative task	Focus	Expressing and justifying opinions, negotiating a decision, suggesting, agreeing/disagreeing, etc.
	Task	You are given a task to discuss with another candidate, based on the prompts on the task card. Then you discuss a second question on the same topic for a minute and make a decision together.
Part 4 Follow-up discussion	Focus	Expressing and justifying opinions, agreeing/disagreeing, etc.
	Task	The interlocutor asks you questions related to the topic in Part 3. You discuss them with the other candidate.

For more information see the **Writing reference** (page 185), the **Exam focus** (page 197) and the **General marking guidelines** (page 206).

Where we live

1

Speaking

1 **Discuss the questions.**

1 What do you like most about the area where you grew up?

2 What are the advantages and disadvantages of living abroad for a short time?

3 If you could live in another country, where would you choose? Why?

Interview (Part 1)

talking about yourself

▶ **EXAM** FOCUS: p.204

2 ▶01 **Listen to two candidates talking to an examiner. Which of the questions in Activity 1 does the examiner ask?**

3 **Which of the candidates, Karl or Elena, provides responses of an appropriate length?**

EXAM TIP

Don't just give single-word answers to the examiner's questions. Try to use introductory phrases like *Well, ...*, *Actually, ...*, *Now I come to think of it, ...*.

4 **Look at responses to the questions Karl and Elena were asked. They are too short. Make the responses longer and more interesting.**

1 Spain.

2 I'm a student.

3 The weather.

4 My friends.

5 **Work in pairs. Turn to page 152 and do the activities.**

6 **How would you evaluate your own performance? Use the General marking guidelines on page 207 to help you. Can you suggest any ways in which the other students you worked with could improve?**

Multiple-choice cloze (Part 1)

▶ **EXAM** FOCUS: p.197

7 Look at the title of an article about children's dream homes. What other features do you think the children included in their dream homes?

8:35   ☀ ...ıl 🔋 49% ▭

A fairytale castle
with a pool and a water slide, please.

A recent (**0**) ....._B study_..... of children aged between four and eleven years old has (**1**) .... that their notion of the ideal home presents major (**2**) .... to conventional wisdom. More than a quarter of the youngest group (**3**) .... a desire to live in a house made either entirely of sweets or of toys rather than more traditional (**4**) .... One in four boys and nearly half the girls would choose to live in a fairytale castle. Other specifications for the (**5**) .... dream house, unveiled by the research, include the fact that a third of children would like an indoor swimming pool and that more than a quarter of eleven-year-olds, given the choice, would (**6**) .... for water slides over stairs. Fifteen percent of boys also want a football pitch on the (**7**) .... Somewhat surprisingly, only one child in ten wants to live on a giant bouncy castle but almost a third say they would still choose their family home (**8**) .... all other options.

EXAM TIP

When you meet a new word, always record and learn it with its collocates (e.g. _dream + home_).

8 Read the article. Were your predictions correct? Which findings do you think are most and least surprising?

	A	B	C	D
0	research	study	enquiry	inquest
1	exposed	revealed	outlined	uncovered
2	questions	issues	challenges	tests
3	claimed	expressed	uttered	announced
4	substances	components	materials	elements
5	supreme	ultimate	great	fundamental
6	choose	select	decide	opt
7	zone	area	premises	grounds
8	over	rather	instead	between

9 Read the first sentence of the article again and look at the example (0). The correct answer is B. Look at the reasons why the other alternatives are not possible and match them with the incorrect alternatives (A, C and D).

1 possible in the context but followed by the preposition _into_, not _of_

2 an uncountable noun, so cannot be used with the indefinite article

3 often collocates with the phrase '_into the death of_'

10 Read the article again. For questions 1–8, decide which answer (A, B, C or D) best fits each gap. Use the criteria you used in Activity 9 to help you.

11 How closely does the place you live now correspond to your ideal home?

Speaking

1 What are the advantages and disadvantages of living in a small town or village as opposed to a big city?

2 ▶ 02 Listen to a woman talking about moving to a remote village. Does she mention any of the things you talked about?

Perfect and continuous forms

▶ **GRAMMAR** REFERENCE p.181

3 Choose the correct verb form in each sentence. In which sentences are both forms possible? Then listen again. Which form does the speaker use in each case?

1 For years *I'd told/I'd been telling* all my friends that I wanted to get away from the hustle and bustle of London.

2 *I had, in fact, always been/I had, in fact, always been being* a real city person.

3 By the beginning of next month I *will have lived/will have been living* here for exactly a year.

4 *I've looked back, retraced my steps and come/I've been looking back, retracing my steps and coming* to understand just how great a change it has actually been.

5 *I've spent/I've been spending* hours exploring the glorious countryside by bicycle and on foot and *have discovered/been discovering* a taste for silence and solitude I didn't know I had.

6 By the time the first year comes to an end, almost all my London friends *will have been/will have been being* here to stay.

4 Work in pairs and discuss the difference in meaning between the pairs of sentences.

1 A We've been renovating all the bathrooms. It's taking ages!

   B We've renovated all the bathrooms. It cost a fortune!

2 A I'll have walked more than 200 kilometres by the time I get to Santiago.

   B I will have been walking twenty kilometres a day for nearly a month by then.

3 A When it struck midnight, Tim had written the essay.

   B When it struck midnight, Tim had been writing the essay for more than twenty-four hours.

5 Divide the stative verbs in the box into five groups: emotions, knowledge, possession, communication, senses.

agree   believe   belong   care   deny   hear
know   like   love   own   possess   promise
smell   taste   understand

LANGUAGE TIP

Some verbs have both stative and dynamic meanings. They can only be used in continuous forms with a dynamic meaning.

I'm **feeling** unwell. (*feel* = experience a feeling or emotion)

Compare this with the stative meaning.

I **feel** we should give him a chance. (*feel* = have an opinion)

6 Complete the sentences with the correct form of the verb in brackets.

1 I .... (*think*) that living in a small village would be a bit boring.

2 I .... (*think*) of spending a week in Ireland in early June.

3 I .... (*see*) a friend of mine for dinner tomorrow night.

4 I .... (*see*) your point but I think cities can be very lonely places.

5 I .... (*taste*) the sauce to see if it needs more salt.

6 This sauce .... (*taste*) a bit strange.

7 Imagine you have won the lottery and have been living in your dream home for a year now. Tell the class what changes there have been in your life over the last year.

Reading

1 Work in pairs and discuss the questions. Which city noises do you find most irritating? Are there any big city noises you actually like?

2 Read the magazine article. How many of the noises you discussed are mentioned?

Sounds of the city

Cities are noisy places. The <u>whine</u> of scooters, the <u>wail</u> of ambulance sirens, the <u>rumble</u> of an underground train deep in the belly of the earth – all these are part of the city soundscape and contribute to our perception of cities as vibrant places to be.

Perhaps the most characteristic of city noises is the constant <u>buzz</u> of traffic. But that could be about to change. Newer electric and hybrid vehicles are actually completely silent and, as attractive as that may sound, it represents a safety problem

– they creep up on unsuspecting pedestrians and on one another, and that means accidents.

One way to prevent this happening is to give them a voice. And it seems we will be able to choose just what kind of voice that should be. Since city dwellers often miss the sound of the wind in the trees, the laughter of children or birdsong, these are all sounds that acoustic engineers are considering. Imagine a fleet of electric taxis chirping happily like sparrows, <u>sighing</u> like a summer breeze in long grass or <u>giggling</u> like toddlers. Sounds pretty good to me!

Figurative language

3 Complete the sentences with the correct form of the underlined words in the article in Activity 2.

1 The teacher said it wasn't funny and she should stop ....
2 The child kept .... that she had a smaller cake than her sister.
3 He .... with sadness over all the old friends he had lost.
4 When the little girl's ice cream dropped into the gutter, she started to .... in distress.
5 I hadn't eaten anything all day and my stomach kept ....
6 The fly .... against the window made it difficult to concentrate.

LANGUAGE TIP

We also use verbs that describe sounds animals make for human speech.
*'Get out of there!' he **roared**.*

4 Decide which of the words in the box are associated with humans (H), animals (A) or both (B).

bark clap cough groan purr roar
shudder sigh stutter tremble

5 Complete the sentences with the literal meaning of the words in Activity 4. Change the form of the words if necessary.

1 Her hands .... as she handed him the letter.
2 Our cat only .... if you massage his ears.
3 He .... when he said words beginning with *t*.
4 Everyone .... when Dad told that terrible old joke again.
5 Only a few people in the audience .... at the end of the recital.
6 I had no idea a lion's .... could be so loud.
7 My neighbour's dog only ever .... at the postman.
8 I'm allergic to pollen – it makes me ....
9 Even the idea of eating liver makes me ....
10 He was safe! He breathed a .... of relief.

6 Choose the correct alternative in each of the sentences.

1 There was a sudden *clap/bark* of thunder and all the lights went out.
2 I couldn't hear a word he was saying over the *roar/purr* of the plane taking off.
3 The earth *groaned/coughed* and then began to *shudder/clap* violently.
4 The sergeant *barked/purred* a command and the troops sprang into action.
5 We were in the centre of the lake when the motor *coughed/groaned* and then *stuttered/sighed* a couple of times before cutting out altogether.
6 The leaves *trembled/shuddered* in the autumn breeze.

7 Work in pairs. Turn to page 161 and do the activity.

Speaking

1 Discuss the questions.

1 How well do you know your way round your town or city?

2 What do you do to help you navigate in a town or city you don't know well?

3 Have you ever got completely lost?

Multiple choice (Part 5)

▶ **EXAM** FOCUS p.199

2 Read the title and the first paragraph of the newspaper article and guess what it will be about. Then read the rest of the article to see if you were right.

EXAM TIP

Don't answer questions using your beliefs or experience. Always look for evidence in the text.

3 Read the article again. For questions 1–6, choose the answer (A, B, C or D) which you think fits best according to the text.

1 The writer suggests that it is difficult to find your way round London

   A if you are from Manhattan.

   B if you are used to cities that are laid out differently.

   C if you don't have a good map or street directory.

   D if you are not familiar with the one-way system.

2 The writer's view of people who pass The Knowledge is that they

   A are very fortunate.

   B are very studious.

   C deserve the right to drive a taxi.

   D should learn even more about their city.

3 What aspect of The Knowledge does the writer find most surprising?

   A Candidates cannot use anything but their visual memory during the test.

   B Candidates have to describe a number of different routes.

   C The length of time it takes candidates to prepare for the test.

   D The quaint name that has been given to the oral examination.

4 Why does the writer give three examples of groups of people whose brains have not changed?

   A to show how surprised she is that a person's brain can change

   B to highlight the results found in similar studies

   C to show that cabbies have a very special ability

   D to show that cabbies have superior intelligence

5 The writer suggests studies done on the Paris and Chicago cab driver are surprising because the researchers

   A copied what Eleanor Maguire had done.

   B chose to study two such different cities.

   C didn't check to see if the cabbies had passed a test.

   D didn't find what they had expected.

6 What is the writer's attitude to stories about taxi drivers around the world?

   A She is appalled that such poor drivers could exist.

   B She is uncertain how far the stories can be relied upon.

   C She thinks these criticisms of drivers are without justification.

   D She thinks potential passengers should take them as a warning.

4 Work in pairs and discuss the questions.

1 How well do taxi drivers know their way around the city or town where you live?

2 Have you ever encountered a taxi driver who actually got lost?

Vocabulary

working out meaning from context

5 Match the underlined words in the article with meanings 1–8.

1 a feeling of great respect

2 more than a little but not very much

3 a terrible or painful experience that continues for a period of time

4 confused

5 confusing

6 an impressive achievement

7 be successful

8 extremely worried and frightened

6 Write one sentence for each of the words in Activity 5. Compare your sentences with a partner.

More than just STREETWISE

London is not a good place for fans of right angles. People who like the methodical grid system of Manhattan are <u>baffled</u> by the <u>bewildering</u> network of knotted streets. It's entirely possible to take two right turns and end up in the same place. Even with a map, some people manage to get lost. And yet there are thousands of Londoners who have committed the city's entire layout to memory – cab drivers. Piloting London's distinctive black cabs is no mean <u>feat</u>. To earn the privilege, drivers have to pass an intense intellectual <u>ordeal</u>, known charmingly as The Knowledge. Ever since 1865, they've had to memorise the location of every street within six miles of Charing Cross. Today this implies familiarity with all 25,000 of the capital's arteries, veins and capillaries. They also need to know the locations of 20,000 landmarks – museums, police stations, theatres, clubs and more – and 320 routes that connect everything up.

It can take two to four years to learn everything. To prove their skills, prospective drivers do oral examinations called 'appearances' at the licencing office, where they have to recite the best route between any two points. Incredible as it may seem, they have to do this without any reference to maps aside from the mental map they have in their head. They have to narrate the details of their journey, complete with passed landmarks, road names, junctions, turns and maybe even traffic lights. Only after successfully doing this several times over can they earn a cab driver's licence.

Given how hard it is, it shouldn't be surprising that The Knowledge changes the brains of those who acquire it. Eleanor Maguire from University College studied those changes and showed that the brains of London taxi drivers do indeed undergo a change which makes them very different from those of mere mortals like us. Doctors, for example, with their extensive knowledge of human anatomy and physiology, don't exhibit the change Maguire found. You don't see it in memory champions who have trained themselves to remember seemingly impossible lists and who go on to win quizzes and competitions. You don't see it in London's bus drivers who have similar driving skills but work along fixed routes. Among all of these groups, only the London cabbies, with their heightened spatial memories, have the change Maguire was looking for.

One reason this might be is that London, as a cluster of what were once villages, simply demands higher order skills. Cab drivers in Paris and Chicago face similar challenges when it comes to traffic and navigation and also have to get through a test that demands an in-depth knowledge of the city concerned. Strange as it may seem, though, when researchers looked at drivers in these cities in a bid to replicate Maguire's London study, they found none of the same changes in brain structure. Even among cabbies, the Londoners who pass The Knowledge are unique. But it's not just their skills and the ways in which these have changed their brains that set the London cabbies apart.

Their passengers generally trust them and can even be <u>somewhat</u> in <u>awe</u> of their navigation skills. Their colleagues elsewhere in the world do not <u>fare</u> so well when it comes to passenger attitudes. Rudeness, impatience and poor driving skills are among their many sins if the many customer complaints on the internet are to be believed.

Cabbies in other countries also find themselves accused of possessing too limited a knowledge – or no knowledge whatsoever – of the cities where they ply their trade. Stories abound of drivers making <u>frantic</u> appeals on their radios for guidance or relying too heavily on GPS. Believe these tales if you choose to but should you find yourself going round in circles in the labyrinth that is London for many a foreign visitor, don't hesitate to hail a cab. The cabbie may not ooze charm but will certainly know the quickest and most direct way of getting you where you want to go.

Speaking

1 **Draw a floor plan of the flat or house where you live. Then work in pairs.**

1 Explain your floor plan to your partner.

2 Explain how you use the space available to you.

3 Say whether you need more space than you currently have. Why/Why not?

Multiple matching (Part 4)

▶ **EXAM** FOCUS p.203

2 **Look at the exam tasks. Tick (✓) the things that you like least about the place where you live. Then tick the advantages it has over other places you have lived in. Compare your answers with a partner.**

Task 1

For questions 1–5, choose from the list (A–H) what each speaker likes least about the place where they live.

A feeling unsafe

B the absence of a garden

C the smell of other people's cooking

D the uninspiring view

E the lack of space for preparing meals

F being obliged to get rid of favourite possessions

G the sense of claustrophobia

H the noise from other people living in the building

Speaker 1 **1** [ ]

Speaker 2 **2** [ ]

Speaker 3 **3** [ ]

Speaker 4 **4** [ ]

Speaker 5 **5** [ ]

Task 2

For questions 6–10, choose from the list (A–H) what each speaker sees as the main advantage of the place where they live.

A plenty of storage

B entertainment facilities nearby

C the freedom to furnish the home without limitations

D spending less time on domestic chores

E having a close friend next door

F social contact with others living nearby

G being able to make good use of the entire space

H knowing you can always ask a neighbour to help

Speaker 1 **6** [ ]

Speaker 2 **7** [ ]

Speaker 3 **8** [ ]

Speaker 4 **9** [ ]

Speaker 5 **10** [ ]

3 ▶ 03 **Do the exam tasks in Activity 2. You will hear five short extracts in which people are talking about the places where they live. While you listen, you must complete both tasks.**

4 **What kind of person do you imagine each of the speakers is?**

Vocabulary

expressions with *space* and *room*

5 **Decide if it is possible to complete the sentences with *space*, *room* or both words.**

1 That chest of drawers takes up too much .... We ought to get rid of it.

2 I don't think I've got enough .... in my suitcase for these boots.

3 Could you make .... for people to get past, please?

4 It was such a popular event that there was standing .... only by the time we got there.

5 There isn't really enough .... here to do aerobics.

6 I like cities with plenty of open ....

7 That was delicious but if I have any more, I won't have any .... for dessert.

8 The only explanation she gave for breaking up with him was that she needed more ....

6 **Work in pairs. Turn to page 161 and do the activity.**

Speaking

1 **Work in pairs and discuss the questions.**

1   What attracts visitors to your town or city?
2   Does it have any landmarks?
3   Are they well-known to people who have never been there?

2 **Read the extract from an article about branding cities. Does your town or city have any of the characteristics mentioned in the extract?**

City brands

Does your city have a famous landmark, a rich cultural tradition or is it home to a major industry, a world-renowned hotel or even a distinctive way of getting around like London's black cabs or Amsterdam's barges? Perhaps it's a mecca for theatre-goers, musicians or party animals. Or maybe it's just a nice place to be. Top brand cities seem to have it all. <u>Not only can they boast lists as long as your arm of magnificent buildings, museums and galleries, they are also home to famous restaurants, glorious parks, iconic sports stadiums and all sorts of places to see and be seen.</u>

For cities and towns less favourably endowed the first step in establishing a brand is to identify assets and find a way of communicating these, usually by means of a logo and slogan. But getting the logo and slogan right is no mean feat. <u>Under no circumstances should visitors be led to believe a city can promise something it cannot deliver.</u>

No one is impressed if a place calls itself the 'sunshine capital' but is in fact cold, wet and windy, or claims to 'never sleep' when by-laws oblige all bars and restaurants to close by midnight. ◼

Emphasis with inversion

▶ **GRAMMAR** REFERENCE p.175

3 **Look at the underlined sentences in the article. What do you notice about the verb forms? Rewrite the sentences so that they are less emphatic.**

LANGUAGE TIP

You are more likely to find structures with subject-verb inversion in more formal or literary written contexts than you are in speech.
***Hardly had he** arrived **when** Jo rushed in.*

4 **Rewrite the sentences using inversion. Start with the word given.**

1   This city has seldom been in greater need of energy-efficient public transport than it is today.
    Seldom ....
2   We had just ordered our meal when the waiter rudely asked us if we would mind paying the bill.
    Scarcely ....
3   I have rarely seen such a brilliant display of artistry and expertise.
    Rarely ....
4   You have failed to hand in your essay on time and you have also copied several paragraphs directly from the internet.
    Not only ....
5   You should not let people who don't respect the dress code into the club under any circumstances.
    Under no circumstances ....
6   She posted the letter and then began to regret what she had said.
    No sooner ....
7   My client has never revealed the contents of this document to the media.
    At no time ....
8   I had only just finished the assignment when my boss asked me to do something else for her.
    Hardly ....

5 **Work in pairs. In which situations would you expect to hear or read the sentences in Activity 4?**

6 **Write sentences beginning with the words in italics in Activity 4. Compare your sentences with a partner.**

Listening

1 ▶ **04 Work in pairs and listen to a podcast about a way to improve contact between neighbours. How would people react to a scheme like this where you live?**

Essay (Part 1)

using the task input to help you plan

▶ **WRITING** REFERENCE p.186

2 **Work in pairs and imagine that you have been asked to write an essay on promoting greater contact between neighbours.**

1 Brainstorm ideas, including the ones in the podcast and your own ideas.

2 Think of points for and against your ideas.

3 Choose three ideas and include a supportive and a critical comment for each one.

3 **Look at two plans for a similar essay and then turn to the checklist on page 185. Which plan do you think would produce the better essay?**

A

PLAN

Introduction: Say why the move to the suburbs has been such a big problem.

Solution 1: Invest in urban renewal schemes in the centre of the city.

+ It will attract businesses that had moved out to the shopping malls.

– Money should be spent on schools and hospitals, not prettying up the centre of town.

Solution 2: Offer incentives for moving back to the centre.

+ If there are financial and lifestyle benefits, people will come back.

– Unless life in the suburbs is made harder for them, no one will bother to make the move.

Conclusion: Say which solution I believe will be most effective.

PLAN

Introduction: Reasons we have to get people to move back to the city centre.

Paragraph 1: The government should invest more money.

Paragraph 2: People should realise that infrastructure for suburban living is too costly.

Conclusion: If all these things are done, people will move back.

4 **Write a plan for the essay in Activity 2. Show it to other students. Can they suggest improvements to your plan?**

5 **Look at the task input and use it to help you write another plan.**

1 Think of what specific ideas might be connected to each of the three headings (legislation, education and special taxes).

2 Use the opinions expressed to give you a clue.

3 For each opinion expressed, think of a supportive or critical comment to balance the opinion.

> Your class has attended a panel discussion on what methods governments should use to discourage the use of private cars in the centre of the city. You have made the notes below.
>
> Methods governments could use to discourage the use of private cars in the city centre
> • investment
> • education
> • taxes
>
> Some opinions expressed in the discussion
> 'Make businesses pay parking levies for their employees and they'll move out of the city centre.'
> 'Improve the public transport system, then people won't need their cars.'
> 'If people understood how much better pedestrianised city centres are, they wouldn't want to bring their cars in.'
>
> Write an essay for your tutor, discussing **two** of the methods in your notes. You should **explain which method you think is more important** for governments to consider, **giving reasons** to support your opinion.
>
> You may, if you wish, make use of the opinions expressed in the discussion but you should use your own words as far as possible. Write your essay in **220–260** words in an appropriate style.

EXAM TIP

Try to avoid copying phrases from the input in Part 1. Use your own words.

6 **Write a draft of the essay in Activity 5. Show it to two other students and see if they can offer any advice on ways of improving your work.**

1 Complete the second sentence so that it has a similar meaning to the first sentence, using the word given. Do not change the word given. You must use between three and six words, including the word given.

1 I only managed to buy my own place after years of sharing with other people. **DID**

Only after years of sharing with other people .... my own place.

2 The neighbours are really noisy and they are not very friendly either. **ONLY**

Not .... really noisy, they are also not very friendly.

3 You shouldn't ever put your full address on a luggage label. **TIME**

At .... put your full address on a luggage label.

4 It will be six years since I moved here next Saturday. **FOR**

By next Saturday I will .... six years.

5 You shouldn't tell anyone about this under any circumstances. **NO**

Under .... tell anyone about this.

6 I closed the door and immediately realised I had left my keys inside the house. **SOONER**

No .... the door than I realised my keys were inside the house.

2 Complete the sentences with the present simple or continuous form of the verb in brackets.

1 I .... (*smell*) smoke. Is there something burning?

2 The soup is almost ready. Dad .... (*taste*) it to see if it's hot enough.

3 I .... (*see*) Josh on Friday evening but perhaps you and I could get together on Saturday.

4 Look at the cat! He .... (*smell*) the roses!

5 We .... (*think*) of renting a small plot of land to grow our own vegetables.

6 This tea .... (*taste*) of mangoes.

3 Read the article and decide which answer (A, B, C or D) best fits each gap.

	A	B	C	D
1	draw	create	make	come
2	reverse	back	rear	underside
3	led	brought	produced	saw
4	history	past	ages	time
5	holding	storing	bearing	exhibiting
6	seems	looks	resembles	reminds
7	appealed	charmed	attracted	enticed
8	get	bring	set	put

Weekly Herald

The logo that *everyone* loves

It was 1977 and the American graphic designer Milton Glaser had been asked to **(1)** .... up with a logo for New York State. He pulled a red crayon from his pocket and began to sketch on the **(2)** .... of an envelope: first an I , then the simple outline of a heart, followed by two letters, N and Y. Glaser's doodle **(3)** .... to the development of one of the most successful advertising campaigns of all **(4)** .... It was so successful, in fact, that the torn envelope **(5)** .... his original idea is now in a permanent collection in a museum. The upbeat message of Glaser's design, which **(6)** .... the kind of joyful graffiti that a young lover might carve into a tree, **(7)** .... to New Yorkers as well as tourists. Glaser himself acknowledges that it seems strange that a logo could have such an impact but it seems his design really did **(8)** .... about a change in people's attitudes at a time when the city had been going through difficult times.

The art of conversation

2

Long turn (Part 2)

giving opinions

▶ **EXAM** FOCUS p.204

1 **Work in pairs. What would be the worst thing about being stuck somewhere without a phone or internet access?**

2 ▶ 05 **Listen to four students giving their opinion about the statements. Do they agree (A) or disagree (D) with them?**

1 I feel anxious if I don't receive a text every few minutes.
2 It's important to respond to text messages immediately.
3 There are some things you should never communicate by text.
4 I find it easier to express myself in texts than face-to-face.

3 **Listen again and write down the expressions for giving opinions you hear. Compare your answers with a partner. Then turn to page 161 and check your answers.**

4 **Work in pairs and discuss which of the statements in Activity 2 you agree/disagree with. Use some of the expressions for giving opinions.**

5 **Look at the exam task and underline the three things the examiner asks the candidate to do.**

> Look at the pictures. They show people using their phones. I'd like you to compare two of the pictures and say why people might be communicating in this way and how effective this form of communication might be.

EXAM TIP

Don't focus on factual descriptions of the pictures. Make sure you answer the examiner's questions.

6 ▶ 06 **Listen to a candidate doing the task and answer the questions.**

Does the candidate

1 use a variety of expressions to give her opinion?

2 answer by comparing the pictures?

3 follow the examiner's instructions fully?

4 focus too much on factual descriptions of the pictures?

7 **Work in pairs. Turn to page 152 and do Task 1. Then turn to page 158 and do Task 2.**

Word formation (Part 3)

▶ **EXAM** FOCUS p.198

8 **What part of speech is missing in the sentences? Complete the questions with the correct form of the word in capitals and then discuss them with a partner.**

COMMUNICATE

1 Apart from being excellent .... , what other characteristics should politicians have?

2 Do you think shy people are necessarily .... ?

3 Do you agree that texting is a great form of .... ?

EXAM TIP

Read the whole of each sentence through carefully to make sure it makes sense with the form of the word you have chosen – don't just read line by line.

9 **For questions 1–8, read the text on the right. Use the word given in capitals at the end of some of the lines to form a word that fits in the gap in the same line.**

Texting champion

Fifteen-year-old American Kate Moore
(0) _narrowly_ defeated the other   NARROW
(1) .... to win the National   FINAL
Texting Championships after the
(2) .... of a series of bizarre tasks   COMPLETE
that included texting blindfolded and texting
while negotiating her way along a moving
obstacle course. In the final showdown Miss
Moore out-texted fourteen-year-old Morgan
Dynda after both girls had to text three
lengthy phrases without making any mistakes
on the **(3)** .... abbreviations,   REQUIRE
capitalisation or punctuation. The teenager
was **(4)** .... of the idea that she   DISMISS
focuses too much on virtual communications,
saying that she is a very **(5)** ....   SOCIAL
person and prefers to spend time
face-to-face with her friends rather than
talk to them via a screen. Still, she manages
to find time to send an **(6)** ....   ASTONISH
400 texts a day. Kate claims this is for studying,
which she says is more **(7)** ....   EFFECT
done by text because she can store the
messages and use them for **(8)** ....   REFER
purposes later.

Q W E R T Y U K P

10 **Check your answers by answering the questions about the missing word.**

1 If it is a noun, should it be singular or plural?

2 If it is an adjective, does it need a negative prefix?

3 If it is a verb, is it singular or plural, past or present?

11 **How well do you think you would do in a texting competition?**

Speaking

1 Answer the questionnaire and compare your answers with a partner. Then turn to page 162 to find out if you're an introvert.

Are you an introvert?

1 When you're at a party, do you sometimes long to escape to somewhere quiet?

2 Do you prefer online relationships to face-to-face ones?

3 Do you prefer listening to talking?

4 Do you dread going to parties where you don't know many people?

5 Do you feel uncomfortable speaking in front of groups of people?

6 Do you immediately put in earphones and start listening to music when you're in a public place in case anyone tries to talk to you?

Multiple choice (Part 1)

▶ **EXAM** FOCUS p.202

EXAM TIP

Read the question and options for each extract carefully before you listen. Don't expect to hear exactly the same words used in the options and the listening text – often, these will be paraphrases.

2 ▶ 07 **You will hear three different extracts. For questions 1–6, choose the answer (A, B or C) which fits best according to what you hear. There are two questions for each extract.**

Extract 1

You hear two friends discussing a book about introverts.

1 How did the book make the man feel?
  A unsure what makes him an introvert
  B positive about his personality
  C relieved that his behaviour is normal

2 The speakers agree that the book
  A contained too much detailed research.
  B was written in an academic style.
  C presented an unbalanced argument.

Extract 2

You hear two friends discussing online friendships.

3 What do the speakers agree about the way people use social networking sites?
  A Too much personal information is provided.
  B People aren't honest enough.
  C There is very little privacy.

4 What is the man's attitude to his online friendships?
  A He is irritated by online friends' lack of sensitivity.
  B He is concerned that he still maintains online relationships.
  C He is worried about losing online friendships.

Extract 3

You hear part of a discussion with two people who decided to stay offline for a month.

5 How did the woman feel after the first week offline?
  A content to be able to focus on other things
  B disturbed by the isolation
  C used to the lack of contact

6 Why would the man recommend the experience?
  A It changed his attitude to online friendships.
  B It made him realise that he was addicted to the internet.
  C It helped him to have self-discipline.

3 Listen to Extract One again and look at question 1. Are there any paraphrases in the recording for *unsure, positive* or *relieved*? Which words in the recording are summarised by the word *normal*?

4 Match phrases A–E from the recording with the correct answers to questions 2–6 in Activity 2.

A … everyone presents a certain cultivated image of themselves online, which isn't always accurate.

B … so not worth devoting so many pages to them.

C … it was weird – almost like being invisible.

D I've had to learn to be strict with myself.

E What gets me is people who insist on going on and on about their perfect life.

Articles

definite, indefinite and zero articles

▶ **GRAMMAR** REFERENCE p.171

1 **Read the first paragraph of an article and choose the best summary.**

1 The best conversations take place in groups.

2 It requires effort to have a good conversation.

How to avoid competitive conversation

Good conversation with **(1)** *the/(-)* friends not only brings **(2)** *the/(-)* happiness and enjoyment, it fulfils a special need **(3)** *the/(-)* human beings have wherever they live in **(4)** *the/(-)* world. What I'll always remember about **(5)** *a/the* night I met my wife is the wonderful conversation we had and how we connected instantly. But it can't be a solely individual endeavour – it has to be **(6)** *a/the* group effort. Each individual has to sacrifice a little for the benefit of **(7)** *a/the* group as a whole and, ultimately, to increase the pleasure each individual receives. It's like singing in **(8)** *a/the* choir where the harmony and rhythm of a song depends on each individual to keep it going. One person who keeps singing **(9)** *a/the* sour note can ruin it for everyone. That's why it's so important that **(10)** *the/(-)* conversations are co-operative instead of competitive.

2 **Read the paragraph again and choose the correct alternatives, *a, the* or zero article (-) .**

LANGUAGE TIP

Some adjectives can be used as nouns, to refer to all the peole who have a particular characteristic. They are used with the definite article and are followed by a plural verb: ***the rich, the poor, the Swiss, the Chinese***, etc.

3 **Find one or more examples of each rule in the paragraph in Activity 1.**

1 We use the definite article (*the*) before all nouns

A when something has already been mentioned.

B when only one of something exists.

C when referring to something/someone specific.

2 We use the indefinite article (*a/an*) before singular countable nouns when referring to something or someone general or non-specific.

3 We use zero article (-)

A before plural and uncountable nouns when talking about something in general.

B when referring to something abstract or general.

4 **Complete the next part of the article with *a/an*, *the* or zero article (-).**

But too many people are competitive in conversation. They turn **(1)** .... attention of **(2)** .... others to themselves using quite subtle tactics. The response a person gives to what someone says can take two forms: the 'shift response' and the 'support response'. The support response keeps **(3)** .... focus on **(4)** .... speaker and on **(5)** .... topic he has introduced. The shift response allows the other person to 'shift' the focus to themselves. For example:

Support-response

| James: | I'm thinking of buying a new car. |
| Rob: | Yeah? Are you looking at any particular model? |

Shift-response

James:	I'm thinking about buying a new car.
Rob:	Yeah? I'm thinking about buying **(6)** .... new car too.
James:	Really?
Rob:	Yep, I test drove **(7)** .... Mustang yesterday and it was awesome.

We're all guilty of using the shift response from time to time. We sometimes can't wait for **(8)** .... other person to finish speaking so we can jump in. We pretend to be listening intently but we are really focusing on what we are going to say once we find **(9)** .... opening, hoping we will be asked **(10)** .... question.

Speaking

5 **Work in pairs and discuss the questions.**

1 Suggest some ways of dealing with people who use the shift response in conversation.

2 What kind of conversations do you enjoy the most?

Gapped text (Part 7)

▶ **EXAM** FOCUS p.200

1 **Work in pairs and discuss the statement** *Technology is having a negative effect on the quality of conversation.* **Give reasons for your answers.**

2 **Look at the title and read the article quickly, ignoring the missing paragraphs. How useful did the writer find the class on how to have a conversation?**

3 **Read the first two paragraphs of the article again carefully and look at the words in bold. What information do you think the missing paragraph will contain?**

1 some information about the teacher
2 some background information
3 some information about the other participants

4 **Read paragraphs A–G and look at the words in bold. Which one contains the right kind of information for the first gap?**

EXAM TIP

Read each paragraph, followed by each possible missing paragraph A–G, to see which one fits best in the gap. Think about meaning, reference words, grammar, etc. Check that the option you choose also fits with the paragraph that follows.

5 **Six paragraphs have been removed from the article. Choose from the paragraphs A–G the one which fits each gap (1–6). Use the words in bold to help you. There is one extra paragraph which you do not need to use.**

6 **Work out the meanings of the underlined words in paragraphs A–G from the context. Compare your answers with a partner.**

Speaking

7 **Work in pairs and discuss the questions.**

1 Do you think you would enjoy a class like this?
2 How would you answer the 'opener' questions in the sixth paragraph? What do you think of them?
3 What do you think of the six ways to have a better conversation in paragraph B? How similar are they to Cicero's rules in paragraph G?

A
These aims seemed disappointingly unambitious to me. I had hopes of becoming a <u>witty</u> and intellectual conversationalist. But none of my new friends shared this desire. It was the simple act of talking and listening and learning that my classmates sought.

B
Some useful advice **followed** on the 'six ways to have a better conversation'. These, according to the school, are:
(1) Be curious about others.
(2) Take off your mask.
(3) <u>Empathise</u> with others.
(4) Get behind the job title.
(5) Use adventurous openings.
(6) Have courage.

C
Haynes **went on** to explain that the Enlightenment was the age of conversation, when ladies and gentlemen in English dining rooms and French salons could become famous through <u>eloquence</u> alone.

D
Then we were told to break off into pairs and answer the question: Which three words describe your conversations with (a) friends, (b) family and (c) colleagues? My partner said *banter*, *sarcastic* and *sporadic* were the words he would use to describe all three types of conversation. Before I had a chance to share my three words, it was time for a **break**.

E
There was general <u>unease</u> about how email, instant messaging and texting had crept into the space formerly occupied by conversation. 'What was the point,' asked a **young man**, 'of asking how someone's day was when you've been emailing them from the office?'

F
After **this** enjoyable burst of role play Haynes put up a slide that said: *What conversation are you not having?* and then it was all over. Once the class structure had been dismantled, conversation seemed to <u>dwindle</u>.

G
The basics of **this** were first described by the ancient Roman writer Cicero, which can be summarised as follows: speak clearly, do not interrupt, be courteous, never criticise people behind their backs, stick to subjects of general interest, do not talk about yourself and, above all, never lose your temper.

How to have a conversation

Is conversation a dying art, struck down by text, email and messaging? And do we really need to be taught how to talk to each other? I enrolled in a class at the School of Life, an academy of 'self-help', to find out. The topic was *How to have a **conversation***.

1

I had arrived about twenty minutes early but the rest of the class was already there. **One woman** kindly invited me into her circle. She was finding it hard to have meaningful relationships. Technology was partly to blame: 'Sometimes you feel the smart phone is like a third person,' she said. **Another new acquaintance** agreed and described how immediate access to Google had blocked off avenues of conversation with her boyfriend. 'Before we would argue about this or that but now we just look it up on Wikipedia,' she said.

2

My classmates also spoke of more personal reasons for their attendance. An IT worker in her fifties had found that her conversations with her husband 'wandered' and wanted to learn ways to become a better partner. A man in his late twenties said he wanted to have fewer rows with his girlfriend.

3

Our discussion was interrupted by the arrival of our teacher, Cathy Haynes. Haynes flicked to the first slide in her PowerPoint presentation and we sat attentively as she talked about how the nature of conversation had changed over the past 300 years.

4

After an enjoyable ten minutes spent chatting to my classmates and discovering more about their motives for joining the class, we were told to retake our seats. Haynes continued her PowerPoint presentation, asking us to reflect on a René Magritte painting, a comedy sketch and a book about marriage. All of these examples were meant to encourage us to stop seeing conversations as a means to an end and to avoid stereotyping the other person.

5

Then it was time to put some of these ideas into practice. In groups, we had to try out ideas for unusual openings. A man in his early twenties, who joked that he had thought of this before, suggested as a chat-up line: 'Tell me something I want to know.' A more challenging opener came from another group member: 'If you were coming to the end of your life, what would you have wanted to have achieved?'

6

Despite our excellent teacher, I suspect the class was too abstract to be useful. Nearly three-quarters of the session were spent listening to theories of conversation. Genuine discussions were stopped in mid-flow, with the class asked to return its attention to the presentation. There was a touching eagerness to share ideas but frustration grew as our time ran out. What I suspect my classmates had hoped to find was that most basic thing: human connection. But I doubt the class had made this any more achievable.

Speaking

1 Work in pairs and discuss which of the statements you agree with.

1 You should never raise your voice during a discussion.
2 People who shout the loudest tend to get heard.
3 How you say something is as important as what you say.
4 Gossip is never harmless.

Communication collocations

2 Match the verbs *make*, *have*, *give* and *hold* with the nouns in the box to make collocations. Some nouns can be used with more than one verb.

a chat	(a) conversation	a debate
a discussion	a gossip	a presentation
a speech	a statement	a talk

3 Choose the correct alternative in each sentence.

1 He delivered an interesting *debate/speech* at the conference.
2 We had to make polite *talk/conversation* with the director of the company.
3 Most people hate making small *talk/gossip* at parties.
4 The *discussion/speech* was led by the CEO.
5 His controversial ideas have stimulated a lot of *debate/talk*.
6 It was difficult to keep the *chat/conversation* going because the connection kept breaking up.
7 How to improve the system is a matter for *debate/conversation*.
8 They were deep in *gossip/conversation* and didn't notice the restaurant had closed.

Adjectives: ways of speaking

4 ▶ 08 Listen and answer the questions. Then compare your ideas with a partner.

1 Do you agree with the information given?
2 What are your impressions of each speaker?
3 Which person is the easiest to understand?
4 Which accent do you prefer?
5 Which person do you think sounds the most trustworthy and authoritative?

5 Work in pairs. Look at the adjectives in the box and answer the questions.

deep	flat	harsh	high-pitched
husky	lively	mellow	monotonous
nasal	soft	soothing	squeaky
warm	wobbly		

1 Which of the adjectives are positive and which are negative?
2 Which of the adjectives have a similar meaning?
3 Which are attractive in a man or a woman?
4 Which do you think match the voices of the speakers in Activity 4?

6 Work in pairs and discuss the questions.

1 How important do you think someone's voice is?
2 Do you think it's possible to fall in love with someone from the sound of their voice?
3 Which celebrities do you agree have attractive voices?

7 Complete the sentences with words from Activity 5.

1 She speaks in such a mellow and .... manner that it makes me feel drowsy.
2 Most people find a .... tone the most annoying because it sounds like the person is complaining all the time.
3 Actresses with deep, ... voices are considered to be very attractive.
4 You can often tell if someone is nervous by their .... voice.
5 I don't think he means to but he always sounds bored because he speaks in such a .... monotone.
6 Some languages sound soft and soothing, while others can sound .... – as if people are arguing all the time.

8 Which of the adjectives in Activity 5 can be used to describe

1 a colour?
2 a landscape?
3 a person?
4 an actor's performance?

Defining and non-defining relative clauses

▶ GRAMMAR REFERENCE p.178

1 Can you think of a politician or a person in the public eye who has an unpleasant voice? Compare your ideas with a partner.

2 Read the article and choose the correct alternatives.

Like it or not, people are judged not by what they know or do and not by the content of their speech, but simply by the way they sound. A University of California study found that when it comes to first impressions, it was visual impact **(1)** *which/who* was the most important consideration, followed by vocal impact. On the telephone, **(2)** *whose/where* appearance is irrelevant, the sound of your voice accounts for a full 83% of how others judge you.

Clearly, your voice is a key communication tool. It speaks volumes about who you are and determines how the world hears and sees you. Many professionals **(3)** *which/who* have the talent and motivation to move ahead, find common speaking problems block their success. Take the advertising executive, for example, **(4)** *whom/whose* soft, breathy voice makes her otherwise inspired presentation seem weak and lifeless, or the talented IT consultant with a strong regional accent **(5)** *which/whose* people find difficult to understand.

How you use your voice can make others view you as decisive, confident, trustworthy and likeable – or insecure, weak, unpleasant, boring, crude or even dishonest. In fact, **(6)** *when/why* trying to get their message across, people pay little, if any, attention to the effect their voices have on other people. Instead, it's the content **(7)** *which/who* they are much more concerned about.

So you may never know the reason **(8)** *when/why* you failed to land that dream job because people are unlikely to explain that every time you speak up, you may be letting yourself down.

3 Match sentences 1–2 with meanings A–B.

1 She listened to the second message in her phone inbox, which was in English.

2 She listened to the second message in her phone inbox which was in English.

A Message number 1 was in another language. She listened to message number 2, which was in English.

B She had received lots of phone messages; the fifth and eleventh messages were in English. She listened to message number 11.

4 Which sentence makes it clear that Paul has more than one brother?

1 Paul's brother whose girlfriend is from Argentina speaks good Spanish.

2 Paul's brother, whose girlfriend is from Argentina, speaks good Spanish.

5 Complete the sentences with the words in the box. In some sentences more than one option is possible.

that	when	where	which (x2)	who
whom	whose			

1 The man .... was speaking loudly on his mobile phone was a journalist.

2 I will never forget .... I was when I heard the news.

3 The person with .... I have most in common is my sister.

4 The man .... phone I found sent me £100!

5 The time .... I spent without internet access was terribly hard.

6 My mobile phone, ... I lost on the train last week, had all my contacts on it.

7 It was early in the morning .... I received a call from my aunt in Australia.

8 I had to take an urgent call, ... was why I walked out of the restaurant.

LANGUAGE TIP

That and *which* can often be used interchangeably in defining relative clauses. *That* rather than *which* is usually used after quantifiers such as *everything, something, all.*

*Something **that** most people find annoying ...*

6 Which sentences in Activity 5 contain defining (D) and which contain non-defining (ND) relative clauses? In which sentence is it possible to omit the relative pronoun?

Proposal (Part 2)
organising your ideas

▶ **WRITING** REFERENCE p.192

1 **Which statement refers to a proposal and which refers to a report?**

1 This looks to the future, giving specific plans for a particular situation.

2 This makes recommendations that are based on a current situation.

2 **Look at the exam task and the tips for writing a proposal. Then read a candidate's answer. The candidate has not followed one of the tips. Which one?**

You see this announcement on a notice board where you work.

IMPROVE OUR COMMUNICATION

The Staff Training and Development Department has decided to spend part of its budget on a programme to improve workplace communication.

The Staff Training and Development Officer invites you to send a proposal outlining any problems with current workplace communication and explaining how it can be improved. A decision will then be made about how the money should be spent.

Write your **proposal** in **220–260** words in an appropriate style.

Tips for writing a proposal

1 Begin by stating the purpose of your proposal.

2 Use an impersonal, semi-formal style.

3 Use clear layout with headings.

4 Express opinions and make recommendations in the last section of your proposal.

5 Include a final sentence summarising your opinion.

6 Use bullet points but not too many.

<u>Improving workplace communication: a proposal</u>

<u>Introduction</u>

In this proposal I will assess the current situation with regard to workplace communication, go on to identify the needs which should be addressed by a staff training programme and conclude by describing this training programme.

<u>Current situation</u>

Feedback from other members of staff suggests that the volume of email messages we receive has become a problem. Many people find that they spend several hours a day responding to these messages. A second but related complaint concerned poorly written emails. Many of us receive messages that cause offence, are difficult to understand or are simply far too long.

<u>Key needs to be addressed</u>

Both the number of email messages we receive and the quality of the messages have a negative impact on our productivity. People feel disinclined to respond to rude, confusing or excessively lengthy messages. This issue must be addressed.

<u>Recommendations</u>

I would suggest the following to the Staff Training and Development Department:

• All members of staff should be encouraged to communicate by phone whenever possible.

• Any information that needs to be communicated to the entire staff should be presented in a face-to-face meeting rather than through email.

• A training course on writing effective email messages should be offered to all staff members.

3 **Look at the exam task and prepare to write your answer.**

Students at your college have to give a spoken presentation as part of their final assessment and need some help. The school director has invited you to send a proposal outlining any problems students have with presentations and suggesting how these problems could be overcome.

---

1 Begin by brainstorming ideas. Write them down in any order and don't worry about language at this stage.

2 Group your ideas under headings for each section of your proposal.

3 Write a first draft, paying attention to the level of formality of the language.

1 Complete the sentences with the correct form of the word in capitals.

1 That's the total cost of the holiday, ... all meals.　**INCLUDE**

2 I'm afraid there's been an .... error.　**ADMINISTRATE**

3 Texting can be a problem if it becomes an ....　**ADDICT**

4 .... is a problem which affects many people – they can't decide what to do, so they end up not doing anything.　**DECIDE**

5 Their music is easy to recognise because the sound is quite ....　**DISTINCTION**

6 The technology museum is very .... – there are lots of gadgets you can try out.　**INTERACT**

7 Alex is not a very good .... – he often struggles to express himself.　**COMMUNICATE**

8 I found her immediate .... of all my suggestions really offensive.　**DISMISS**

2 Complete the article with *a/an*, *the* or zero article (-).

▶ Search

TEXTING your way to the TOP

Texting Your Way to the Top is quite **(1)** .... good book but it's a bit heavy-going in some ways. A lot of the information is from **(2)** .... recent research that's been done and that makes it rather hard to read at times. We all write **(3)** .... texts but I'm not sure they're so important as to justify **(4)** .... whole book on **(5)** .... subject. It might have been better to make it into a chapter in a book on **(6)** .... good business communication or something like that. Another thing is, who's going to read it? If you are **(7)** .... kind of person who ends a relationship by sending a text, you certainly wouldn't be reading **(8)** .... book like this. I suppose you might find it useful if you had just moved to **(9)** .... English-speaking country and didn't really know what **(10)** .... conventions were about this sort of thing there but it's quite expensive at €40.

3 Complete the article with the correct relative pronoun.

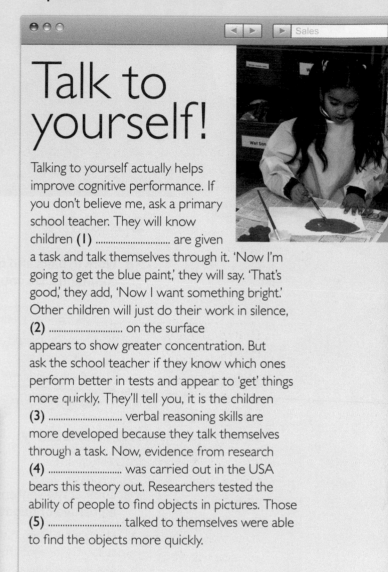

● ● ●　◀ ▶　▶ Sales

Talk to yourself!

Talking to yourself actually helps improve cognitive performance. If you don't believe me, ask a primary school teacher. They will know children **(1)** .... are given a task and talk themselves through it. 'Now I'm going to get the blue paint,' they will say. 'That's good,' they add, 'Now I want something bright.' Other children will just do their work in silence, **(2)** .... on the surface appears to show greater concentration. But ask the school teacher if they know which ones perform better in tests and appear to 'get' things more quickly. They'll tell you, it is the children **(3)** .... verbal reasoning skills are more developed because they talk themselves through a task. Now, evidence from research **(4)** .... was carried out in the USA bears this theory out. Researchers tested the ability of people to find objects in pictures. Those **(5)** .... talked to themselves were able to find the objects more quickly.

4 Choose the correct alternative in each sentence.

1 She had such a *monotonous/high-pitched* voice that students often used to fall asleep in her lectures.

2 I didn't catch what Tom said. He's got a really *soft/harsh* voice.

3 Some women prefer their voice when they have a cold because it sounds *husky/wobbly*.

4 When she gets overexcited, her voice is quite *mellow/squeaky*.

5 The colours in this painting are so *warm/flat* and soothing.

6 I couldn't concentrate on what the actor was saying because his *nasal/lively* tone was so off-putting.

Ages and stages

Speaking

1 **Work in pairs and discuss why someone might have made each of the comments. Do you agree with them?**

> Youth is wasted on the young.
> (*George Bernard Shaw*)

> You can live to be a hundred only if you give up all the things that make you want to live to be a hundred.
> (*attributed to Woody Allen*)

Vocabulary
stages of life

2 **Look at the sentences and decide whether the underlined words have a positive or negative connotation.**

1 Much as I like him, his rather <u>juvenile</u> sense of humour makes me question his suitability for a job that requires a degree of tact.

2 She has a <u>childlike</u> innocence about her that is rather surprising.

3 Like many actors of his generation, he has retained a <u>youthful</u> demeanour, despite his advancing years.

4 We are both <u>mature</u> enough to discuss this without getting emotional.

5 I think most practical jokes are humourless and <u>puerile</u>.

6 Some of these <u>geriatric</u> rock stars should really think twice before going on tour. It's just embarrassing!

3 **Which of the words in the box could you use to replace the underlined words in Activity 2? Which one has a different connotation?**

adolescent   adult   aging   boyish   childish   infantile

4 **Work in pairs. Think of other near synonyms for the words in Activities 2 and 3. Do they have positive, negative or neutral connotations?**

Speaking

5 What books or TV series were you interested in when you were younger? Are you still interested in them now?

6 Read the article about the teenage obsession with vampires. Do you agree with the writer?

Sunday *Review*

Lust for blood

why are teenagers obsessed with vampires?

The recent teenage obsession with vampires is nothing new. They have long been a source of <u>fascination</u>. One of the first vampire stories in English was written 200 years ago by John Polidori, barely out of his teens himself at the time. Vampires appealed to teenagers as much then as they do now but why should this be so? One theory connects their <u>attraction</u> to the myth of eternal <u>youth</u>. The character Polidori described in his *The Vampyre* has a lot in common with those we find in today's hugely popular books, films and TV series. He embodied all that we might consider cool, had a great <u>sense</u> of <u>style</u> and was also deeply mysterious. He always knew what to say and when to say it and had, of course, complete <u>freedom</u> to roam the city by night. These are all qualities that many teenagers lack. They often feel tongue-tied and awkward, frequently have little <u>self-confidence</u> and their movements, especially after dark, are subject to their parents' <u>will</u>. So the vampire is, in a sense, everything the teenager would like to be but is not. At the same time, the vampire's sense of <u>alienation</u> from 'normal' or adult <u>society</u> is something many teenagers share. There is <u>risk</u> and <u>danger</u> involved in being a vampire or a vampire's girlfriend or boyfriend, though that too has its <u>appeal</u> – they've often waited more than 100 years to be with the one they love.

Countable and uncountable nouns

▶ **GRAMMAR** REFERENCE p.174

7 Read the article again and put the underlined nouns into the correct category.

1 nouns that are always uncountable
2 nouns that are uncountable when they are used in this way

8 Decide if one or both alternatives are possible in each sentence. If both are possible, is there a difference in meaning?

1 I suggest we stop for *coffee/a coffee* in half an hour if that's alright with you.
2 He published his *research/researches* into the origin of the vampire myth.
3 The classrooms all have excellent audio-visual *equipment/equipments*.
4 I must remember to buy *some paper/a paper*.
5 Spain is famous for its *wine/wines*.
6 It was actually just *luck/a luck* that decided the match.

LANGUAGE TIP

Some uncountable nouns that refer to emotions and mental activity can be used with the indefinite article (*a/an*) when their meaning is limited in some way.
*She has **a pathological fear** of spiders.*

---

9 Insert an indefinite article in the sentences if necessary.

1 Some teenagers have profound mistrust of adults.
2 The first candidate demonstrated good knowledge of grammar and vocabulary.
3 My grandfather still enjoys very good health.
4 He speaks perfect Italian.
5 My friends really wanted their daughter to have good education.
6 She has good understanding of all the issues.
7 I hope you have good weather in Venice.
8 She did excellent work in the final year of her Art degree.

10 Work in pairs. Turn to page 165 and do the activity.

Speaking

1 Answer the questions. Then compare your answers with other students.

1 Do you keep a diary or have a blog? Why/Why not?
2 What are the main differences between blogs and diaries?
3 What are the potential risks of keeping a diary?

Cross-text multiple matching (Part 6)

▶ **EXAM** FOCUS p.200

2 Read extracts A–D from articles about keeping a diary. Which extracts provide answers to question 3 in Activity 1?

3 Read questions 1–4 and underline the main ideas. Which questions ask you to find extracts with the same opinions? Which questions ask you to find extracts with different opinions?

Which columnist

shares a similar opinion to columnist A about the risks of keeping a diary? **1** [ ]

regards diaries as superior to social networking sites for a different reason to columnist D? **2** [ ]

has a similar view to columnist B about teenagers' contradictory behaviour? **3** [ ]

has a different attitude to columnist D about the reaction older people have to reading teenage diaries? **4** [ ]

4 Read the extracts again. Which texts mention issues 1–4 in the table?

Issue	Texts
1 diary keeping is risky	*A* , ...
2 diaries are superior to social networking sites	.... , *D*
3 teenagers' behaviour can seem contradictory	.... , ...
4 reactions of older people when rereading their teenage diaries	.... , ...

5 For questions 1–4, choose from the extracts (A–D). The extracts may be chosen more than once.

6 Complete the sentences with the correct form of the underlined words and phrases in the extracts.

1 Tony is always .... of his younger brother. I don't know why he puts up with it.
2 Every time I hear my voice on a recording, it makes me .... – I can't stand it!
3 Ironing has to be one of the most .... tasks there is.
4 The weather was absolutely .... when we were on holiday. It didn't stop raining once.
5 There is a very real .... that our team won't qualify for the World Cup.
6 In the interview she did her utmost to .... her role in the disastrous election result.

7 Which of the opinions about diary writing do you agree with? Work in pairs and discuss your answers.

EXAM TIP

Don't worry if you do not choose all of the extracts as answers to the questions. You often need to use one extact more than once, which means you don't need to use another extract at all.

ADVICE RESPOND NEWS

What diaries can and can't do for you

Four columnists comment on the benefits and dangers of diary writing

A

Diaries are embarrassing. Even as adults, though we might pretend to feel nothing more than mild amusement on rereading our teenage diaries, more often than not we secretly cringe with embarrassment over their raw emotion and trivial content. Why, I wonder, when they are nothing more than records of the childish hopes and ambitions we've now outgrown? But keeping a diary has advantages over other modes of expression. For one thing, a conventional diary is wonderfully impermanent. It can be quickly and completely destroyed if the writer so chooses, something that does not hold true for digital media. Diaries are also intended to be confidential, though younger siblings can, and do, often find them a huge temptation. If found, a diary will be read and its contents certainly made fun of and possibly shared with the very people one would least like to know about them.

B

Though they're perfectly happy to post all sorts of details about their personal lives on Facebook, the prospect of somebody finding and reading a secret diary is enough to put many teenagers off the idea of keeping one. While those fears might be well-founded, discovery is not the main threat diaries pose. They might actually induce writers to tell themselves something they didn't want to know. It might be an admission of jealousy, a confession of a secret infatuation or even an outpouring of pent up resentment and rage. Threatening as this might be, there is real power in writing these sorts of things down. We can't begin to change the things we find most irksome about ourselves without first accepting them, and writing openly and honestly is the first step. We might ultimately burn the pages but we should use them first to confront the things that trouble us.

C

Teenage writers may come to regard their diary as a shoulder to cry on or even as a rather poor substitute for a boyfriend or girlfriend. That's fine, of course, as long as the diarist really doesn't secretly hope that any boyfriend or girlfriend will ever read the diary. They may believe they would actually like this to happen but they would be horrified if it really did. But even just fantasising that someone else will read a diary can distort the whole process. Writers who imagine an audience try to impress, to persuade or perhaps to protect their own and others' feelings. They exaggerate the positive and downplay the negative. In short, they lie. As I see it, once a diary is anything but completely honest, the whole activity is rendered pointless. If you intend to address your friends and acquaintances directly, keep a blog or write your autobiography. A diary should be written, without reticence, for your eyes only.

D

Diaries with locks and keys have retained their popularity among teenage girls, despite the fact that they happily keep what amounts to digital diaries through posts on Facebook, Twitter or Tumblr. Posts on such sites are effectively publications intended to produce a reaction and a response even if it is just approval or disapproval. Attracting disapproval in the extreme form of cyber bullying stops many teenagers expressing their feelings on such sites. They are not safe places for baring one's soul. The diary, for all its old-fashioned sentimentality, can, and should, be a place for such honesty. People who reread their teenage diaries are understandably appalled to discover how little space they gave to what really matters and how much time they dedicated to the boy or girl on the bus who might or might not have fancied them. But at least diaries are truly private places where such things can be expressed.

Reading

1 Work in small groups. Make a list of five things you think all adults should be able to do.

2 Look at a similar list from a blog. Tick (✓) the things that you can do. Add two more items from your list in Activity 1.

| Profile | Blog | Articles |

Things every adult should be able to do

1 Perform CPR and the Heimlich Manoeuvre

One day it may be your partner or child who needs your help.

2 Do basic cooking

I find it appalling that so many young people live on pot noodles and toast. Learn to cook – you might even enjoy it.

3 Speed read

The average person reads a couple of thousand words a day and the average student reads a lot more. Sometimes you need to get the gist superfast. Speed reading can take the pressure off.

4 Use tools like hammers, screwdrivers and saws

Learn basic carpentry and it could end up saving you money. Why buy bookshelves if you can build them yourself?

5 Make a simple budget

It's no fun being in debt. A simple budget is the key.

6 Look good in front of a camera

It's amazing how many people don't know how to find their most beguiling smile.

Introductory *it*

▶ **GRAMMAR** REFERENCE p.176

3 Look at the four uses of the introductory *it* and find more examples of each one in the list in Activity 2.

1 to avoid beginning a sentence with an infinitive or gerund
It's always good to have a chance to catch up with old friends.

2 to emphasise a relative clause (cleft sentence)
It was James who left the lights turned on in the building, not me.

3 when the subject of a clause is another clause
It's shocking how many people don't bother to recycle their rubbish.

4 in the structure: subject + verb + *it* + adjective + infinitive/clause
I found it embarrassing to have to tell her how I felt.

> ### LANGUAGE TIP
>
> We do not normally use subject + verb + *it* + adjective + infinitive/clause if there is no adjective.
> *I cannot bear **it** to hear a baby crying.*
> We can use introductory *it* with *like, love, hate,* etc. in sentences like:
> *I hate **it** when you keep changing the channel like that.*

4 Rewrite the sentences using the introductory *it*.

1 That we have become so disconnected from the natural environment is sad.

2 To learn basic first aid skills is vital for school children.

3 How dependent people have become on mobile phones worries me.

4 That you were bitten by an insect of some kind is likely.

5 To make new friends was difficult for me.

6 For people to contact a member of staff first is vital.

7 Not to throw away letters with your name and address on them makes good sense.

8 That you should never tell anyone your password is common knowledge.

5 Look at the list you wrote in Activity 1 and choose four items that you consider important or would like to learn. Rewrite the items using the introductory *it*. Compare your choices with a partner.

Collaborative task and discussion (Parts 3 and 4)

responding to and expanding on your partner's ideas

▶ **EXAM** FOCUS p.205

1 ▶ 09 **Listen to two candidates, Daniela and Martin, doing both parts of the Part 3 task. Which candidate responds to and expands on what the other candidate says?**

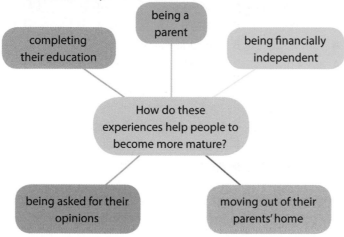

- being a parent
- completing their education
- being financially independent
- How do these experiences help people to become more mature?
- being asked for their opinions
- moving out of their parents' home

EXAM TIP

In Parts 3 and 4 your ability to interact with the other candidate is assessed. Express your opinion and make sure you pick up on what the other candidate says.

2 **Listen again and look at some of the exchanges between the two students. Underline the phrases that Daniela (D) uses to respond to what Martin (M) says. Then underline the phrases she uses to expand on what Martin says.**

1 **M:** If you are still reliant on your parents for money, you are never entirely free to make your own decisions, so, in some senses, you remain in the position that you were in when you were a child.

   D: You mean, because you're having to ask your parents for money and possibly also having to justify what you spend it on?

   M: Yes.

   D: There's a lot to be said for that argument. In many cases, I think it does make people less able to take responsibility for their own decisions and it often creates tensions in a family.

2 **M:** Apart from earning your own living, I think the thing that really gives you adult status is having your own family. With children of your own, you grow up fast.

   D: Yes, you're forced to mature by having to make sacrifices and by being responsible for other people, aren't you?

3 **Look at some of Daniela's ideas. Use the suggestions in brackets to respond to and expand on them. Then act out the conversation with another student.**

1

> It's more and more common for people to return to study throughout their lives.

(Agree and give an example of someone who has returned to study.)

2

> I don't think moving into your own flat or house necessarily makes you an adult, either. A lot of people move out when they start university – I did – but, although I probably thought of myself as very grown up, I wasn't, really.

(Express interest in Daniela's comment about not being grown up and then comment on your own experience.)

3

> That's why the real transition from childhood to adulthood is being treated as an adult. Do you see what I mean?

(Say that you do and give an example of being treated like an adult to check that this is what Daniela means.)

4 ▶ 10 **Listen to the candidates doing the Part 4 task and answer the questions.**

1 Which of them has ideas that are closest to your point of view?

2 How would you respond to and expand on these ideas?

3 Is there anything either of the students says that you disagree with?

5 **Work in groups of three. Turn to page 156 and do the activity.**

News

Blue Zones

Although the aging process isn't fully (0) ...B. understood..., scientists do know that health and longevity (1) .... a complex interplay of genetics and environment. Researcher Dan Buettner has spent years visiting areas of the world where people tend to live longer, healthier lives in an attempt to (2) .... what these environmental factors might be. He identified areas he calls 'Blue Zones', where people live particularly long and happy lives. Sardinia, for example, has the highest (3) .... of male centenarians in the world, Okinawa the longest disability-free life (4) .... and Costa Rica's Nicoya Peninsula middle-aged residents who are four times more likely to (5) .... their ninetieth birthday than their (6) .... in the United States. As diverse as the people in the Blue Zones may be, they share a number of characteristics. Their homes (7) .... physical activity, they avoid overeating, have purposeful lives and are surrounded by others who value and appreciate them. As Buettner observes, these patterns not only (8) .... in lives that are longer but in lives well led.

Multiple choice cloze (Part 1)

▶ **EXAM** FOCUS p.197

1 Work in pairs. What's the average life expectancy for people in your country? What environmental factors do you think contribute to longevity?

2 Read the article about parts of the world where longevity is particularly common. Are any of the places or factors you talked about mentioned?

0	**A** appreciated	**B** understood	**C** known	**D** identified
1	**A** involve	**B** demand	**C** beg	**D** need
2	**A** sort	**B** conclude	**C** settle	**D** determine
3	**A** amount	**B** instance	**C** concentration	**D** figure
4	**A** anticipation	**B** hope	**C** probability	**D** expectancy
5	**A** reach	**B** arrive	**C** achieve	**D** complete
6	**A** equals	**B** peers	**C** colleagues	**D** partners
7	**A** promote	**B** drive	**C** insist	**D** push
8	**A** result	**B** produce	**C** lead	**D** make

3 Which option would you choose to complete these two sentences? Compare your answers with a partner.

1 A large .... of the students felt their needs would be better served by an on-campus health centre.

   A quantity   **B** proportion   **C** amount   **D** figure

2 He had withdrawn a large .... of money earlier that morning.

   A number   **B** proportion   **C** amount   **D** figure

4 Work in pairs and look at the questions in Activity 2. Which one depends on whether the noun that follows is countable or uncountable?

5 Read the article again. For questions 1–8, decide which answer (A, B, C or D) best fits each gap.

EXAM TIP

Sometimes the choice between the options depends on whether the noun that follows is countable or uncountable.

Speaking

6 Answer the questions. Then compare your answers with other students.

1 What do the three places mentioned in the article have in common?

2 If you could live anywhere when you retire, would you choose one of these places or somewhere else? Why?

3 If it became possible to live to be 150, would you want to?

Speaking

1 **Work in pairs. Do you agree with these statements? Explain your answers.**

1 If your parents live to be over eighty-five, you probably will too.

2 People in past centuries seldom lived beyond early middle age.

3 Having a stressful job reduces your life expectancy.

4 Married people are more likely to live longer lives than single people.

Multiple choice (Part 3)

▶ **EXAM** FOCUS p.203

2 ▶ **11** **You will hear an interview with Angus Johnson, who does research into longevity. For questions 1–6, choose the answer (A, B, C or D) which fits best according to what you hear.**

EXAM TIP

Many of the questions in Part 3 are concerned with the speaker's opinions. Listen out for phrases that indicate the speaker is about to express an opinion (e.g. *It strikes me that …* , *As I see it, …* , *In my view, …*).

1 What does Dr Johnson think about people who attribute longevity to genetic factors?

   A They are deliberately ignoring the evidence.

   B They are unwilling to face reality.

   C It may lead them to take silly risks.

   D They lack confidence in this belief.

2 How does Dr Johnson respond when people say most people died young in the past?

   A He explains that this was due to the prevalence of untreatable illnesses.

   B He agrees on the basis that so many people died in their infancy.

   C He says that people should look at examples from the past.

   D He explains that people aged much more quickly in the past.

3 When, according to Dr Johnson, can a job shorten life expectancy?

   A When it is so disagreeable that people are really unhappy at work.

   B When the burden of responsibility is too great.

   C When there is a demand to meet unrealistic deadlines.

   D When workers are paid in accordance with how much they produce.

4 How does Dr Johnson explain the role of conscientiousness in longevity?

   A It makes people feel anxious about their health.

   B It forces people to change the way they live.

   C It makes people consider simplifying their lives.

   D It ensures that people take good care of themselves.

5 Dr Johnson says that marriage contributes to women's longevity

   A if they are content with the relationship.

   B if their partner is happy about their being together.

   C if they get married when they're young.

   D if their partner also lives for a long time.

6 What is Dr Johnson's attitude to the theory about the longevity of widows?

   A He is not fully convinced but hopes it is valid.

   B He believes future research will prove it to be false.

   C He acknowledges the possible existence of alternative theories.

   D He dismisses it as mere speculation that requires proper study.

3 **Work in pairs. What surprises you most about the longevity factors mentioned in the interview? Would you describe yourself as conscientious? Why/Why not?**

Vocabulary

working out meaning from context

4 **Work in pairs. Look at the sentences from the interview and discuss the meaning of the underlined words and phrases.**

1 Putting so much emphasis on genetics is just <u>wishful thinking</u>.

2 … a completely <u>foolhardy</u> attitude, as far as I'm concerned.

3 <u>Granted</u>, a miserable job you dislike causes the wrong kind of stress.

4 But doesn't that contradict the idea that <u>laid-back</u> people live longer?

5 They'll also be more inclined to avoid very fattening foods but they won't <u>veer</u> to the other extreme of starving themselves.

6 Sadly, <u>when the boot is on the other foot</u> – that is, if a woman is happily married and her partner is not …

3 Look at three more plans for the task and answer the questions.

1 Which is most similar to the plan you made?

2 Which two plans are missing an important element in the task? Which element is it?

A

1 questions I asked
2 descriptions of people I asked
3 problems with survey
4 analysis of survey results

B

1 description of problem
2 survey results
3 reasons why young people feel positive towards older people
4 reasons why young people are not looking forward to growing old themselves

C

1 introduction
2 attitudes to older people
3 attitudes to growing old
4 recommendations

Speaking

1 Work in pairs and discuss the questions.

1 How much contact do you have with people of different generations in your family or neighbourhood?

2 What might younger people enjoy or find difficult about talking to older people?

3 What might older people enjoy or find difficult about talking to younger people?

Report (Part 2)

dos and don'ts

▶ **WRITING** REFERENCE p.192

2 Look at the exam task and write a plan for your answer.

An international development agency has been looking into attitudes to aging around the world. The research director has asked you to conduct a survey and write a report. Your report should discuss how young people where you live feel about older people in the community and the prospect of growing old themselves. You have also been asked to make recommendations about how attitudes could be changed.

Write your **report** in **220–260 words** in an appropriate style.

4 Look at the advice for writing reports. Which piece of advice should start with *Don't*?

1 Begin by stating the purpose of your report.

2 Use invented statistics to provide a succinct summary of your results.

3 Use lists of points where appropriate.

4 Divide your report into sections according to the input.

5 Develop the ideas in the task input.

6 Use a clear layout with headings.

7 Make your report look the same as an essay.

8 Use an impersonal, formal style.

5 Look at the model report on page 192 and check your answers in Activity 4. Which of the plans in Activity 3 is most similar to the structure of the model report?

6 Look at the useful language for report writing on page 193. Choose expressions to use for the task in Activity 2.

7 Write a draft of your report and show it to another student. Then work in pairs and use the advice in Activity 4 to check each other's work. Can you make any suggestions about how your reports could be improved?

1 Complete the second sentence so that it has a similar meaning to the first sentence, using the word given. Do not change the word given. You must use between three and six words, including the word given.

1 We really must learn to use less water.
VITAL
It is _a vital requirement_ to use less water. _in water shortage_ _cantrys with_

2 Elderly people sometimes deeply mistrust technology.
HAVE
Elderly people sometimes _have problems with new_ technology.

3 The council are the ones that should do something about graffiti.
THAT
It's _important that the council do_ something about graffiti.

4 Very few people make an effort to recycle their rubbish, which I find astonishing.
HOW
It's _astonishing how a few people_ make an effort to recycle their rubbish.

5 Adults behaving like teenagers really embarrass me.
FIND
I _find it really embarassing_ when adults behave like teenagers.

6 He knows a lot of colloquial English.
EXCELLENT
He _'s knowledge is excellent_ of colloquial English. _ti_

2 Choose the correct option to complete the sentences.

1 Her _infantile_ behaviour caused a lot of problems in the group.
A mature   B infantile   C geriatric   D childlike

2 His _D_ good looks and great singing voice made him an immediate hit with teenagers.
A childish   B immature   C boyish   D adolescent

3 Europe's _C_ population presents considerable problems for governments trying to find a way of cutting spending on healthcare and pensions.
A aging   B mature   C adult   D grown-up

4 They say that being happy is one of the keys to looking _D_ , even in late middle age.
A adolescent   B teenage   C puerile   D youthful

5 I am really tired of your _C / D_ jokes. Grow up!
A childlike   B youthful   C puerile   D boyish

6 I think the really _A_ way of going about this would be to sit down and discuss it calmly.
A adult   B aging   C elderly   D older

3 Read the article and decide which answer (A, B, C or D) best fits each gap.

News10

Who invented teenagers?

There is some debate about who coined the **(1)** _term_ or when it was first used but teenagers have, of course, always **(2)** _existed_ . Even so, until the 1930s no one paid them much **(3)** _attention_ . It was then that we began to see teenage actors, many of whom were **(4)** _prior_ child stars, on cinema screens. Initially the films were comedies, but later teenage actors starred in dramas depicting the conflicts **(5)** _arising_ from the so-called 'generation gap'. The clothing and food industries quickly jumped on the bandwagon and began to produce goods **(6)** _____ this newly-discovered social group. These same fashions and foods still **(7)** _maintain_ their own today. How many people, after all, can claim they have never owned a pair of jeans or eaten a hamburger, both of which were originally products **(8)** _offered_ at the teenage market? Teenagers rule but it seems strange to think that their reign began less than a century ago.

1	A name	B idea	C term	D idiom
2	A been	B existed	C subsisted	D endured
3	A notice	B thought	C mind	D attention
4	A former	B earlier	C prior	D past
5	A causing	B happening	C arising	D occurring
6	A aiming	B seeking	C focussing	D targeting
7	A hold	B maintain	C stand	D occupy
8	A offered	B pitched	C delivered	D proposed

No gain without pain

Sentence completion (Part 2)

▶ **EXAM** FOCUS p.202

1 Work in pairs and add three more statements to the questionnaire. Then ask and answer questions to find out whether anyone in your class is a perfectionist.

Are you a perfectionist?	Yes	No
1 I get upset if I get less than 99% in a test.	○	○

EXAM TIP

Before you listen, read the exam task carefully to get an idea of what you will hear. You may hear more than one word which could fit grammatically, so make sure that you choose the word (or words) which also make sense.

2 You will hear part of a radio talk by a psychologist called Mary Shaw on perfectionism. Look at the exam task and predict what kind of information is missing.

Why perfectionism isn't perfect

Mary thinks that because it is only a '**(1)** *fantasy / goal*..........', perfectionism cannot be achieved.

Mary thinks that musicians who are primarily concerned with their musical **(2)** ....*technique*........ may underperform.

Mary says that becoming obsessed with **(3)** .....*detial*..... is a problem experienced by many perfectionists.

Mary is convinced that language learners who concentrate on communication will find that their **(4)** .....*accuracy*..... also gets better.

Mary is concerned that some young athletes may be so worried about **(5)** ....*failure*....... that they are unwilling to participate.

Mary's tip for perfectionists is to set a **(6)** ......*timelimit*...... for every task.

According to Mary, it's useful to remember the phrase '**(7)** .....*less is more*.....' when doing tasks such as giving a presentation.

Mary thinks that people should be satisfied with achieving their **(8)** .....*potential*..... without worrying about being perfect.

3 ▶ 12 Listen to the first part of the talk and look at Question 1 on page 36. Which words do you hear that could fit grammatically? Which word makes sense?

4 ▶ 13 Listen to the whole talk. For questions 2–8, complete the sentences.

5 Do you agree with the advice given?

Verb patterns: -ing/infinitive

6 Work in pairs. Think of four qualities you need to be a high achiever. Then read the article. Does the writer mention them?

24 | **LIFESTYLE**

HIGH achievers

Very few people can claim that they have achieved all that they'd ever **hoped (1)** to achieve (achieve). So what is stopping you right now from making a much greater contribution to society? What is **preventing you from (2)** fulfil' (fulfil) your potential? You don't want to look back in twenty years' time and **regret** not **(3)** having (have) tried hard enough. Here are some possible reasons:

- You do not have enough belief in yourself. All successful people have enormous self-belief. They know that they have something special to contribute and they **expect (4)** to make (make) their mark.

- You are too comfortable where you are. Why try something new when you are already doing what you are good at? High achievers go further. They grab every opportunity and are **prepared (5)** to take (take on) difficult challenges. This means that they **risk (6)** to fail (fail) again and again. Do you **dare (7)** _____ (leave) your comfort zone or do you **avoid (8)** to take (take) risks?

- You're not **forcing yourself (9)** to work (work) hard enough. Either that or you **keep (10)** doing (do) unproductive tasks. If you have clear goals but are not making progress towards them, **consider (11)** increasing (increase) your activity level. Picasso painted over 20,000 pictures. Persistence pays dividends.

- You are not mixing with high achievers. Let's face it – your friends and family are really nice people but they are not challenging you enough. Spend more time with high flyers and positive thinkers who understand what it takes to succeed. They will **help (12)** to turn (turn) your dreams into reality.

7 Do you think the advice in the article is helpful? Which of the advice applies to you?

8 Complete the article with the correct form of the verbs in brackets.

9 Match the verbs in bold in the article with patterns 1–5. Some verbs can be used in more than one pattern.

1 verb + -ing   consider + risk
2 verb + infinitive
3 verb + infinitive without to
4 verb + object + infinitive
5 verb + object + -ing

LANGUAGE TIP

Some verbs such as *start*, *love*, *hate*, *prefer*, *attempt* and *continue* can be followed by either –*ing* or an infinitive with very little difference in meaning.
*I started **to watch**/**watching** the film at 9 p.m.*

---

10 Work in pairs and answer the questions.

1 Which sentence means Frank no longer buys a newspaper?
   A Frank stopped to buy a newspaper. ✓
   B Frank stopped buying a newspaper.

2 Which sentence expresses regret for something that was said in the past?
   A I regret saying you were wrong. ✓
   B I regret to say you were wrong.

3 Which sentence refers to the time before Alice booked the appointment?
   A Alice remembered to book an appointment at the dentist.
   B Alice remembered booking an appointment at the dentist. ✓

Speaking

11 Work in pairs and discuss the questions.

1 How are you going to turn your dreams into reality?
2 What ambitions have you fulfilled so far?
3 How do you feel about leaving your comfort zone?
4 What do you think is the best way to make a contribution to society?

Reading

1 **Work in pairs and discuss the questions.**

1 Why do you think people find successful entrepreneurs so inspiring?

2 Do you think you've got what it takes to be a successful entrepreneur?

2 **Read the article and say what is unusual about the success of Levi Roots.**

Investor	Trader

Levi Roots: My recipe for success

When I was making Reggae Reggae Sauce in my kitchen, I knew it was going to be popular because I had sold the sauce at the Notting Hill Carnival and to local businesses. But I did not imagine I would get to where I am now. I don't think I could have become so big without the exposure of *Dragons' Den* on the BBC. That TV programme had about 4.5 million viewers. Until this, the banks weren't interested in a forty-nine year-old Rastafarian who produced a sauce in his kitchen and called it *Reggae Reggae*.

No one could have envisaged then the level of success that my business has had in the past five years. Sales reached more than one million pounds within the first year. My first order

from a large supermarket of 250,000 bottles sold out within a week, outselling Heinz tomato ketchup.

My basic business philosophy is a quote from Shakespeare's Julius Caesar: *We must take the current when it serves or lose our ventures.* I always say this is an entrepreneur's mantra. You must grab an opportunity when it comes.

I don't think I want to work until I drop – not at all. I want to enjoy the success I have been granted. I have been going to Jamaica recently and I would like to retire there. I have just started distributing Reggae Reggae Sauce in Jamaica but it is not made there. It is my dream to set up a factory in Clarendon, the sugar cane community where I grew up with my grandmother.

3 **Match words 1–6 with meanings A–F.**

1 exposure   **A** a project or enterprise

2 envisage   **B** be given or rewarded with

3 mantra   **C** imagine or visualise

4 granted   **D** a repeated phrase, e.g. in meditation

5 venture   **E** take hold of something

6 grab   **F** publicity or attention

Verb/Noun collocations

4 **Answer the questions about the verbs *grasp*, *grab*, *take* and *seize*.**

1 Which is the most formal word? *seize*   *seize grab/grasp*

2 Which words suggest doing something suddenly? *grab/grasp*

3 Which of the verbs can be used in each sentence?

A Entrepreneurs *all of them* every opportunity.

B The military *seize* power in 1927.

C The government failed to *take/seize* control of the situation.

D They didn't *grasp* (*means that understand*) the fact that the business was doomed to fail.

E We *grab (took/seize)* the chance to meet the president.

5 **Look at the underlined verbs in the collocations. Which verbs from the box also collocate with the nouns?**

doubt	exceed	follow	fulfil	gain
realise	receive	rely on	suffer	

1 <u>encounter</u> a setback   *suffer, receive (problem)*

2 <u>trust</u> your intuition   *rely on, follow*

3 <u>get</u> exposure   *receive gain (It getting know everybody) advertisement*

4 <u>get</u> inspiration   *gain, receive exceed fulfil*

5 <u>have</u> an expectation

6 <u>achieve</u> an ambition   *fulfil, realise*

LANGUAGE TIP

Many words that you are familiar with may have additional collocations that you don't yet know. You need to keep extending your knowledge of collocations of both familiar words and new words.

6 **Think of as many verbs as you can that collocate with the nouns in the box. Then turn to page 162 and compare your list.**

advantage	argument	difficulties
dreams	perfection	popularity
potential	praise	target	thanks

7 **Write six sentences using some of the collocations in Activity 6.**

Speaking

8 **Work in pairs and discuss the questions.**

1 Why do you think Reggae Reggae Sauce has been such a success?

2 Would you like to start your own business? Why/Why not?

Key word transformations (Part 4)

▶ **EXAM** FOCUS p.199

1 **Look at the exam question and answer the questions.**

positive, negative + Aim

> No one could have envisaged the success the business would have.
>
> **POSSIBLE**
>
> *It could not be possible*
> It .... to envisage the success the business would have.

1 Do you need to use an active or passive form? *A*
2 Do you need to use a negative or a positive form? *N*
3 Which of these options fits best?
   A wouldn't have been possible *past*
   B couldn't be possible
   C could have been possible

2 **Choose the correct option to complete the second sentence so that it has a similar meaning to the first sentence.**

1 Unfortunately, they failed to achieve their ambitious goals.
   SUCCESSFUL
   They .... their ambitious goals.
   A were not successful in
   B weren't successful in achieving *(in doing)*
   C are not successful to achieve

2 I wish I had started my own business sooner.
   REGRET
   I .... my own business sooner.
   A have the regret not to have started
   B regret I hadn't started
   C regret not having started *(looking back in the time)*

3 Jack is completely trustworthy as a business partner.
   RELIED
   Jack .... as a business partner.
   A is relied completely
   B can be relied on completely
   C relied on completely

3 **For questions 1–6, complete the second sentence so that it has a similar meaning to the first sentence, using the word given. Do not change the word given. You must use between three and six words, including the word given.**

1 Some people doubt whether Martin's new business venture will do well.
   EXPECTED *not being is / expected to do*
   Martin's new business venture .... well by some people. → *is not expected to do*

2 Unfortunately, I couldn't visit my brother in Australia as I didn't have enough money.
   ABLE *3rd cond. would had / would be able*
   If I'd had more money, I .... to visit my brother in Australia. *would have been able*

3 It's possible that his ambition to be a doctor will fail if he doesn't work hard.
   REALISED *couldn't / may not be*
   His ambition to be a doctor .... if he doesn't work hard. *might not be realised →2* *realised into fail*

4 Learning to drive is a waste of time unless you already have a car. *(in)*
   POINT *is no point learning*
   There .... to drive unless you already have a car.

5 The sales director thinks it might be a good idea to take on new sales staff. *taking on*
   CONSIDERING *were considering to take on*
   The sales director *is* .... new sales staff. *ING→*

6 My parents wouldn't allow me to go to the party.
   PREVENTED *prevented me from going ✓*
   My parents .... to the party. *(ing)* *NEGATIVE / not / NOT x / PAST / preposition*

EXAM TIP

Make sure you don't write more than six words. Contractions (e.g. *won't*) count as two words.

IMPROVING → WRITE REVIEW, ARTICLE
WRITING WRITE IT DOWN

Speaking

1 **Work in pairs and discuss the questions.**

1 How important is it to you to have the latest mobile phone, laptop, TV, etc.? Will designers ever stop updating these gadgets?

2 What are the two best and worst inventions of the twenty-first century so far?

3 What do you think these sayings mean? Do you agree?
There is nothing new under the sun.
Necessity is the mother of invention.

Multiple choice (Part 5)

▶ **EXAM** FOCUS p.199

> **EXAM TIP**
>
> You will need to read the text containing the answer for each question very carefully to check that there is evidence for each option you choose. Also check that it actually answers the question.

2 **Read the title and the article quickly. In what way is the Museum of Failed Products similar to or different from a normal museum?**

3 **Look at question 1 in Activity 4 and the first paragraph of the article.**

1 Are options A–D all mentioned in the text? *NO?*

2 Underline the sentence which compares the museum to a supermarket. Which of the options answers the question?

4 **For questions 2–6, choose the answer (A, B, C or D) which you think fits best according to the text.**

1 According to the writer, what is the reason why the storehouse does *not* resemble a supermarket?

A its appearance on the outside

B the dimly-lit space

C the size of the building

D the range of products on each shelf

2 What is the writer's main purpose in the second paragraph?

A to provide an idea of what the museum contains

B to give reasons why these products were rejected by consumers

C to explain how obvious it should have been that these products would fail

D to illustrate how the museum is organised

3 What is Carol Sherry's attitude to the failed products?

A She feels particularly attached to some products.

B She has sympathy for the people who invented them.

C She prefers failed products to successful ones.

D She appreciates the concepts behind the products.

4 According to the writer, Mr McMath failed to realise that his collection would

A be better if it were more selective.

B grow so quickly.

C contain so many failed products.

D be so difficult to store.

5 According to the writer, what is remarkable about the product developers who visit GfK?

A their ignorance of the existence of the collection

B the lack of attention paid to previous failures

C the way they dismiss their own companies' failures

D their tendency to repeat past failures

6 What point is the writer making in the last paragraph?

A that failure should have been prevented

B that failure is an acceptable part of life

C that people are afraid to talk about failure

D that thinking negatively often leads to failure

5 **Work in pairs. Why do you think 'most products fail'?**

Working out meaning from context

6 **Look at the underlined words in the article and use the context to help you choose the correct meaning.**

1 poignant

  A sad   B significant

2 haphazardly

  A logically   B randomly

3 fleeting

  A passing quickly   B durable

4 indiscriminately

  A in a planned way   B in an unplanned way

5 aversion

  A willingness   B unwillingness

6 doomed

  A bound to fail   B might fail

The Museum of Failed Products

Our business editor paid a visit to the graveyard of good ideas

In an unremarkable business park outside the city of Ann Arbor in Michigan stands a <u>poignant</u> memorial to humanity's shattered dreams. It doesn't look like that from the outside, though. Even when you get inside, it takes a few moments for your eyes to adjust to what you're seeing. It appears to be a vast and <u>haphazardly</u> organised supermarket; along every aisle, grey metal shelves are crammed with thousands of packages of food and household products. There is something unusually cacophonous about the displays and soon enough you work out the reason: unlike in a real supermarket, there is only one of each item.

The storehouse, operated by a company called GfK Custom Research North America, has acquired a nickname: the Museum of Failed Products. This is consumer capitalism's graveyard or, to put it less grandly, it's almost certainly the only place on the planet where you'll find A Touch of Yogurt shampoo alongside the equally unpopular For Oily Hair Only. The museum is home to discontinued brands of caffeinated beer and self-heating soup cans that had a regrettable tendency to explode in customers' faces.

There is a Japanese term, *mono no aware*, that translates roughly as 'the pathos of things'. It captures a kind of bittersweet melancholy at life's impermanence – that additional beauty imparted to cherry blossoms, for their <u>fleeting</u> nature. It's only stretching the concept slightly to suggest that this is how the museum's manager, an understatedly stylish GfK employee named Carol Sherry, feels about the cartons of Morning Banana Juice in her care or about Fortune Snookies, a short-lived line of fortune cookies for dogs. Every failure, the way she sees it, embodies its own sad story on the part of designers, marketers and salespeople. It is never far from her mind that real people had their mortgages, their car payments and their family holidays riding on the success of products such as A Touch of Yogurt.

The Museum of Failed Products was itself a kind of accident, albeit a happier one. Its creator, a now retired marketing man named Robert McMath, merely intended to accumulate a 'reference library' of consumer products, not failures per se. And so, starting in the 1960s, he began purchasing and preserving a sample of every new item he could find.

Soon, the collection outgrew his office in upstate New York and he was forced to move into a converted granary to accommodate it. Later, GfK bought him out, moving the whole lot to Michigan. What McMath hadn't taken into account was the three-word truth that was to prove the making of his career: *most products fail.* According to some estimates, the failure rate is as high as ninety percent. Simply by collecting new products <u>indiscriminately</u>, McMath had ensured that his hoard would come to consist overwhelmingly of unsuccessful ones.

By far the most striking thing about the museum, though, is that it should exist as a viable, profit-making business in the first place. You might have assumed that any consumer product manufacturer worthy of the name would have its own such collection – a carefully stewarded resource to help it avoid making errors its rivals had already made. Yet the executives who arrive every week at Sherry's door are evidence of how rarely this happens. Product developers are so focused on their next hoped-for success, so unwilling to invest time or energy thinking about their industry's past failures that they only belatedly realise how much they need to access GfK's collection. Most surprising of all is that many of the designers who have found their way to the museum have come there to examine – or been surprised to discover – products that their own companies had created, then abandoned.

It isn't hard to imagine how one downside of the positive-thinking culture, an aversion to confronting failure, might have been responsible for the very existence of many of the products lining its shelves. Each one must have made it through a series of meetings at which nobody realised that the product was <u>doomed</u>. Perhaps nobody wanted to contemplate the prospect of failure; perhaps someone did but didn't want to bring it up for discussion. By the time the truth became obvious, the original developers would have moved to other products or other firms. Little energy would have been invested in discovering what went wrong. Everyone involved would have conspired, perhaps without realising what they're doing, never to speak of it again. Failure is everywhere. It's just that most of the time we'd rather avoid confronting that fact.

Reading

1 Read the article about Roger Black and decide if the statements are true (T) or false (F).

1 His biggest mistake had a positive outcome.
2 He should have done better in the maths exam.
3 He regrets not studying medicine.
4 He wishes he'd known he was going to be an athlete.

24 **SPORTSCENE**

An unexpected turn of events

In many ways, my whole career has been shaped around the biggest mistake of my life. At school I played a lot of rugby and cricket but I never really did much athletics. My primary aim was to do well in my final exams so I **(1)** *could/will* read medicine at university. I **(2)** *needed to/must* do well in the maths exam, but when it came to it, there was one question I got stuck on. I just **(3)** *couldn't/can't* work it out, so I left it and went back to it later. The more I looked at it, the more confused I got. I started to panic and when the time was up, I **(4)** *mustn't/couldn't* complete the whole paper.

I **(5)** *can/must* still recall it vividly. I was absolutely devastated. I **(6)** *had to/must* stay behind at school for a year and retake that maths exam. Because of the year off, I **(7)** *couldn't/didn't have to* go travelling or join in any of the things my friends were doing and so I ended up joining my local athletics club in Hampshire.

My school said I **(8)** *could retake/could have retaken* the exam and, eventually, I started reading medicine at Southampton University but by then my life had changed. I was European junior 400 m champion and I left university after the first term because there was no way I **(9)** *could have done/needn't do* both. I **(10)** *should have realised/had to realise* sooner that I would have to choose between the two.

I never knew I was going to be an Olympic athlete when I was at school, even though people assume I **(11)** *might be able to/must have done*. It's easy to believe that we're programmed on a path in life but it **(12)** *doesn't have to/mustn't* be like that. It took that one mistake for me to find mine.

2 Work in pairs and answer the questions.

1 In what way might this story help young people?
2 What has turned out differently from how you expected in your life so far?

Modal verbs

▶ **GRAMMAR** REFERENCE p.176

3 Read the article again and choose the correct alternatives.

4 Find one or more examples in the article of modals used to express

1 ability.
2 criticism.
3 logical deduction.
4 permission.
5 possibility.
6 obligation/necessity.
7 lack of obligation/necessity.

LANGUAGE TIP

Need has two past forms with slightly different meanings.

She **didn't need to catch** the early flight. (It wasn't necessary to do this. It's not clear if she did or not.)

She **needn't have caught** the early flight. (She did this but it wasn't necessary.)

5 Which of the modal verbs in the article could be replaced by *be able to*, *be allowed to* or *ought to*?

6 Complete the questions with the correct form of the verb in brackets. Then ask and answer them with a partner.

1 Is there anything you feel you ___should have achieved___ (should/achieve) by now that you haven't?
2 What ___had to___ (have to) do that you hated doing at school?
3 Which of your dreams do you think ___might have come___ (might/come) true?
4 Is there anything that you ___needn't do___ (not need/do) that you have done recently?
5 What do you think your parents ___could have done___ (could/do) differently when you were a child?
6 How do you think your teachers ___must have seen___ (must/see) you when you were in primary school?

ABC

Collaborative task and discussion (Parts 3 and 4)

justifying an opinion

▶ **EXAM** FOCUS p.205

1 Have you ever given up a sport or a hobby? If so, why did you give it up?

2 ▶ 14 Look at the exam task and listen to two candidates, Jan and Marisol, doing both parts of the task. Do you agree with their opinions?

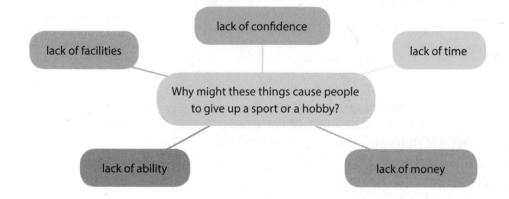

lack of confidence

lack of facilities

lack of time

Why might these things cause people to give up a sport or a hobby?

lack of ability

lack of money

3 Complete the phrases the speakers use when justifying an opinion. Then listen again and check.

1 In my opinion, ... *the reason* many people give up a sport or hobby is because of the costs involved.
2 I believe that .... *there is a long way* to explaining why people have to give up. *could be wrong*
3 I .... but I imagine many people get demotivated because they realise they're never going to be an amazing pianist or guitar player.
4 I know from .... *my own experience* that that's quite common.

4 Which of the phrases in Activity 3 is used by the candidates

2 **A** to introduce a point?
4 **B** to emphasise a point?
1 **C** to give personal evidence?
3 **D** to speculate without evidence?

5 ▶ 15 Listen to Marisol and Jan answering these questions. Which candidate answers the question well?

1 What do you think is the value of having a hobby?
2 Do you believe playing computer games is a good hobby?

6 Work in pairs. Turn to page 152 and do the activities.

7 How would you evaluate your own performance? Use the General marking guidelines on page 207 to help you. Can you suggest any ways in which the other students you worked with could improve?

EXAM TIP

Discuss each of the options on the task sheet in some detail with your partner. Don't dismiss any as being insignificant or unimportant too early in the discussion or you may run out of things to say. Also, don't be afraid to state the obvious.

Speaking

1 **How useful are these tips for helping people to achieve more in their lives?**

- Smile more.
- Never use negative words such as *fail* or *lose*.
- Expect only positive outcomes.
- Use visualisation techniques to imagine yourself succeeding.

Essay (Part 1)

effective introductory and concluding paragraphs

▶ **WRITING** REFERENCE p.186

2 **Look at the exam task below and the introductions on the right. Which one is better? Think about appropriate academic style and inclusion of specific examples.**

> Your class has attended a seminar on the benefits of training students to think positively. You have made the notes below.
>
> **The benefits of training students to think positively**
> - reduces stress
> - improves productivity
> - increases creativity
>
> **Some opinions expressed during the seminar**
> - 'The training is empowering. I feel I can achieve so much more.'
> - 'Having a positive outlook helps people to put their problems into perspective.'
> - 'It gives people the tools they need to find alternative solutions to their problems.'
>
> Write an essay for your tutor, discussing **two** of the benefits in your notes. You should **explain which benefit you think is more important**, **giving reasons** to support your opinion.
>
> You may, if you wish, make use of the opinions expressed during the seminar but you should use your own words as far as possible.
>
> Write your essay in **220–260** words in an appropriate style.

A It is undoubtedly true that there are many benefits to training students to think positively. Many students struggle with problems such as time management or feeling demotivated when they get a lower mark than they were hoping for. These types of problems can have a very negative impact on their performance and may sometimes lead to them dropping out of college.

B Training students to think positively is a very good idea, in my opinion. It's very easy to become negative when things aren't going well and you're not enjoying the course for whatever reason. I know from my own experience that students can find this very hard, especially if they have no one to help them deal with their problems.

EXAM TIP

In the introduction, give a brief outline of the issue, saying why it is important or why people have different opinions about it.

3 **Work in pairs and write a plan setting out your ideas for the main body of the essay in Activity 2. Make sure you include some evidence to support your ideas.**

4 **Decide if the statements about writing a conclusion are true (T) or false (F).**

1 You should give your opinion.
2 You should add some more examples to support your opinion.
3 You should briefly explain which benefit is more important.
4 You should summarise your main point(s).

5 **Complete the phrases that are often used in concluding paragraphs.**

1 To .... up, I would argue that reducing stress is of the greatest benefit.
2 It .... to me that everyone could benefit from this type of training.
3 Above .... , I think that positive thinking creates a better attitude.
4 The main point I would like to .... can be summarised as …

6 **Work in pairs. Turn to page 162 and do the activity.**

7 **Write your essay and check your work using the checklist on page 185.**

ALL PAGE

1 Choose the correct alternative in each sentence.

1 Nobody *might/could* have predicted how successful the company would be.

2 You *shouldn't/mustn't* have given up so easily when you had a chance of winning.

3 Dan *didn't need to/shouldn't have* be told what his mistake was.

4 The company *should know/must have known* that there would be serious losses.

5 We *would/will* never have expected that things would turn out so well.

6 That *can't/mustn't be* Sophie. She's supposed to be in Australia.

2 Complete the second sentence so that it has a similar meaning to the first sentence, using the word given. Do not change the word given. You must use between three and six words, including the word given.

1 It wasn't necessary for Emma to book her train ticket so far in advance because there were plenty of seats available.

BOOKED

Emma _have not booked_ her ticket so far in advance because there were plenty of seats available.

2 Unfortunately, I didn't have enough money to go travelling with my friends.

WOULD

If I'd had more money, I _would have to go for_ travelling with my friends.

3 Lucy was sorry she hadn't applied for the course in time.

REGRETTED

Lucy _____ for the course in time.

4 I realised I hadn't booked an appointment when I got to the hair salon.

FORGOTTEN

I realised I _had forgotten to book_ an appointment when I got to the hair salon.

5 As children, we were forbidden from watching TV until all our homework was done.

ALLOWED

As children, we _had not allowed to watch_ TV until all our homework was done.

6 Kevin thinks it might be a good idea to sell the house.

CONSIDERING

Kevin _was considering to sell_ the house.

3 Choose the correct option to complete the sentences.

1 Great business leaders always ___C___ adversity.
A suffer B overcome C exceed

2 Don't expect to ___B___ any thanks for speaking the truth.
A win B receive C earn

3 We were able to ___A___ an advantage over the competition.
A gain B exceed C beat

4 We were so lucky to be able to ___C___ our ambition of travelling the world.
A recognise B find C realise

5 I was really happy when I ___C___ my target of running ten kilometres in thirty minutes.
A followed B overcame C reached

6 The book ___B___ a lot of praise from critics.
A achieved B received C gained

7 Sometimes it's hard to ___A___ the lecturer's main argument.
A receive B find C follow

8 The idea is beginning to ___A___ popularity, although it was unpopular at first.
A gain B follow C reach

4 Read the text below. Use the word given in capitals at the end of some of the lines to form a word that fits in the gap in the same line.

BUSINESS

Advice for budding entrepreneurs

It's nearly impossible to succeed without people to help you. Nobody can do everything on their own and being friendly and (1) _helpful_ is **HELP**
one of the most important (2) _characters_ for a **CHARACTER**
young entrepreneur to have. Without the ability to network and work with people, you won't be able to develop the (3) _relationships_ that you need to **RELATION**
provide the support you'll need.
Many young entrepreneurs get (4) _motivation_ **MOTIVATE**
when things do not live up to their (5) _expectation_ **EXPECT**
. It's a mistake to believe you can instantly start making millions of dollars. Most ideas will end in (6) _failure_. Don't take this to heart, treat it **FAIL**
as a (7) _misfortune_ from which you will recover. **FORTUNE**
Remember that luck plays a major part in the success of any project. You may think you have the perfect idea but luck may not be on your side and you may not always get the (8) _recognition_ that **RECOGNISE**
you deserve.

The feel-good factor

Open cloze (Part 2)

▶ **EXAM** FOCUS p.198

1 **Work in pairs and discuss the questions.**

1   Is there a particular activity that makes you feel happy?
2   What one change to your current lifestyle would make you happier?
3   What has been the happiest period of your life so far?

2 **Read an article about a new way to investigate happiness. How does the writer feel about using technology in this way?**

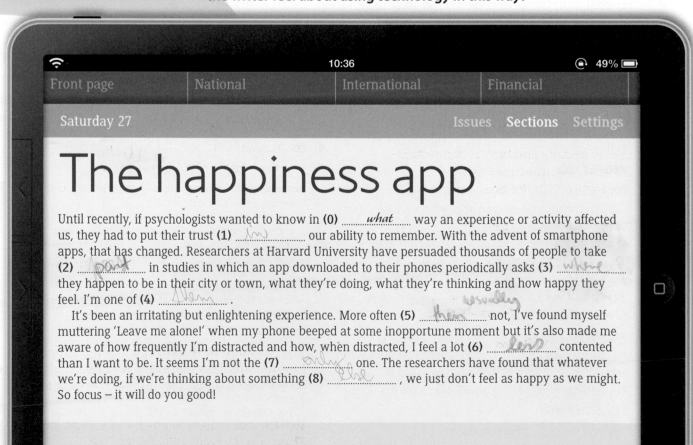

Front page	National	International	Financial

Saturday 27   Issues   **Sections**   Settings

The happiness app

Until recently, if psychologists wanted to know in **(0)** _____*what*_____ way an experience or activity affected us, they had to put their trust **(1)** _____in_____ our ability to remember. With the advent of smartphone apps, that has changed. Researchers at Harvard University have persuaded thousands of people to take **(2)** _____part_____ in studies in which an app downloaded to their phones periodically asks **(3)** _____where_____ they happen to be in their city or town, what they're doing, what they're thinking and how happy they feel. I'm one of **(4)** _____them_____ .

It's been an irritating but enlightening experience. More often **(5)** _____than_____ not, I've found myself muttering 'Leave me alone!' when my phone beeped at some inopportune moment but it's also made me aware of how frequently I'm distracted and how, when distracted, I feel a lot **(6)** _____less_____ contented than I want to be. It seems I'm not the **(7)** _____only_____ one. The researchers have found that whatever we're doing, if we're thinking about something **(8)** _____else_____ , we just don't feel as happy as we might. So focus – it will do you good!

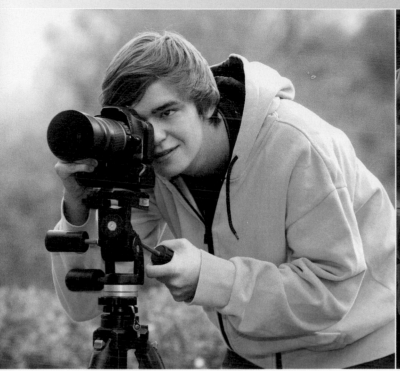

3 Read the article again. For questions 1–8, think of the word which best fits each gap. Use only one word for each gap.

EXAM TIP

Try reading the text 'aloud' in your head. That may help you to work out what some of the missing words are.

Long turn (Part 2)

speculating (1)

▶ **EXAM** FOCUS p.204

4 Work in pairs and look at the pictures. Discuss the questions using the expressions in the box.

I can't be completely sure
I don't know why
I may be wrong about this
I suppose it/he/she/they could
One possible explanation might be
This is just a guess, but

1 What do they have in common?
2 In what ways are they different from one another?
3 Is there anything in the pictures that is difficult for you to identify or explain?

EXAM TIP

Don't worry if there are things in the pictures that you cannot identify or explain. The Speaking exam is not intended to test your general knowledge. You are supposed to speculate about things like where the people are or what they are doing.

5 ▶ 16 Listen to the instructions an examiner gives a candidate. Which things does he *not* ask them to do?

1 talk about all three pictures
2 choose two of the pictures
3 describe each of the pictures   *whereas*
4 compare the pictures   *while*
5 decide where the pictures were taken
6 generalise about people in situations similar to those in the pictures

6 Work in pairs.

Student A: compare two of the pictures according to the examiner's instructions.

Student B: listen and make a note of the phrases Student A uses to speculate.

7 ▶ 17 Listen to the next part of the examiner's instructions. What does the other candidate have to do? Discuss the question with a partner.

8 Work in pairs. Turn to page 153 and do Task 1. Then turn to page 158 and do Task 2.

Multiple choice (Part 3)

▶ **EXAM** FOCUS p.203

1 Work in pairs and order the professions in the box according to how interesting you think they are (1 = very interesting, 7 = boring). Which career would be most satisfying?

---

banking   health care   hospitality
law   marketing   media   teaching

---

2 You will hear a radio interview with Diana McLeod, a careers advisor at a university. Look at question 1 in Activity 4 and underline the key words in the question and options.

3 ▶ 18 Listen to the first part of the interview and look at question 1 in Activity 4. Answer the questions.

1 Which key words or words with a similar meaning did you hear?

2 Which option is correct?

4 ▶ 19 Read through questions 2–6 and underline the key words. Then listen to the interview and choose the answer (A, B, C or D) which fits best according to what you hear.

1 What does Diana say the results of the survey show about teaching as a career?

  A Teachers find their work makes them happy.

  B People working in the media are a lot less happy than teachers.

  C Teaching doesn't offer opportunities for creativity.

  D Teachers find their work stimulating.

2 According to Diana, which cause of unhappiness at work is rising?

  A fear of being sacked

  B not having many friends at work

  C having to move to an unfamiliar place

  D being obliged to do overtime

3 Diana says job satisfaction is better in small and medium-sized businesses because

  A employers are much stricter about bullying.

  B employers treat staff as individuals.

  C employers don't demand as much from staff.

  D employers run lots of staff training programmes.

4 Diana says people who are thinking of becoming self-employed should

  A make sure they've got enough money first.

  B learn to take responsibility for their own decisions.

  C try to keep at least one day a week free.

  D be prepared to work longer hours.

5 Diana says bonus payments sometimes fail to give workers a sense of satisfaction because

  A they only provide for the bare essentials.

  B they are not always seen as a reward for good work.

  C there is no element of surprise.

  D employers use them to make people work harder.

6 Diana thinks the secret to success at work is

  A making sure that your work is noticed.

  B getting into a position of authority.

  C benefitting others through your work.

  D doing work that is creative.

EXAM TIP

The interviewer's questions will help you to follow the discussion so you know which question you should be listening for.

5 Answer the questions. Then tell a partner about your answers.

1 What might make you stay in a dead-end job?

2 Do you find it difficult to keep your nose to the grindstone?

3 Have you ever worked for a real slave driver?

4 If you are up to your ears in work, what do you generally do about it?

5 Would a carrot and stick approach make you work harder?

6 Do you think taking an unpaid internship is a good way of getting a foot in the door?

6 Work in pairs. Turn to page 165 and do the activity.

Speaking

1 **Work in pairs and discuss which three things would most affect your levels of job satisfaction.**

- working long hours
- a long commute
- being in control of your own destiny
- lack of job security
- having to move away from home to get a job
- feeling that you are making a contribution

Hypothetical meaning

▶ **GRAMMAR** REFERENCE p.175

2 **Choose the correct alternative in each sentence.**

1 I wish my boss *wouldn't/couldn't* keep criticising me.

2 I wish I *could stop/stopped* sleeping through my alarm!

3 If only I *could/would* find a better work-life balance.

4 I'd rather he *doesn't/didn't* always make the decisions.

5 I wish I *had chosen/chose* to study something scientific or technical.

6 If only they *would give/give* me a chance to show them what I can do.

7 It's high time the government *do/did* ~~do~~ something to prevent further job losses.

8 *Would/Had* you rather we finished the report next week?

3 **Complete the sentences about hypothetical meaning with the terms in the box.**

---
past simple (x2)   past perfect   *if only*
rather   *would* + infinitive   *could* + infinitive
---

1 We use *wish* + ... to express a wish that is not true in the present. We also use it to express something that might come true in the future.

2 We use *wish* + ... to talk about other people's irritating habits. This form is only rarely used with *I* or *we*.

3 We use ..*if only*.. with the same verb forms as *wish* but to express stronger feelings.

4 We use *wish* + ..*past perfect*.. to refer to things we are sorry about in the past or to express regret.

5 We use *wish* + ..*could + infinitive*.. to talk about an ability we would like to have.

6 We use *it's (high/about) time* + ..*past simple*.. to talk about the present or the future. We mean that the action should have been done before.

7 We use *would* ..*rather*.. + past simple to talk about our preferences for the present or the future.

4 **Complete the second sentence so that it has a similar meaning to the first sentence, using the word given. Do not change the word given. You must use between three and six words, including the word given.**

1 I regret having quit my job.
WISH
I ..*wish I had not*.. quit my job.

2 It really gets on my nerves when my colleague borrows my stapler.
STOP
I wish my colleague ..*would stop* ~~~~ *borrowing*.. my stapler.

3 I don't want to hear every single thing that happened in the meeting.
YOU
I'd rather ..*you wouldn't tell*.. me every single thing that happened in the meeting.

4 Things would be so much better if people learnt to be a bit kinder.
ONLY
If ..*only*.. *people could* ~~would~~ *learn* to be a bit kinder, things would be so much better.

5 I have to spend so long answering emails and I hate it!
WISH
I ..*wish I didn't have*.. to spend so long answering emails.

6 I should have written long before this and told you about my new job.
HIGH
It's ..*high time I wrote to you*.. and told you about my new job.

5 **Complete the sentences so they are true for you. Then tell a partner your answers and answer any questions they may have.**

1 I know my friend wishes that ..*I were less stupid*..

2 If I had the choice, I'd rather that my life ..*were easier*..

3 I really wish I wasn't ..*so clumsy*..

4 It's high time people in my country ..*start taking*..

5 I sometimes wish I hadn't ..*left my country* ~~responsibility~~..

6 I wish I could ..*speak fluent english for the environment*..

Multiple matching (Part 8)

▶ **EXAM** FOCUS p.201

1 Work in pairs and discuss the questions.

1 How much does an average person in your country need to earn in order to live comfortably? *depends where he lives – living situations*

2 If someone has more money than that, what do you think they should do with it? *– donate – help others*

2 You are going to read an article about the relationship between money and happiness. Read the headings and the article quickly. In which section does the writer talk about

1 students and the relationship between money and happiness? *E*

2 a clever new way of finding out exactly how money contributes to happiness? *D*

3 why money sometimes fails to make people happy? *A*

4 two different categories of spending money and their impact on happiness? *B*

5 how a change in financial circumstances affected people's happiness? *C*

3 Look at question 1 in the exam task. The correct answer is *D*. Find words or phrases in section D that correspond to the underlined words in question 1.

In which section of the article does the writer

describe a study in which <u>subjects</u> were <u>given a strict time limit</u>? **1** *D*

<u>praise the researchers</u> for something they did? **2** *E*

describe precisely how the <u>researchers chose the subjects</u> of one of their studies? **3** *B*

give <u>details</u> about the way the subjects were <u>divided into groups</u>? **4** *D*

regret a missed opportunity in the research? **5** *B*

state what Dunn, Aknin and Norton originally wanted to establish? **6** *A*

report results of a study of people from the same social group? **7** *E*

describe a study where subjects received money from people other than the researchers? **8** *C*

point out the negative consequences of spending patterns for spenders and for others? **9** *A*

state that more should be done to help people learn to use their money wisely? **10** *E*

4 Read the article again. For questions 2–10, choose from the sections (A–E). The sections may be chosen more than once.

> **EXAM TIP**
>
> If a question uses the verb *state*, you should look for a sentence in the text that says the same thing in different words.

Vocabulary

working out meaning from context

5 Find words and phrases in the article that match meanings 1–8.

1 have just enough money to buy the things you need (Section A) *make ends meet*

2 interesting but strange and surprising (Section A)

3 carelessly waste (Section A)

4 without any definite plan (Section B)

5 think of an idea (Section C) *come*

6 easy to be certain about (Section C)

7 in two ways (Section E)

8 demand (Section E) *call for*

6 Use forms of the words and phrases in Activity 5 to complete these sentences.

1 A lot of travel agencies in town have closed because there isn't as much .....*demand*..... for them as there used to be.

2 I was rather .... by what you said the other day about your ancestors. Were they all from Ireland?

3 The difference between being happy and contented is not always .....*clear cut*.....

4 He inherited a lot of money from his great aunt but he .....*squandered*..... it all on cars and holidays in the Caribbean.

5 As far as the police could tell, the burglars were not targeting particular houses or flats but just choosing them .... *randomly*

6 I've been trying to think of a really original present for Greta but I haven't managed to .....*come up with*..... anything yet.

7 A lot of my friends have ended up having to take two or even three jobs to be able to .....*afford*..... his basics needs *make ends meet*

8 I understand what you're saying, but I disagree with you .... Firstly, I don't think she meant what she said and secondly, I know it isn't true.

7 Work in pairs and discuss the questions.

1 Which of the studies in the article do you find the most convincing? Why?

2 If someone gave you $20, what would you spend it on?

3 Describe the happiest person you know.

The price of happiness

A When does money buy happiness?

Can money buy happiness? Yes, but only to a very limited extent unless you learn how to put it to good use. A large body of research shows that if your income meets your basic needs, this will make you relatively happy. Curiously, though, if you have more than you need to to make ends meet, you won't necessarily be any happier, even if you have a lot more than is necessary.

One of the most intriguing explanations for this paradox is that people often squander their wealth on the very things that are least likely to make them feel good, namely, consumer goods. Furthermore, the more they indulge in consumer goods, the more likely they are to obsess about money and the less inclined they will be to use that money to help others. And it is doing just that – using money to help others – that three Canadian researchers, Elizabeth Dunn, Lara Aknin and Michael Norton set out to prove was the key to happiness.

B Personal versus social spending

The researchers started out by randomly selecting a group of just over 600 people from the local telephone directory. They asked them four questions: *How much do you earn? How happy are you? How much of your income is devoted to personal spending on bills and expenses or gifts for yourself? And how much goes on 'social spending', that is, gifts for others and donations to charity?* They then looked at the relationship between income, happiness and the two types of spending. Unfortunately, the researchers couldn't claim that it was the type of spending that made people happy or not, though their study did show that spending seems to have more to do with happiness than income alone.

C The effects of bonuses and spending

But Dunn, Aknin and Norton needed to come up with another kind of test which would show a change in happiness levels over time. To do this, they chose sixteen people and asked them how happy they were before and after receiving a bonus at work. The bonuses varied in amount and, once again, after some time had passed, the researchers asked their informants how they had spent the money. Thanks to the care the researchers took, this time the relationship between social spending and happiness was much more clear-cut, so much so, in fact, that they could state definitively that the way people spent the bonus played more of a role in their happiness than the size of the bonus itself. But there was still work to be done.

D A novel experiment that ties it all together

Once the research group had both the results of a large survey and a study of how levels of happiness changed, they went on to design a novel experiment. This time they chose forty-six people whom they asked to rate their happiness first thing in the morning. Each of them was then given either $5 or $20 and told they had to spend it by five in the afternoon of the same day. Half the people were told to spend the money on themselves and the other half were told they should buy a gift for someone else or donate the money to a charity. The participants were called after 5 p.m. that day and asked to rate their happiness again. This time around, the statistics proved Dunn, Aknin and Norton's hypothesis even more clearly. It didn't matter how much the participants had been given; if they had spent it on someone else, they tended to feel happier.

E A role for education

Even though it is so easy to observe the positive effects of social spending, most people just don't know they are there. The researchers asked over 100 university students which of the four conditions from the final experiment would make them happiest. Most were wrong on two counts. They believed they would be happiest with $20 and happiest spending it on themselves. There is clearly a call for teaching people the facts of money and happiness. Dunn, Aknin and Norton's research would make an excellent starting point.

Reading

1 Read an extract from a book review. What is the reviewer's overall impression of the book?

52 **HEALTHY YOU**

Naturally High

A friend had been telling me to read Jean Rossner's *Naturally High* but it took me ages to actually get round to doing **(1)** it and **(2)** ↑ even longer to try to put some of the book's excellent advice into practice.

Despite my inherent cynicism, I found *Naturally High* extraordinarily helpful in many ways – so many **(3)** ↑ , in fact, that I'm emulating my friend and **(4)** ↑ recommending **(5)** it to almost everyone I meet. All the usual suggestions are there; you know the **(6)** ones I mean: meditation, eating foods that boost the feel-good hormone serotonin and training for the marathon to get those endorphins pumping.

But if you're not much of an athlete, you might prefer to just get your taste buds used to really hot chillies. Rossner explains that we get a similar endorphin boost after the agony of eating **(7)** them fades. **(8)** ↑ Misgivings about eating chillies? Try chocolate instead. It will do the endorphin trick too and **(9)** ↑ painlessly into the bargain.

For those **(10)** ↑ who live in colder parts of the world, Rossner explains how to banish. 'Seasonal affective disorder' or SAD. Giving yourself a blast with a special sunlamp first thing on those dark winter mornings apparently turns SAD into happy. Even hardened misanthropes need the occasional natural high.

If you're one of **(11)** them, then why not try curling up on the sofa with a pet dog or cat? Rossner tells us that pet patting reduces stress and **(12)** ↑ will make both pet and person purr with contentment. Well, maybe **(13)** not if it's a dog but **(14)** they keep you warm too!

2 Would you be interested in reading this book? Why/Why not?

Substitution and ellipsis

▶ **GRAMMAR** REFERENCE p.180

3 Look at the underlined words and phrases in the review. What do they refer to?

4 Look at the review again. Where you see the symbol ↑, decide which word or words have been left out by the writer.

LANGUAGE TIP

Ellipsis is used a lot in informal spoken English. For example, we often omit the auxiliary verb and even the subject pronoun in questions about future plans and our responses.

A: *(Are you) Going on holiday this year?*
B: *(I'm) Not sure – (it) depends how much money I save.*

5 Work in pairs. Read the sentence aloud and discuss how to replace the underlined words.

My friend Susan wanted me to buy <u>my friend Susan</u> a book for <u>my friend Susan's</u> birthday but I couldn't find the <u>book</u> that <u>my friend Susan</u> wanted in our local bookshop, so I got <u>my friend Susan</u> another <u>book</u> that I found <u>in our local bookshop</u> instead of the <u>book</u> <u>my friend Susan</u> had asked for.

6 Complete the sentences with the words in the box.

do	either	it	not	one	so
that	there				

1 **A** Are you and Janna going to come to that meditation course with us?
   B I'm not sure. We might ...... *not/do*

2 **A** We'll probably have something quick to eat in that new café on the corner.
   B Great! I'll meet you ...... *there* ....

3 **A** Will someone meet you at the airport in Zurich?
   B I hope ...... *so* .... I've never been there before.

4 I'm not sure whether to get a black jacket or a red ...... *one* ....

5 I finally read the book last month. ...... *It* ...... was far better than I had expected.

6 She wanted to know whether we were coming to the party or ...... *not* ....

7 Simon and Clare say they can't manage next weekend and I can't ...... *either* ....

8 He won quite a big prize in the lottery. ...... *That* ...... meant he could finally give up work and write a novel.

Prefix *mis-* and false opposites

1 What does the prefix *mis-* mean? Complete the sentences with the correct form of the word in brackets. Use the prefix *mis-*.

1 I think there must have been some kind of misunderstanding (*understand*). That's not what I meant.

2 Some of their decisions have been misguided (*guide*), to say the least.

3 There are some important misconception (*concept*) about what counts as a natural high.

4 Some of the evidence about the effects of herbs is particularly .... (*lead*).

5 I had serious misgivings (*give*) about going to the meditation course but I really enjoyed it in the end.

6 The predictions were based on a serious misinterpretation (*interpret*) of the results of the survey.

7 My only other criticism of the book is that there is at least one misprint (*print*) in every chapter.

8 Some people are very mistrustful (*trust*) of conventional medicine but are happy to try the strangest natural remedies.

LANGUAGE TIP

Not all negative prefixes added to words make them the opposite of a base word. In some cases they mean something quite different, e.g. *disease*. In others, no base form exists, e.g. *misanthrope*.

2 Work in pairs. Look at the underlined words in the sentences and discuss their meaning.

1 He's quite <u>unassuming</u> and never seems to want any credit for all the wonderful work he does. F

2 I <u>inadvertently</u> picked up someone else's suitcase in baggage reclaim and I don't have any of my own clothes. A

3 I've never really liked watermelon juice – it's rather <u>insipid</u> if you ask me. B

4 He was such a <u>nondescript</u> little man that no one would ever have imagined him capable of painting surrealist masterpieces. E

5 'Does Joe have a girlfriend?' she asked, trying to look as <u>nonchalant</u> as she could. C

6 A group of <u>disgruntled</u> students had occupied the main administration block. D

3 Match the underlined words in Activity 2 with meanings A–F.

A without realising what you are doing

B without much taste

C behaving calmly and not seeming interested in anything or worried about anything

D annoyed or disappointed, especially because things have not happened in the way that you wanted

E very ordinary and not interesting or unusual

F showing no desire to be noticed or given special treatment

4 Answer the questions. Then tell a partner about your answers.

1 Have you ever felt disgruntled about conditions at your school or college or in your workplace?

2 What would you do if you inadvertently took something that belonged to someone else?

3 Are there any foods or drinks that you find insipid?

4 Can you think of any famous people who are actually rather nondescript?

5 Have you ever tried to appear nonchalant even though you were actually very curious about something?

6 Do you know anyone that you would describe as unassuming?

7 Have you ever misunderstood something someone said to you? What happened?

8 Would you agree that there is a lot of misleading information about health care on the internet? Can you think of any specific examples?

Vocabulary

sentence adverbs

1 **Work in pairs and discuss the questions.**

1 Do you normally read film reviews before you see a film? Do you ever read them afterwards?

2 Have you ever seen a film that the critics hated but you really loved or vice versa?

3 What information do you look for in a film review?

2 **Cross out the adverb that does *not* make sense in each review extract.**

1 *Sadly/Hopefully/Ironically*, this was to be the last time the two friends would meet.

2 *Understandably/Oddly enough/Surprisingly*, in the foreword, the authors are praised for their extensive referencing but there were only a couple of mentions of other people's work.

3 *Oddly enough/Curiously/Sadly*, the lead, Tyler Swan, is from the south of the United States, though I for one could not detect any trace of an accent.

4 *Thankfully/Happily/Naturally*, they were able to replace him with the absolutely stunning new talent, Kieran O'Halloran.

5 *Hopefully/Thankfully/Ironically*, the next time she directs, she will not have to deal with the bunch of miscast has-beens she was stuck with in this case.

6 *Unfortunately/Thankfully/Sadly*, the script writer has not been able to reflect the detailed information about the invasion of Singapore we find in the novel.

7 *Thankfully/Understandably/Happily*, the disastrous performance finally came to an end and we were all able to head for nearby restaurants.

8 *Understandably/Naturally/Oddly enough*, a director of his calibre wanted to work with a much more experienced cast.

Review (Part 2)

covering key features

▶ **WRITING** REFERENCE p.194

3 **Match extracts 1–8 in Activity 2 with key features of reviews A–D.**

A information about the writer, actors, director, etc.

B comments on the plot or contents

C critical comment on what the reviewer liked or disliked

D final evaluation

4 **Work in pairs. Look at the exam task and discuss which two films you would review.**

> You see this announcement in an international magazine called *Cinefilia*.
>
> ## The most uplifting and the biggest downer
>
> It's sometimes hard to choose a film that fits your mood purely on the basis of the poster or the description on the cover of the DVD. That's why we want to publish reviews of the most uplifting and the most depressing films our readers have seen, so that others know what to watch and what to avoid.
>
> Send in a review which describes the most uplifting film you've ever seen and the one you found the biggest downer. Make sure you give reasons for your choices.
>
> Write your **review** in **220–260** words in an appropriate style.

EXAM TIP

When you plan your review, think about what you are trying to achieve. You need to inform your readers so they can decide whether to see the film, read the book, etc. Don't tell them the whole plot.

5 **Make notes about each of the films you chose using the features in Activity 3.**

6 **Write a draft of your review. Use sentence adverbs, substitution and ellipsis.**

7 **Show your draft to a partner to see what they like most about your reviews. Suggest any improvements, particularly to sentences where it would be better to use sentence adverbs, substitution and ellipsis.**

1 Complete the sentences with the correct form of the verb in brackets.

1 I wish the papers _stopped_ (stop) reporting nothing but bad news. It's really depressing me.

2 It's high time you _started_ (start) taking more responsibility for your own well-being.

3 If only I _had realised_ (realise) the job was going to be so difficult! I would never have accepted it – I'd have kept my old job.

4 I love it here but I sometimes wish it _wouldn't rain_ (not rain) so much.

5 If only I _could get_ (get) out of the habit of going to bed so late. I'm always so tired in the mornings.

6 I'd rather we _didn't go_ (not go) out tonight. Let's stay in and watch a movie.

2 Choose the correct option to complete the sentences.

1 He was a genius in many ways but somewhat ___C___ when it came to his very poor choice of friends.

  A misinterpreted   C misguided
  B misunderstood   D mistrusted

2 Much as I liked the first candidate, I do have some ___A___ about offering her the job.

  A misgivings   C misinterpretations
  B misunderstandings   D misspellings

3 They live in a rather ___A___ little grey house on the outskirts of town.

  A unassuming   C insipid
  B nondescript   D nonchalant

4 Some of the participants' names had been ___A___ in the conference programme.

  A misspelt   C misled
  B misunderstood   D misinterpreted

5 The student representatives were more than a little ___B___ about the school director's refusal to see them.

  A disturbed   C disillusioned
  B disgruntled   D disinclined

6 The idea that bread is fattening is a common ___A___ that many people have.

  A misconception   C misprint
  B misinterpretation   D misgiving

3 Read the article below and think of the word which best fits each gap. Use only one word for each gap. There is an example at the beginning (0).

Happiness

NEWS   REVIEWS   FEATURES

Getting the measure of the happiest man on earth

Matthieu Ricard, 'the happiest man on earth', abandoned a successful scientific career **(0)** _to_ become a Buddhist monk. Since **(1)** _then_ , this unassuming man has taken a host of stunning photographs of the Himalayas, acted **(2)** _as_ the Dalai Lama's interpreter and meditated for many thousands of hours.

According to Ricard, there are a number of misconceptions about meditation, the most common **(3)** _one_ being the idea that it's all about making the mind go blank. Instead, he explains, what we should be doing is learning to let our thoughts pass without holding on to **(4)** _them_ . If Ricard himself is anything to go by, **(5)** _this_ is an approach which produces some fairly extraordinary results. When scientists recently measured the activity of the French monk's brain, they found that the parts known to generate positive emotions were far **(6)** _more_ active and highly developed in Ricard than they were in others, so much **(7)** _so_ that the scientists thought their equipment might be faulty. **(8)** _It_ wasn't. When it comes to measuring happiness, Matthieu Ricard is simply right off the scale.

4 Read the questions and choose the option that is not possible in each response.

1 Do you think Tina will come to the party?

  A She might.   B She might do.   C She might do it.

2 Are you and Max going to have a holiday this year?

  A We hope.   B We hope we are.   C We hope so.

3 Would your daughter like a drink?

  A No, thank you. She's just had it.
  B No, thank you. She's just had one.
  C No, thank you. She doesn't want one.

4 Were you thinking of coming into the office tomorrow?

  A No, but I can.   B No, but I can do.   C No, but I can be.

5 Which of your brothers is it who works as a scriptwriter?

  A The eldest.   B The eldest one is.   C The eldest one.

6 How many times have you been to Formentera?

  A Three.   B Three times.   C They are three.

Multiple-choice cloze (Part 1)

5 For questions 1–8, read the text below and decide which answer (A, B, C or D) best fits each gap. There is an example at the beginning (0).

Be a better listener

Listening is the most important of all skills for successful conversations at work, college or in social **(0)** _A situations_. Generally, people are very **(1)** _B frail_ listeners. The reason for this is that when talking to a colleague or a friend, they are often already preparing their **(2)** _response_ while the colleague or friend is still speaking. But effective listening requires that you listen as though there were nothing else in the world more fascinating to you than what that person is saying.

Even in the **(3)** _middle_ of an extremely noisy party, the very best listeners seem to have **(4)** _achieved_ the gift of making the person who is speaking feel as if he or she were the only person in the room. They do this by paying **(5)** _strong_ attention and asking lots of questions.

One very useful technique to **(6)** _put make_ the conversation going is to ask, 'What do you mean, exactly?' It's impossible for the other person not to **(7)** _attach_ more detail. You can then follow **(8)** _____ with other open-ended questions and keep the conversation rolling along.

0	**A** situations	**B** locations	**C** places	**D** settings
1	**A** faint	**B** poor	**C** frail	**D** hopeless
2	**A** speech	**B** response	**C** reaction	**D** expression
3	**A** heart	**B** depth	**C** middle	**D** peak
4	**A** possessed	**B** achieved	**C** received	**D** acquired
5	**A** strong	**B** close	**C** hard	**D** deep
6	**A** give	**B** put	**C** get	**D** make
7	**A** provide	**B** participate	**C** contribute	**D** attach
8	**A** along	**B** in	**C** up	**D** after

Open cloze (Part 2)

6 For questions 1–8, read the text below and think of the word which best fits each gap. Use only one word for each gap. There is an example at the beginning (0).

Failure leads to success

Success takes time, patience and commitment. **(0)** _In_ the digital age of 'overnight' success stories, this hard graft is easily overlooked. **(1)** _More_ often than not, success is the result of months and years of consecutive all-nighters, involving trial and error, setback after setback. There is often nothing quite **(2)** _like_ failure to make people strive harder for success.

A worrying trend in some schools is the pretence that there are **(3)** _come no_ winners or losers in school sports. It may be hard for children to accept failure but, equally, it's unfair not to encourage and reward talent. This applies **(4)** _to_ all subjects, including sport. Removing the competitive spirit from schools crushes the incentive to improve and does not prepare young people **(5)** _to fea_ the trials ahead. In school, let **(6)** _us__?_ reward those high achievers but at the same time encourage those that **(7)** _had_ failed to do better. **(8)** _what_ we mustn't forget is that the keen sting of failure can spur on greatness.

Word formation (Part 3)

7 For questions 1–8, read the text below. Use the word given in capitals at the end of some of the lines to form a word that fits in the gap in the same line. There is an example at the beginning (0).

Message in a bottle

News that a bottle **(0)** ....*containing*.... a message sent by two twelve-year-old French-Canadian girls has been found on a beach in Ireland, eight years after it had first set sail from Canada, has been met with **(1)** ..amazed..~~ment~~. The story has captured the **(2)** ..Imagination.. of people all over the world.

CONTAIN

AMAZE

IMAGINE

The girls threw the bottle into the St Lawrence River in Quebec while on holiday. But the chances of it being picked up by ten-year-old Oisin Millea eight years later on the other side of the world were **(3)** ..unlikely.. The message, which was placed in a two-litre Sprite bottle, was written in French and is still **(4)** ..expected..~~unexpectedly~~ legible.

LIKE

EXPECT

Oisin made the **(5)** ..discovering..~~my~~ while walking on the beach near his home in County Waterford. His mother said Oisin was an **(6)** ..enthusiastic.. treasure-hunter but this was by far the most incredible find he'd yet made. She added that one of the most **(7)** ..remarkable.. things about this story was the amount of media attention it has attracted from news **(8)** ..agencies.. all over the world.

DISCOVER

ENTHUSIASM

REMARK

AGENT

Key word transformations (Part 4)

8 For questions 1–6, complete the second sentence so that it has a similar meaning to the first sentence, using the word given. Do not change the word given. You must use between three and six words, including the word given.

1 I sat down and immediately my mobile started ringing.

SOONER

No ..Sooner i took a seat.. my mobile started ringing.

2 Sue understood the theory described in the lecture really well.

GOOD

Sue ..is good in understanding.. the theory described in the lecture.

3 I am embarrassed whenever a friend pays me a compliment.

FIND

I ..find it embarrassing.. to receive compliments from friends.

4 I was ill, so I couldn't go to the festival.

PREVENTED

Illness ..prevented me to go.. to the festival.

5 The villagers were profoundly suspicious of strangers.

HAD

The villagers ..had.. ..profoundly suspicious.. of strangers.

6 Many people resent having to pay so much tax.

WISH

Many people .... to pay so much tax.

Living with the past

Word formation (Part 3)

▶ **EXAM** FOCUS p.198

1 **Work in pairs and discuss the questions.**

1 Why do you think many people are so fascinated by dinosaurs?
2 What is the appeal of searching for ancient remains such as coins or fossils?

2 **Work in pairs. Read the article quickly and see how many facts about the mammoth you can remember.**

A mammoth find

	SPOTLIGHT

A mammoth, named Jenya after the eleven-year-old boy who made the **(0)** *astonishing* find, is thought to be the most **(1)** _perfectly_ preserved animal of its kind. The last great mammoth was unearthed in 1901, so this finding has caused great excitement among zoologists. Jenya's **(2)** _remains_ were excavated from the Siberian permafrost and taken to St Petersburg for **(3)** _analysis_ Tests show that Jenya was fifteen years old, two metres tall and weighed 500 kilograms, which is **(4)** _considerably_ smaller than other mammoth finds. What probably killed Jenya was not his size but a missing left tusk that made him **(5)** _unfit_ for fights with other mammoths or human **(6)** _hunters_ who were settling the Siberian marshes and swamps 20,000–30,000 years ago. So Jenya's death might have been the result of a **(7)** _confrontation_ with an Ice Age man. Zoologists now believe that mammoths were driven to **(8)** _extinction_ by humans as well as by the changing climate.

ASTONISH
PERFECT
REMAIN
ANALYSE
CONSIDER
FIT
HUNT
CONFRONT
EXTINCT

EXAM TIP

Get into the habit of keeping an organised record of your vocabulary learning. Remember not just to record the meaning but also information about word formation (e.g. noun/adjective forms).

3 **Which of the words in capitals in Activity 2**

1 form a noun ending in the suffix -*tion*?
2 form a word with the prefix *un*-?
3 have two noun forms with different meanings?

4 **Read the article again. For questions 1–8, use the word given in capitals at the end of some of the lines to form a word that fits in the gap in the same line.**

5 **Should objects of historical significance in foreign museums be returned to their country of origin? Why/Why not?**

Multiple choice (Part 1)

▶ **EXAM** FOCUS p.202

6 ▶ **20** **You will hear three different extracts. For questions 1–6, choose the answer (A, B or C) which fits best according to what you hear. There are two questions for each extract.**

Extract 1

You hear two friends discussing an excavation project in their town.

1   What has the woman found surprising?

   A that there is such a large team of archaeologists

   B that residents were previously unaware of the site

   C that the excavation hadn't taken place sooner

2   In what way do the speakers agree their attitude to the town has changed?

   A They feel more connected to the past as a result.

   B They would like to find out more about the town's history.

   C They think it gives the town a special character.

Extract 2

You hear two friends discussing a visit to a dinosaur exhibition at a natural history museum.

3   The man compares the exhibition unfavourably with a computer game

   A to emphasise its poor value for money.

   B to show its lack of appeal for children.

   C to highlight its limited educational value.

4   What do they agree is the problem with the exhibits?

   A They covered only a limited period.

   B The model dinosaurs were unconvincing.

   C The information wasn't presented clearly.

Extract 3

You hear two family members discussing staying at an old holiday house as children.

5   How did the woman feel about staying at the house?

   A curious about previous inhabitants

   B frustrated by the lack of modern comfort

   C scared by stories she heard about the house

6   The speakers express the hope that the house will

   A be available for holidays.

   B retain its character.

   C become a museum.

7   **Which of the adjectives in the box can be used with the prefix *in*-? Which can be used with *un*-?**

accurate	believable	changed	convincing	covered	discovered
favourable	informative	modernised	significant		

Speaking

1 **Work in pairs and discuss which of the quotes about history you agree with.**

1 'The distinction between the past, present and future is only a stubbornly persistent illusion.' *Albert Einstein*

2 'We learn from history that we never learn anything from history.' *GWF Hegel*

3 'Happy people have no history.' *Leo Tolstoy*

Comparing

▶ **GRAMMAR** REFERENCE p.172

2 **Look at the sentences and decide if there is any difference in meaning between the phrases in italics. Tick the statements which are true for you and compare your ideas with a partner.**

1 I'm *far more/a great deal more* interested in the past than I used to be.

2 I'm *just as/nowhere near as* likely to visit a museum as a shopping mall when I'm on holiday.

3 I think most kids learn *easily/quite* as much about the past from computer games.

4 I find it's *not as much fun/much less fun* going to a museum by yourself.

LANGUAGE TIP

Like is used with nouns or gerunds to make comparisons.
*He's tall **like** his father.*
*Watching cricket is **like** watching paint dry.*
As is only used in comparisons in the phrases *as … as* and *not so/as … as.*

---

3 **Complete the sentences with one word. In some sentences more than one answer may be possible.**

1 Museums are .... more interactive than they used to be.

2 Museums used to be .... less interesting than they are now.

3 .... of the most frequently visited museums in the world is the Louvre in Paris.

4 Most people would rather listen to a guide .... read a guidebook.

5 When I was younger, museums were nothing like as crowded .... they are now.

6 .... far the best museum I've ever visited is the Air and Space Museum in Washington.

---

4 **Read the article. Does the writer approve of museums as places for entertainment?**

TheReporter

Blog feed

HOME NEWS WORLD SPORT FINANCE **COMMENT** BLOGS C

Museums as entertainment

The past three decades have seen a huge museum building boom all over the world. Museums are popular as **(1)** *ever/never* before. Visitors are now **(2)** *far more/ so much* willing to stand in queues for hours in order to have **(3)** *the briefest/the briefer* of encounters with an old master painting. Some museums have been obliged to stay open round the clock to meet the demand. **(4)** *More than ever/By far*, museum attendance is seen as a routine part of a modern lifestyle. Overall, the number of people visiting museums gets **(5)** *higher and higher/just as high* each year. But are museums in danger of becoming just another leisure activity ending in yet another consumer opportunity at the museum shop? Does **(6)** *a great deal/considerably* wider accessibility inevitably mean a decline in the quest for serious reflection and deeper understanding?

5 **Read the article again and choose the correct alternatives.**

6 **Work in pairs and discuss the question.**

If you were asked to choose something that represented your generation for a museum, what would it be?

1 Think of an object and say what it would tell future generations about life today.

2 Present your museum object to the class.

7 **Work in pairs. Turn to page 163 and do the activity.**

Long turn (Part 2)
comparing

▶ **EXAM** FOCUS p.204

1 ▶ 21 Look at the pictures and listen to the examiner. What three things do you have to do?

2 ▶ 22 Listen to Alessandra doing the task. Which of the pictures does she compare?

3 Tick the information about the pictures that Alessandra includes.

- weather
- nationality
- location
- clothes
- possible reasons for the visit
- historical significance of the place
- what might happen next
- how the people are feeling

4 Work in pairs and discuss Alessandra's answer. Is there anything you both agree/disagree with her about?

5 Listen again. Which of the words/expressions for comparing and contrasting do you hear?

On the other hand, …   Having said that, …
Nevertheless, …   Similarly, …   Whilst …
Whereas …   Although …   However, …
One significant difference is …
What both photos have in common is …

6 Compare the picture that Alessandra didn't discuss with one of the other pictures. Use some of the expressions in Activity 5.

7 Work in pairs. Turn to page 153 and do Task 1. Then turn to page 159 and do Task 2. Check whether your partner uses a good range of expressions for comparing and contrasting.

EXAM TIP

To give yourself the best opportunity to show what you can do, don't worry about the timing – just keep speaking until the examiner says *thank you*.

Multiple choice (Part 5)

▶ **EXAM** FOCUS p.199

1 **Work in pairs and discuss questions.**

1 How much do you know about your ancestors?

2 Are you interested in finding out more about them? Why/Why not?

2 **You are going to read an article about a journalist called Lucy Kellaway and her investigation into her family history. For questions 1–6, choose the answer (A, B, C or D) which you think fits best according to the text.**

EXAM TIP

Underline the part of the text which gives the answer for each question and double-check that the option you choose both answers the question and matches what the text says.

1 Why did Kellaway accept the invitation by Ancestral Footsteps?

   A She felt it was time she caught up with a popular pastime.

   B She was curious to discover the appeal of ancestor research.

   C She felt it was a more attractive option than doing the research herself.

   D She was tempted by the idea of a luxury holiday mixed with research.

2 What overall point is Kellaway making about the TV programme in the second paragraph?

   A She thinks it teaches people nothing about their identities.

   B She admits to secretly enjoying it despite disapproving of it.

   C She thinks it is only providing good publicity for celebrities.

   D She is concerned that it only presents a sensational view of history.

3 Kellaway's family is uninterested in ancestor research because they believe

   A they would find the process of carrying out the research dull.

   B there was little of interest to discover about their own ancestors.

   C people are interested in ancestor research for the wrong reasons.

   D people should focus more on their own achievements.

4 What is Kellaway's attitude to the researchers in the national archives?

   A She admires their dedication.

   B She is envious of their absorption in their task.

   C She is impressed by the strength of their obsession.

   D She is amazed by the kind of information being discovered.

5 What was Kellaway's initial reaction to Amos's story?

   A disappointed that his story had a predictable end

   B upset by his misfortune

   C proud of his achievements

   D concerned for the welfare of his family

6 In the final paragraph Kellaway admits that she

   A feels embarrassed about her feelings for her ancestors.

   B has changed her mind about the attraction of ancestor research.

   C regrets knowing so little about her family history.

   D was surprised by her family's reaction to the story.

3 **Work in pairs. Has reading this article made you more or less interested in genealogy?**

Vocabulary

adjective/noun collocations

4 **Work out the meanings of the underlined compound adjectives in the article from the context. Compare answers with a partner.**

5 **Underline the nouns that collocate with the adjectives in italics.**

1 *a tailor-made*
   trip   house   course   suit   service

2 *consumer-driven*
   fashion   technology   money   design

3 *a high-minded*
   person   school   ambition   reason   principle

6 **Match the adjectives in the box with the nouns to make collocations. Some adjectives can be used with more than one noun.**

close	common	direct	distant
early	extended	immediate	nuclear

1 a/an .... relative   3 close .... family

2 a/an .... ancestor

7 **Use some of the collocations in Activity 6 to describe your family tree.**

Dead *interesting*

Lucy Kellaway investigates her family history.

Ancestral Footsteps, a travel company that organises exclusive <u>tailor-made</u> holidays to help people to investigate their family history, had invited me on a heritage tour of my roots. I'd accepted the invitation gladly, not because I had any particular interest in my forebears but to <u>understand the bizarre modern craze of ancestor worship.</u> Genealogy tourism, combining holidays with ancestor hunts, is on the rise. A recent study by the University of Illinois argued that the trend was the fastest-growing sector of the travel market and a response to our <u>consumer-driven</u> lifestyle – a search for connection and authenticity in an inauthentic world.

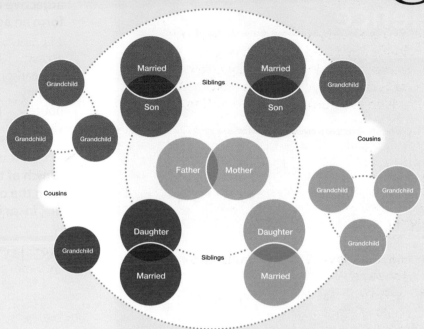

Maybe. But I think there's a more obvious and less <u>high-minded</u> cause at work, too: the runaway success of the BBC reality TV programme *Who Do You Think You Are?* The format, which has been copied in twelve countries, involves a famous person finding his or her roots and watching their emotional reaction as they discover that a distant relation was a villain or a hero. <u>The show is good celebrity TV,</u> with a nice bit of colourful social history thrown in, if you like that sort of thing. But <u>the name of the programme is a bit of a sham. Who we actually are is a matter of our own personality, luck, circumstances, education</u> and that of our parents.

Ancestor scepticism is in my blood. When I told my dad I was going on a genealogical holiday, he quoted something his father used to say to him: 'It's more important to be an ancestor than to have them.' My sister and I were brought up to dismiss people who were obsessed with family trees. <u>For a start, it's boring.</u> Any sentence that begins with 'my great-great-uncle' is never going to go anywhere interesting. <u>People should try to make something of themselves</u> rather than piggy-back on the fact that a distant and long-dead relative was a prince or a prisoner.

As I awaited the results of my own ancestor research, I decided to research other people doing theirs. In the crowded upstairs room at the National Archives at Kew in south-west London, every desk was occupied by someone staring at a screen in a sort of rapture. They were poring over microfiches with a focus more intense than any I've ever seen in any other library or anywhere else at all. I realised I'd got it all wrong. <u>For them, the fun isn't in the facts, it's in the hunting.</u> With obvious delight, the woman nearest me explained that she'd just discovered an ancestor who'd been convicted of stealing.

A few months later I travelled to Wareham in Dorset to meet my personal researcher, Jo Foster. Jo showed me a series of documents explaining how the Kellaways arrived in Australia: my great-grandfather's death certificate says that Alfred Charles Kellaway, son of Amos and Jane, was born in Dorset, England and died in Australia. But the 1861 census reveals that while Alfred and Jane Kellaway were living in Swanage, Dorset, of Amos there was no trace at all. I tried instantly to resist the modern urge to apply psychobabble to explain Amos's disappearance. Would I have been able to forgive him for abandoning his family?

But then I discovered that what actually happened was rather different. Ships' records recounted that my great-great-grandfather deserted ship in Sydney in 1857 to go in search of gold. He didn't find any. But he found New World riches of another sort. After six years in Australia, he had made enough money as a farmer for Jane and their six-year-old son Alfred to sail out to join him. Their story ended happily ever after. The <u>boy received an education and became a clergyman.</u> His son, my grandfather, became a doctor, discovered a treatment for snakebite and lost all interest in his roots.

My father and sister predictably swallowed the story hungrily, along with a big side order of humble pie. And although I still don't think of them as my family, I was more interested than I'd expected to be in the fate of Amos, Jane and Alfred and I'm only sorry I ignored them for so long. So who do I think I am now? The truth is that I'm not who I thought I was six months ago. I still <u>maintain that who I am does not include deserting sailors and failed gold diggers.</u> Time has washed them away. But it does include something less expected. <u>Who I am now is a born-again ancestor bore.</u>

Speaking

1 Read the article. Was the writer surprised by the 'genetic revelations'?

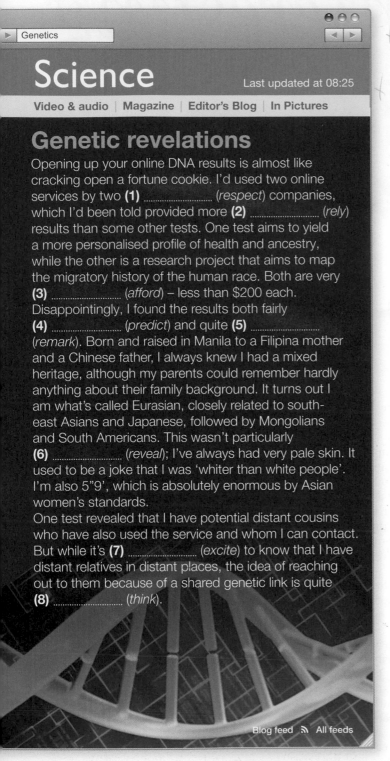

Genetics

Science
Last updated at 08:25

Video & audio | Magazine | Editor's Blog | In Pictures

Genetic revelations

Opening up your online DNA results is almost like cracking open a fortune cookie. I'd used two online services by two **(1)** .... (*respect*) companies, which I'd been told provided more **(2)** .... (*rely*) results than some other tests. One test aims to yield a more personalised profile of health and ancestry, while the other is a research project that aims to map the migratory history of the human race. Both are very **(3)** .... (*afford*) – less than $200 each. Disappointingly, I found the results both fairly **(4)** .... (*predict*) and quite **(5)** .... (*remark*). Born and raised in Manila to a Filipina mother and a Chinese father, I always knew I had a mixed heritage, although my parents could remember hardly anything about their family background. It turns out I am what's called Eurasian, closely related to south-east Asians and Japanese, followed by Mongolians and South Americans. This wasn't particularly **(6)** .... (*reveal*); I've always had very pale skin. It used to be a joke that I was 'whiter than white people'. I'm also 5"9', which is absolutely enormous by Asian women's standards.

One test revealed that I have potential distant cousins who have also used the service and whom I can contact. But while it's **(7)** .... (*excite*) to know that I have distant relatives in distant places, the idea of reaching out to them because of a shared genetic link is quite **(8)** .... (*think*).

Blog feed 🔊 All feeds

2 Work in pairs. Would you consider doing a DNA test to discover more about your ancestry? What do you think people might be hoping to prove from the results of DNA tests?

Prefixes and suffixes

3 Complete the article with the correct adjective form of the words in brackets. Two of the adjectives require negative prefixes.

4 Which of the nouns in the box form an adjective ending in the suffix *-able*? Which form an adjective ending in *-ible*?

access	belief	change	comfort
comparison	comprehension		excitement
identity	imagination		movement
notice	profit	resistance	reverse
variety	vision		

5 Which of the words in Activity 4 form a word with the opposite meaning with the prefix *un-*, *in-* or *ir-*? Can you think of more examples?

LANGUAGE TIP

Words beginning with *l-*, *m-* or *r-* take the prefixes *ir-*, *im-* or *il-* (not *in-* or *un-*).

irresponsible   **im**migration   **il**logical

Remember to double the initial consonant.

6 Which of the words in Activity 4 also have an adjective form ending in *-ive* or *-ing*?

7 Choose the correct alternative in each sentence.

1 Realising I have cousins in Mongolia is the weirdest feeling *imaginable/imaginative*.

2 This is an original and *imaginative/imaginable* idea.

3 The weather can be very *changing/changeable* at this time of year.

4 The quality of old black and white films is often *variable/varying*.

5 His grandfather's *exciting/excitable* moods were hard to deal with.

6 It's *comforting/comfortable* to be able to look at photographs of your childhood.

7 Consumers' *changing/changeable* attitudes are difficult to predict.

8 The film guide is selective – it's not intended to be *comprehensive/comprehensible*.

8 Work in pairs.

Student A: turn to page 162.
Student B: turn to page 169.

Modifying adverbs

▶ **GRAMMAR** REFERENCE p.170

1 **Look at the underlined examples of modifying adverbs and answer the questions.**

A I found the results both <u>fairly</u> predictable and <u>quite</u> unremarkable.

B I'm 5'9", which is <u>absolutely</u> enormous by Asian women's standards.

1 What is the purpose of the modifier? Does it make the adjective stronger or weaker?

2 Which of the adjectives is ungradable (an 'extreme' adjective that can't be made stronger or weaker)?

2 **Which of the adjectives in the box are ungradable?**

disappointed	exceptional	furious
impossible	perfect	terrified

3 **Which of the modifiers in the box can be used with the adjectives in Activity 2?**

bitterly	completely	entirely	extremely
practically	pretty	quite	really
seriously	somewhat	totally	

LANGUAGE TIP

When *quite* is used with ungradable adjectives, it means 'completely', not 'fairly'.

*It's **quite** impossible.*

4 **Read the article. What is 'infantile amnesia' and what did the researchers discover about it?**

5 **Read the article again and choose the correct alternatives.**

Speaking

6 **Answer the questions. Then compare your answers with a partner.**

1 What is your earliest childhood memory?

2 How old were you at the time?

3 How reliable do you think this memory is?

7 **Find out how many students' first memory is about**

1 a trip to the dentist.

2 a vacation.

3 a birthday party.

4 their first day at school.

ROUNDUP

First memories

By interviewing small children about the first events they remember, researchers were **(1)** *somewhat/totally* surprised to discover that the earliest memories of children change as they get older. They don't actually form solid memories which are carried throughout life until around the age of ten.

Ask most adults to describe their earliest memories and they can **(2)** *scarcely/slightly* recall any that occurred before they were school age. This phenomenon, known as infantile amnesia, has been recognised for decades. But the forgetting, it now seems, happens **(3)** *rather/perfectly* slowly throughout childhood. The researchers interviewed 140 children aged between four and eleven. The children were asked to think of their earliest three memories. Researchers then confirmed with parents that the events had actually happened or at least seemed **(4)** *highly/deeply* plausible. These interviews were repeated two years after their initial interviews.

They found that that the vast majority of the youngest children, whose ages ranged from four to seven when first interviewed, were **(5)** *virtually/seriously* unable to recall their earlier first memories, even when reminded of their previous answers by the interviewers. These memories were **(6)** *completely/extremely* gone. However, a significant number of children in the two oldest age groups could still provide the same first memories.

As for what kids remembered, the researchers were surprised that **(7)** *strongly/deeply* emotional events weren't mentioned very often. One child remembered waiting for a bus with her mother and noticing a flower growing up through a crack in the pavement. Another child recalled swallowing a tiny piece of yellow Lego while in the back seat of the car and being **(8)** *seriously/bitterly* worried that he was going to die but being too scared to tell his parents.

Essay (Part 1)

structuring an argument

▶ **WRITING** REFERENCE p.186

Work in pairs and decide on the three most important parts of your country's cultural heritage. Think about buildings, archaeological sites, food, music, celebrations and books.

2 **Look at the exam task and underline the key words.**

> Your class has attended a lecture on the action governments can take to make sure cultural heritage is preserved for future generations. You have made the notes below.
>
> ---
> Priorities for governments aiming to preserve cultural heritage
> • increase funding for museums
> • protect old buildings
> • teach the importance of cultural heritage in schools
> ---
>
> Some opinions expressed in the discussion
> 'Cultural heritage isn't just about buildings – it's about a way of life.'
> 'It's the responsibility of the older generation to pass on a cultural heritage to the next generation.'
> 'Museums are the best places to keep shared memories of a community.'
>
> Write an essay for your tutor discussing **two** of the priorities in your notes. You should **explain which priority you think is more important**, **giving reasons** to support your opinion.
>
> You may, if you wish, make use of the opinions expressed in the discussion but you should use your own words as far as possible.
>
> Write your **essay** in **220–260** words in an appropriate style.

EXAM TIP

It's important to provide specific examples which support your arguments.

3 **Read the statements. Which ones do you agree with?**

1 I would argue that it's unreasonable to expect governments to give more money to museums when they've got more important things to spend people's taxes on. *P*

2 It's become clear in recent years that governments can no longer afford to provide generous grants to help people maintain their historically significant houses. *P*

3 Perhaps retired people could offer to go into schools to share their memories and pass their knowledge on to younger generations. *E*

4 I'm sure there are many voluntary organisations which would be prepared to work on conservation projects. *E*

5 An urgent priority is for the government to provide training for teachers on teaching children about the importance of their cultural heritage. *P*

6 For example, it may be that many people will choose not to speak to their children in the local dialect. *E*

4 **Decide whether the ideas in Activity 3 are main points (P) or supporting evidence (E).**

5 **Underline useful phrases in Activity 3 for giving main points and supporting evidence.**

6 **Choose which two priorities you will discuss in your essay. Plan your main points and supporting evidence.**

7 **Write your essay, including some of the phrases in Activity 3. Check for spelling and punctuation errors. Use the checklist on page 185 to help you.**

1 Choose the correct alternative in each sentence.

1 The talk was *so/far* much more informative than I'd expected.

2 Most people would *much/more* rather go online than read a book.

3 It was *nowhere/nothing like* as impressive as I had imagined.

4 English is a *great/considerable* deal easier than Chinese.

5 It's by *far/ much* the best film I've seen this year.

6 He's not interested in money *like/as* his father.

7 He's working harder than *ever/never* before.

8 Reality TV shows are getting *worst and worst/ worse and worse*.

9 People are *just as/more* likely to visit a museum as go shopping.

10 It's easily the *simpler/simplest* of the suggestions I've heard so far.

2 Choose the correct option to complete the sentences.

1 He was .... serious when he suggested buying the castle.

   A considerably   B deeply   C practically

2 I found the story .... believable.

   A totally   B considerably   C highly

3 It's .... incredible to think this building has been here for 800 years.

   A very   B absolutely   C virtually

4 Older people find it .... comforting to be able to talk about the past.

   A entirely   B totally   C extremely

5 The information is .... confusing – there are all sorts of contradictions.

   A rather   B perfectly   C practically

6 I'm not .... sure if the story is true.

   A extremely   B perfectly   C entirely

7 It's .... impossible to find anyone who remembers my great-grandfather.

   A extremely   B practically   C seriously

8 We found it .... unbelievable when we heard the good news.

   A quite   B practically   C seriously

9 She's been working so hard she's .... exhausted.

   A practically   B extremely   C completely

10 Luke's .... content to stay at home and look after the children.

   A perfectly   B seriously   C deeply

3 Complete the sentences with the correct form of the word in brackets.

1 Now is not the most .... (*favour*) climate for starting a new business.

2 He puts forward the most .... (*convince*) arguments I've ever heard – complete rubbish!

3 I think you have been .... (*inform*). All the tickets sold out months ago.

4 Peter should be a writer when he grows up – he's so .... (*imagine*).

5 Unfortunately, the fire caused .... (*reverse*) damage to the oldest part of the castle.

6 The only way to get to the site is on a footpath – it's .... (*access*) by road.

7 The news about the job losses was met with total .... (*believe*).

8 The story was reported .... (*accuracy*) by the press, who got all the basic facts wrong.

9 There are some accents I find .... (*comprehension*), especially when people speak too fast.

10 I hate it when people ignore you at parties and treat you as if you were .... (*vision*).

4 Complete the sentences with the words in the box. There are some words you do not need to use.

ambition	course	design	person
principles	reason	school	service
suit	technology	trip	

1 If I could afford it, I would take a tailor-made safari ....

2 It's rare to meet a politician who is acting out of high-minded ....

3 The most innovative products are not usually the result of consumer-driven ....

4 Wanting to help put an end to hunger in the world is a very high-minded ....

5 It would be interesting to see if you make more progress doing a tailor-made ....

6 The most high-minded .... I know doesn't care what people think.

7 The best advertising companies provide a tailor-made .... for each client.

8 The campaign group had a high-minded .... for objecting to the proposal.

The hard sell

Collocations: sales and marketing

1 Work in pairs. Have you ever been persuaded to buy something by a clever salesperson? What was it?

2 Read the article. Why was Joe Girard's approach to sales so successful?

> ► Sales

A very likeable super-salesperson

Blog feed 🔊 All feeds

A man called Joe Girard still holds the record as 'the World's Greatest Salesperson', even though more than three decades have passed since he retired. Girard was the number one car and truck salesperson in the United States for twelve years running. Between 1963 and 1978 he sold a staggering total of 13,001 vehicles, all of them direct **(1)** .... sales to individual customers. In one year alone, he managed to sell 1,425 vehicles; that means he made four and a half sales every working day.

So how did he do it? Not with a highly sophisticated **(2)** .... strategy or advertising **(3)** .... as you might imagine. He simply believed wholeheartedly that he was selling the world's best **(4)** .... , namely, himself. Girard knew that customers buy from people they know, like and trust, so he focused most of his energy on establishing a **(5)** .... with potential customers and becoming likeable.

Of course, he used a variety of **(6)** .... techniques, one of which was to make sure people who had bought a car from him would never forget him. Once a month he sent them a letter. These arrived in plain envelopes, always a different size or colour so that they didn't look like junk **(7)** .... and get thrown away. All the letters said was 'I like you. Happy Fourth of July!' or whatever special day it happened to be. They were signed simply 'From Joe Girard.' Sending out 13,000 cards a month in the 1970s must have involved an enormous effort, but the payoffs came in repeat sales from **(8)** .... customers. ■

3 Complete the article with the words in the box.

campaign	loyal	mail	marketing	product	rapport
retail	sales				

4 Would you have bought a car from Joe Girard? Why/Why not?

5 How many collocations can you make with *sales*, *product*, *mail*, *business* and *customer*?

Review of conditionals

▶ GRAMMAR REFERENCE p.172

6 Read the article about sales techniques. Has anyone ever used these techniques on you?

⏺ ⏺ ⏺   ▶ Sales

OME NEWS WORLD SPORT FINANCE **COMMENT** TRAVEL LIFE FASHION

Blog feed 🔊 All feeds

Clever sales techniques that you need to be aware of

Suppose you have just agreed to buy something small like a smartphone on special offer. **(1)** If the salesperson is well-trained, he will immediately see an opening for 'the foot-in-the-door' technique. If you have already bought one inexpensive item, you are more likely to comply with a suggestion to buy something bigger and more expensive, like a tablet computer.

(2) Would you be able to resist a technique like this if you happened to be the victim of a savvy salesperson? A lot of people can't. But sales personnel have other tricks up their sleeves for those who can.

(3) If you hadn't actually agreed to buy anything, the salesperson would probably have opted for the 'door-in-the-face' technique instead. This involves trying to sell you something expensive, knowing you'll refuse. You say no and the salesperson then offers you something smaller and cheaper. We want to be liked and **(4)** if we turn down what seems to be a really good offer, we look unreasonable. ■

7 Look at the numbered sentences in the article in Activity 6. Are they examples of the zero, first, second or third conditional?

8 Read the article below. What is the writer's explanation for the recent success of online shopping?

Monday 18   **SEVEN**NEWS

Click 'til you drop

IN RECENT YEARS WE have seen many of our favourite chain stores close down. I often wonder what could have been done to stop this happening. One obvious cause was the rise of online shopping. **(1)** If it hadn't proved so attractive to customers, many retail stores would still be trading today. But what was the attraction? **(2)** I certainly wouldn't have developed my own particular passion for online shopping if it wasn't more fun, less stressful and a lot less tiring than in-store shopping. The only thing you can't do is try on the clothes but if you know your size, that's not a problem.

9 Look at the underlined mixed conditional sentences in the article in Activity 8. Which one describes

A an imagined/real past event (*if* + past perfect) and contrasts it with a present result (*would* + infinitive)?

B a present situation (*if* + past simple/past continuous) contrasted with an imagined or real past event (*would have* + past participle)?

LANGUAGE TIP

The most common type of mixed conditional is mixed third and second conditional.

If I **hadn't bought** that expensive jacket, I **would** still **have** some money left.

A third conditional sentence can often convey the same idea.

If I **hadn't bought** that expensive jacket, I **would** still **have had** some money left.

10 Complete the mixed conditional sentences. Then decide if it would be possible to express them using a normal third conditional sentence. Is there any change in meaning?

1 If they .... (*do*) some more market research, they .... (*understand*) their customers better.

2 I .... (*be*) a better salesperson today if I .... (*have*) the benefit of better training in sales techniques.

3 If she .... (*be*) a more skilled salesperson, she .... (*made*) enough sales to keep her job.

4 If I .... (*not open*) the door to that nice salesman, I .... (*not be*) the happy owner of a brand new Whirlymix today!

5 The customer .... (*get*) in touch with you by now if she .... (*be*) seriously considering your offer.

6 If it .... (*be*) possible to try clothes on virtually, people .... (*stop*) bothering to go out to shop years ago.

11 Complete the sentences so they are true for you. Then compare your answers with other students.

1 If I have a bit of free time this week, I ...

2 If I could start my own business, I ...

3 If I had the chance to live anywhere in the world for a year, I ...

4 If I had been born fifty years earlier, I would probably ...

5 If I were already able to speak another language completely fluently, I ...

Multiple choice (Part 3)

▶ **EXAM** FOCUS p.203

1 **Work in pairs and discuss the questions.**

1 Which of the senses is most likely to evoke memories for you: sight, sound, smell, taste or touch?

2 Which of the senses are more frequently used in marketing?

3 How are they used?

2 **You will hear an interview with Dr Margaret Patterson, a university lecturer, about using the senses in marketing. Look at the questions in Activity 3 and underline the key words.**

3 ▶ **23** **Listen to the interview. For questions 1–6, choose the answer (A, B, C or D) which fits best according to what you hear.**

EXAM TIP

Listen for words or phrases in the conversation that paraphrase the content of the key words in the questions and options.

1 What is Dr Patterson's attitude to the use of sophisticated scent marketing?

  A She is a little concerned about some instances of it.

  B She does not think people should be so anxious about it.

  C She regards it as a brilliant innovation in the world of marketing.

  D She is not terribly impressed by it.

2 According to Dr Patterson, people feel they have been tricked by scent marketing when

  A food smells are used to encourage them to spend more.

  B products on display have a different smell from what they expect.

  C they find out that the smell has no connection to the products on display.

  D the smell is so inviting they find themselves making unplanned purchases.

3 What does Dr Patterson say about the choice of smell in the toy shop?

  A It should have been more subtle.

  B It is known to put people in a good mood.

  C It is not possible to be certain why it was chosen.

  D It would only have worked in a city like London.

4 What is Dr Patterson's attitude to the milk board campaign?

  A She is not surprised it attracted complaints.

  B She shares people's dislike of the smell they used.

  C She thought it was an original concept.

  D She regards it as a skilful use of scent marketing.

5 What is Dr Patterson's reaction to the complaint by allergy sufferers?

  A She is unsure why they complained.

  B She sympathises with them on the grounds that scent marketing poses a health risk.

  C She thinks they should be warned about places where scent marketing is used.

  D She considers more research is necessary to identify scents which cause problems.

6 What is Dr Patterson's opinion of people who design scent logos?

  A She believes all companies need their services.

  B She thinks it's a rewarding profession.

  C She has great admiration for their knowledge and professionalism.

  D She thinks they are unfairly held responsible for a loss of business.

4 **Listen again and write expressions that match these meanings.**

1 find out about (question 2) ....

2 tricked (question 2) ....

3 it's not possible to be certain (question 3) ....

4 complain (question 4) ....

5 poses a risk (question 5) ....

6 have great admiration for (question 6) ....

Speaking

5 **Work in pairs and discuss the questions.**

1 Do you think scent marketing should be more strictly controlled?

2 Do you have any favourite smells? What do they remind you of?

3 Would you choose the scent of cinnamon, lavender or vanilla to

  • cheer you up if you were feeling lonely?

  • wake you up if you were feeling drowsy?

  • help you get to sleep?

Multiple-choice cloze (Part 1)

▶ **EXAM** FOCUS p.197

1 Work in pairs. What are the four tastes?

2 Read the article about a fifth taste quickly to find out what the taste is. Why didn't people see its potential until recently?

Life STYLE

Selling the fifth taste

Up until recently, if you had **(0)** *D asked* most people how many tastes there were, their answer would almost **(1)** .... have been four: sweet, salty, sour and bitter. Nowadays, however, more and more of us **(2)** .... the existence of a fifth taste: umami. Umami has actually been **(3)** .... since 1907, when Japanese chemist Kikunae Ikeda identified it. He had noticed there was a quality shared by foods as **(4)** .... from one another as asparagus and parmesan cheese, a quality he named umami, the Japanese word for 'delicious'. For many years it was believed that human taste buds were **(5)** .... of detecting this fifth taste but it turns out that we can not only detect it, we **(6)** .... mad for it. Today, from the kitchens of the top avant-garde chefs to humble hamburger joints, umami-consciousness is making its **(7)** .... And it sells! You can now buy umami-flavoured paste in a tube at your local supermarket and if the advertising is to be **(8)** .... , try it once and you'll be back for more.

0	**A** questioned	**B** enquired	**C** quizzed	**D** asked
1	**A** absolutely	**B** certainly	**C** surely	**D** clearly
2	**A** acknowledge	**B** understand	**C** allow	**D** grant
3	**A** about	**B** around	**C** along	**D** on
4	**A** contrasting	**B** unalike	**C** different	**D** diverse
5	**A** incompetent	**B** incapable	**C** inefficient	**D** unable
6	**A** become	**B** turn	**C** feel	**D** go
7	**A** point	**B** mark	**C** impression	**D** fame
8	**A** believed	**B** considered	**C** credited	**D** relied

3 Work in pairs. Look at the example (0) in the article and the answer, *asked*. Discuss why the other alternatives are not possible.

4 Read the article again. For questions 1–8, decide which answer (A, B, C or D) best fits each gap.

EXAM TIP

Try to work out what the options have in common and in what ways they might differ in terms of complementation patterns. For example, *question*, *quiz* and *enquire* are similar in meaning and are all followed by *about* but only *question* and *quiz* take a direct object.

5 Work in pairs. What kinds of foods do you find most tempting? What do you like about these foods: their texture or their taste?

Vocabulary

collocations with *go*

6 Look at the adjectives in the box and answer the questions.

bad	bald	bankrupt	deaf
downhill	grey	hysterical	mad
mouldy	off	salty	sour	tired

1 Which adjectives collocate with *go*?

2 What is the meaning of *go* in the collocations: *be*, *become* or *get*?

7 Replace the underlined words with the correct form of collocations from Activity 6.

1 Things have really <u>deteriorated</u> around here since you left – the sales figures have plummeted.

2 If you keep listening to such loud music, you'll <u>impair your hearing</u>.

3 Ugh, look at this bread! It's <u>grown a fungus</u>.

4 The company <u>didn't have enough money to pay its debts</u> and their shareholders lost a lot of money.

5 My friend's hair started <u>losing its original colour</u> when he was only twenty. It makes him look rather distinguished.

6 I think this mayonnaise might have <u>become too bad to eat</u> – it smells a bit strange.

7 My grandfather had <u>lost his hair</u> by the time he was fifty.

8 Our dog <u>gets very agitated</u> every time the postman comes.

Gapped text (Part 7)

▶ **EXAM** FOCUS p.200

1 Work in pairs. Think of brand names for products you use. Why do you think these names were chosen?

2 Read the article about brand names and perceptions. Were any of the reasons that you discussed in Activity 1 mentioned?

3 Read the first two paragraphs of the article and the paragraphs A–G that were removed. Look at the reasons a student gave for correctly choosing one of the missing paragraphs. Which paragraph is the student referring to?

> 'These' at the beginning of the paragraph refers to 'back vowels' just before the first gap. The word 'researchers' links to 'study' in the paragraph after the gap.

4 Read the article again and choose from the paragraphs A–G the one which fits each gap (1–6). There is one extra paragraph which you do not need to use.

EXAM TIP

Look for linking words and phrases in the options with connections to ideas and language in the sentences before and after each gap.

5 Work in pairs and compare your answers. Give reasons for your choices similar to those the student gave in Activity 3.

6 Do words in your language fit this theory? Can you think of any examples?

Vocabulary

working out meaning from context

7 Look at the underlined words and phrases in the article and choose the correct meaning, A or B. Which clues did you use to help you?

1	observed	**A** watched	**B** said	
2	made-up	**A** invented	**B** prepared	
3	turns out	**A** happens	**B** evicts	
4	appeasing	**A** persuading	**B** making less angry	
5	retracting	**A** moving back	**B** denying what you said	
6	shades	**A** dark places	**B** subtly different degrees	

A

So what's going on? Is there any reason why front vowels should be associated with small, thin, light things? By the same token, why do back vowels make us think of big, solid, heavy things?

B

In each case, the participants in the study tended to choose those named by back vowels as larger, heavier, thicker and darker, a finding with important implications for marketing executives. Logically, it would be better for them to give their ice cream brands names with these vowels and thus convey the idea that their products are heavy and rich.

C

It's amusing to think that human language in some ways is a series of grunts, growls and squeaks and that the smile a delicious ice cream will put on a child's face is very much like the purr of a cat or the wag of a dog's tail.

D

But does this hold true for real brand names? Researchers came up with a clever way of finding out whether it does or not.

E

Since larger animals naturally make deeper sounds and smaller animals naturally make high-pitched sounds, the idea is that animals try to appear larger when they are competing or aggressive, but they try to appear smaller and less threatening when they are not.

F

The theory is, thus, that smiling evolved as a way for mammals in competitive situations to make the voice sound more high-pitched, so as to make the smiler appear smaller and less aggressive, and hence friendlier.

G

Linguists have noted that these often occur in words that refer to big, fat, heavy things. They do not, on the other hand, in words that refer to small, thin, light things. This is not always true but it's a tendency that researchers have found in many words in many different languages.

73 | *Food* STYLE

A product
by any other name … might not taste so *sweet, creamy, rich* or *crunchy*.

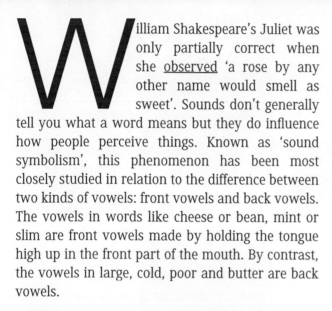

William Shakespeare's Juliet was only partially correct when she <u>observed</u> 'a rose by any other name would smell as sweet'. Sounds don't generally tell you what a word means but they do influence how people perceive things. Known as 'sound symbolism', this phenomenon has been most closely studied in relation to the difference between two kinds of vowels: front vowels and back vowels. The vowels in words like cheese or bean, mint or slim are front vowels made by holding the tongue high up in the front part of the mouth. By contrast, the vowels in large, cold, poor and butter are back vowels.

1 | G | In one study, for example, they created pairs of <u>made-up</u> product names that were identical except for having front vowels or back vowels. People were then asked to say which of a number of hypothetical products seemed bigger or smaller, or heavier or lighter.

2 | B | In fact, it <u>turns out</u> that people do prefer ice creams with names including back vowels. In another study researchers had participants read a description of a new ice cream. Half the participants read a version where the ice cream was called Frish (front vowel) and the other half read a version where it was called Frosh (back vowel), but the descriptions were otherwise identical. Asked their opinions, the 'Frosh people' rated their ice cream as smoother, creamier and richer than the 'Frish people', and were more likely to say they would buy it.

3 | D | They downloaded a list of 81 ice cream flavours and a list of 592 cracker brands from a dieting website. For each list, the total number of front vowels and the total number of back vowels was counted. The result was that the ice cream names indeed had more back vowels and cracker names had more front vowels.

4 | A | The most widely accepted theory, the Frequency Theory, suggests that low frequencies (low pitch) and high frequencies (high pitch) are associated with particular meanings. Mammals and birds tend to use low-frequency sounds when they are aggressive or hostile but use higher-frequency sounds when frightened, <u>appeasing</u> or friendly.

5 | E | This link of high pitch with deference or friendliness may also explain the origin of the smile. We make a smile by <u>retracting</u> the corners of the mouth and this shrinks the size of the front cavity in the mouth, just like the vowels in mint or bean. In fact, the similarity in mouth position between smiling and the vowel *i* explains why we say cheese when we take pictures; *i* is the smiling vowel.

6 | F | Of course, smiling in humans has evolved into a means of expressing many <u>shades</u> of enjoyment and other emotional meanings, just as back vowels have become part of a rich system for expressing complex meanings by combining sounds into words. Something similarly beautiful was created as saltpetre, snow, sherbet and salt were combined to create the sweet lusciousness of ice cream, something that makes us all smile on a hot summer day.

Collaborative task and discussion (Parts 3 and 4)

agreeing and disagreeing

▶ **EXAM** FOCUS p.205

1 **Work in pairs. Look at the picture and discuss the questions.**

1 What is it trying to say about advertising and its effects?

2 How useful do you think anti-advertising campaigns like this are?

2 ▶ **24** **Listen to two students discussing the questions in Activity 1. Which student is most in favour of these kinds of campaigns?**

3 **Listen again and tick (✓) the phrases you hear.**

1 I couldn't agree more.

2 Absolutely!

3 That's not quite the way I see it.

4 I can't argue with that, but …

5 Indeed it is.

6 I'm afraid I just don't see it like that at all.

7 Surely not!

8 We'll just have to agree to differ.

4 **Look at the phrases in Activity 3 and find**

1 three ways of expressing complete agreement.

2 two ways of expressing complete disagreement.

3 one expression to use when you can't reach an agreement.

4 one expression for accepting someone else's point of view reluctantly.

5 one way of expressing partial disagreement.

5 **Add more expressions to the categories in Activity 4. Then compare your answers with a partner.**

6 ▶ **25** **Work in pairs. Look at the exam task and listen to the examiner. Discuss the advantages and disadvantages of each of the ways of promoting products and how effective you think each one would be.**

using social networking sites

making a cool promotional video

How effective would these ways of promoting fashion products be?

sponsoring music festivals

giving free samples

using celebrities in print advertising

7 **Now you have about a minute to decide which method would work best.**

EXAM TIP

You don't have to reach an agreement but you will need to come to a decision. The examiner will ask you to spend a minute doing this at the end of your discussion in Part 3.

8 **Work with another student and compare your answers. Give reasons for saying why a method would be effective or ineffective. Use some of the expressions in Activity 3 to express agreement and disagreement.**

9 **Work in groups of three. Turn to page 154 and do the activity.**

Conditionals: advanced features

▶ **GRAMMAR** REFERENCE p.173

1 ▶ **26 Listen to part of a radio talk on 'stealth advertising'. What do you think of the techniques it describes?**

2 Look at sentences A–D from the recording and find a word or phrase that

1 makes an event seem more hypothetical.
2 is an extremely polite form which is mainly used in writing.
3 makes a request less of an imposition.
4 makes a sentence sound more formal.

A If I were to learn that a friend was being paid to promote a product to me, I would be really angry.

B If you happen to be talking to your friends, can you just mention in passing that you use Lipluxe?

C Should you wish to make a complaint, we suggest you contact the Advertising Control Board.

D Had the company asked my friend's permission to use her blog to promote the product, she would never have agreed to it.

3 Cross out the alternative that is *not* possible in each sentence.

1 *Unless the weather improves/If the weather doesn't improve/If the weather improves*, we won't be able to have the picnic.

2 I'd be really disappointed *if we didn't win/if we won/unless we won* at least one gold medal.

3 You should try to get more sleep, *otherwise/if not/unless* you'll exhaust yourself before the exams have even started.

4 *Provided/Supposing/What if* you don't manage to persuade anyone to sign up for the new phone service, what will you do then?

5 I have nothing against telemarketing, *provided that/as long as/supposing* the people who phone you are willing to take no for an answer.

6 *In the event of/In case of/If* fire, do not use the lifts.

4 Change the meaning of the sentences following the instructions in brackets. Use the conditional forms in Activity 2.

1 If you inherited a lot of money, would you give up working? (more hypothetical)

2 If you require assistance, contact a member of staff. (extremely polite , formal and written)

3 If we had interviewed a larger number of people, we would have obtained more reliable results. (more formal)

4 If you see Joe, can you remind him to give me a call? (less of an imposition)

5 If your brother phones me in the next couple of days, I might be able to arrange an interview. (more hypothetical)

6 If I had known working as a journalist was so demanding, I would have done something else. (more formal)

5 Think of a moral or ethical dilemma. Write your dilemma using one of the new conditional forms in Activity 2. Then exchange with another student and discuss your dilemmas.

Example: Supposing you were asked to promote a product on your blog, what would you do?

Speaking

1 Look at the extract from a survey on attitudes to advertising. Respond to the questions and compare your responses with other students.

Advertising *survey*

For each statement, write: *Agree*, *Disagree* or *Neither*.

1 I like to look at most of the advertisements I am exposed to.

2 Most advertising insults my intelligence.

3 In general, I feel I can trust advertising.

4 Products usually live up to the promises made in their advertisements.

5 In general, I like advertising.

Report (Part 2)

formal language

▶ **WRITING** REFERENCE p.192

2 The survey in Activity 1 was conducted with a large group of people. Look at the results on page 169. Then read the report. Does it give an accurate account of the results?

ATTITUDES TO ADVERTISING

The first question asked respondents about their experience of looking at advertisements. While a little more than a third express dislike, the rest gave either neutral or positive answers. Strange as it may seem, although there were many positive responses to the first question, nearly half the participants in the survey regard advertising as an insult to their intelligence. This apparent contradiction between positive and negative attitudes is reflected once more in the responses to the next two questions. On the one hand, many of those surveyed mistrusted the advertisements they saw. On the other hand, they considered that they provided an accurate picture of the qualities of the products they purchased.

CONCLUSION

Notwithstanding a lack of trust and a feeling of being patronised, many of those whose opinions we sought have a positive attitude to advertising overall.

3 Read the report again and underline

1 four formal ways of expressing contrast between two results or points of view.

2 four formal phrases referring to the people who answered the questionnaire.

3 two formal words for *think*.

4 the ways the writer of the report has reworded the survey questions in a more formal style.

EXAM TIP

Use headings to help you plan and structure your report.

4 Look at the task and some ideas a candidate wrote down while preparing her answer. What headings do you think the candidate used in her report?

> An international market research company has asked you to write a report on advertising in your country. The company that has commissioned the report wants to know about the most common approaches used and how consumers respond to them. You are also asked to suggest changes to current approaches or alternative approaches which you believe would be more effective.
>
> Write your **report** in **220–260** words in an appropriate style.

- telemarketing? advertising hoardings? junk mail? TV advertising? internet pop-ups? giveaways in magazines?
- contrast telemarketing with giveaways in magazines
- contradiction in responses to both: hate telemarketing but buy products/like giveaways (but suffer from giveaway overload)
- better training of telemarketers; fewer, better quality giveaways

5 Look at the model report on page 192. Use the ideas in Activity 4 or your own ideas to write your own report. Use headings, formal ways of expressing contrast and synonyms to refer to 'consumers'.

1 Complete the second sentence so that it has a similar meaning to the first sentence, using the word given. Do not change the word given. You must use between three and six words, including the word given.

1 I don't have much money, so I probably won't go on holiday this year.   **MORE**

If .... , I would go on holiday this year.

2 She didn't get very good marks in the exam, so she didn't get a scholarship.   **BETTER**

She would have got a scholarship if .... marks in the exam.

3 We'll have to save up if we want to be able to afford a new car.   **UNLESS**

We won't be able to afford a new car .... up.

4 I can't play the piano very well because I only studied it for a year.   **LONGER**

Had .... than a year, I would be able to play better.

5 Buy one, get one free.   **CAN**

If .... get one free.

6 I was born in Australia, so I have to apply for visas for some countries.   **NECESSARY**

If I hadn't been born in Australia, it .... for me to apply for visas for some countries.

7 Supposing you saw a friend shoplifting in a supermarket, what would you do?   **WERE**

If .... a friend shoplifting in a supermarket, what would you do?

8 Please feel free to contact me if you require any further information.   **SHOULD**

Please feel free to contact me .... any further information.

2 Choose the correct option to complete the sentences.

1 Smell this milk – I think it might have .... off.

A turned   **B** become   **C** changed   **D** gone

2 That restaurant has really gone .... – the food's terrible now.

A downturn **B** downtown **C** downhill **D** downside

3 Olive oil is on special .... at the supermarket.

A bargain   **B** offer   **C** discount   **D** sale

4 She has a wonderful .... with all her students.

A rapport   **B** empathy   **C** sympathy   **D** identification

5 Have you seen the latest .... figures?

A selling   **B** sales   **C** sale   **D** sold

6 The company .... bankrupt in 2012.

A went   **B** turned   **C** got   **D** became

3 Read the article below and decide which answer (A, B, C or D) best fits each gap.

★Retail Therapy

Time to stop shopping?

Were you aware that clothes are the most rapidly (1) MOUNTING waste item in the UK? Our wardrobes are (2) FULL of things we seldom wear either because they don't fit us anymore or because we've been (3) INFLUENCED that they're no longer in fashion. Rather than having them (4) ALTERED so they do fit or look more up-to-date, we simply go out and buy more. It's not surprising that this overindulgence is now being tackled (5) HEAD ON by people who suggest we should either stop shopping altogether or go on a temporary 'shopping fast'. For example, you might set yourself the (6) TARGET of not buying anything for six months or even a year. For those who really can't stand the (7) THOUGHT of having nothing new to wear, there's always the possibility of (8) SWAPPING your clothes with friends. Why buy two expensive outfits for two special occasions held on different dates when you could share?

1   **A** raising   **B** developing   **C** growing   **D** mounting
2   **A** full   **B** filled   **C** crowded   **D** occupied
3   **A** induced   **B** influenced   **C** persuaded   **D** swayed
4   **A** changed   **B** fixed   **C** mended   **D** altered
5   **A** front-on   **B** head-on   **C** face-on   **D** right-on
6   **A** aim   **B** focus   **C** promise   **D** target
7   **A** concept   **B** plan   **C** notion   **D** thought
8   **A** getting   **B** taking   **C** swapping   **D** giving

Passing through

8

Sentence completion (Part 2)

▶ **EXAM** FOCUS p.202

1 Work in pairs. Think of three reasons for and against using a guidebook during a trip.

2 Look at the exam task in Activity 3. Try to think of some possible answers for questions 2 and 4.

EXAM TIP

Use the time you are given before you listen to try and identify the kind of information you need to listen for. For example, is the missing word or phrase a means of transport, a type of place or something to eat?

3 ▶ 27 **You will hear part of a radio report on a travel show about guidebooks by a travel writer called Tim Cole. For questions 1–8, complete the sentences.**

Travel guidebooks

Tim complains about ending up at a(n) **(1)** .... thanks to misinformation in a guidebook.

Tim recommends checking the **(2)** .... of a guidebook before buying it.

Tim believes that it is when making **(3)** .... that guidebooks can be the most unreliable.

Tim dislikes guidebooks which contain a lot of **(4)** .... because he thinks they aren't useful.

Tim says he has **(5)** .... problems with digital travel guides.

Until digital guidebooks can be individually **(6)** ....,
Tim prefers to use a hard copy.

On his trip to Hawaii, Tim decided to rely on Twitter tourism because he wanted **(7)** .... information.

The most memorable experience Tim had via Twitter was swimming in a(n)
(8) .... at night.

4 Work in pairs. Plan a trip to a world-famous site that you would both enjoy. What preparations would you need to make?

Reported speech

▶ **GRAMMAR** REFERENCE p.178

5 Choose the correct alternative in each sentence to report what Tim said about guidebooks.

1 Tim told people *not to believe/he didn't believe* everything they read in guidebooks.

2 He said that people *don't check/didn't use to check* the date of publication.

3 He said he *wouldn't buy/hadn't bought* a guidebook which had lots of pictures.

4 He said he *couldn't/wouldn't* use a digital guidebook.

5 He was told by Twitter users that he *should visit/had visited* the Ukulele Festival.

6 He says that without Twitter recommendations he *might have missed/might miss* swimming with manta rays.

6 ▶ 28 Work in pairs. Listen and summarise what the speakers say.

7 Choose the correct alternative in each sentence. In which sentences are both alternatives possible?

1 Mia told Matt that her trip to Thailand *had been/was* amazing.

2 Matt asked if Mia *could/can* recommend a guidebook.

3 Mia says *she'll/she'd* never use a guidebook again.

4 Mia said she's considering relying on Twitter recommendations next time she *was travelling/is travelling*.

5 Mia offered to show Matt her photos of Thailand *this/that* evening.

8 Match comments A–E with sentences 1–5 in Activity 7.

A No tense change should be made because the information is still true.

B You only need to make tense changes when referring to a past event if it happened a long time ago or the information is out of date.

C Some modal verbs always change in reported speech.

D You need to make changes to time references if the information is being reported at a later date.

E It isn't necessary to make tense changes if the reporting verb is in the present tense.

9 Read the travel tips and complete the reported statements 1–6.

```
●●●                                    ◄ ►   ► Sales
```

Taj Mahal: visitor tips   ♥ 📎 💬 🔊

1 'I wish I'd been advised to buy my tickets twenty-four hours in advance. You can't get them on the same day.' *Ella, London* ✉

2 'Don't visit between March and October when the weather can be very hot or very wet.' *Sarah, Toronto* ✉

3 'If I go again, I'll definitely make sure I see the Taj Mahal at sunrise or sunset.' *Seamus, Dublin* ✉

4 Don't miss the moonlight viewing if you plan to be in Agra near the time of a full moon.' *Max, Germany* ✉

5 'Has anyone stayed in a good hotel nearby?' *Rosa, Mexico City* ✉

6 'The Taj Mahal is the most beautiful place in the world. Everyone must go there at least once.' *David, New York* ✉

1 Ella said she .... to buy her tickets 24 hours in advance.

2 Sarah told people .... between March and October when the weather can be very hot or very wet.

3 Seamus said if he .... the Taj Mahal at sunrise or sunset.

4 Max said that if you .... near the time of the full moon, you .... the moonlight viewing.

5 Rosa asked .... in a good hotel in nearby.

6 David said the Taj Mahal .... and that everyone ....

LANGUAGE TIP

That is often omitted when reporting statements.
She said (that) she was hungry.

Speaking

10 Work in pairs and plan an itinerary for a visitor to your city or region. Then swap partners and give your recommendations to another student, who should then report what you said to his/her partner. Give recommendations on

• what to visit.

• when to travel.

• tourist traps to avoid.

• managing on a tight budget.

• getting off the beaten track.

Speaking

1 Choose the correct alternative in each sentence. Then tick (✓) the ideas you agree with and compare answers with a partner.

1 I think visiting famous landmarks encourages a *respectful/respected* attitude to the past.

2 I believe travel is the best way to develop an *aware/awareness* of other cultures.

3 I don't find the idea of luxury holidays in remote locations that *appealing/unappealing* – I'd rather camp.

4 I like going back to the same places on holiday – I prefer *familiarity/familiar* destinations.

5 I always make sure my *knowledge/knowledges* of local customs and traditions is good before I travel.

6 I prefer not to use guidebook recommendations to find restaurants because I like to make my own *discovery/discoveries*.

7 I always buy postcards of places I visit as a *remind/reminder* of where I've been.

8 I think it's always best to travel with low *expectation/expectations*; then you'll never be disappointed.

2 Look at the words in italics in Activity 1. Check if they have adjective, verb and noun forms as well as any negative prefixes that can be used with them.

Word formation (Part 3)

▶ **EXAM** FOCUS p.198

3 Read the article. Do you agree with the writer's attitude towards souvenirs?

Souvenir hunting

Souvenirs (0) ....*originated*.... from memento mori, which is a Latin phrase meaning 'Remember you will die'. These were objects which were supposed to focus (1) .... on the spiritual world rather than (2) .... material goods. But nowadays cheap souvenirs such as plastic statues of the Eiffel Tower are bought by people to somehow prove their (3) .... has had some meaning.

   I used to be a (4) .... snob about souvenirs and couldn't understand why people bought such kitsch (5) .... of their travels. But now I'm more respectful. One of the best souvenirs I ever bought was a lolly made in the shape of the Leaning Tower of Pisa, which we bought on a family holiday. I couldn't resist it. It was so colourful and (6) .... – so weird! I also love coming across souvenirs in (7) .... places – like the time I bought a landscape made from driftwood at a boat petrol station in the Bay of Helsinki.

   So my recommendation for buying souvenirs is to keep an open mind because you can find them in the (8) .... locations. ∎

ORIGIN

AWARE
EARTH

EXIST
MASS

REMIND

APPEAL
EXPECT

STRANGE

4 Read the article again. For questions 1–8, use the word given in capitals at the end of some of the lines to form a word that fits in the gap in the same line.

EXAM TIP

Make sure you read the text all the way through to get a general understanding before trying to do the task.

5 Work in pairs and discuss the questions.

1 What kind of souvenirs do you like buying for yourself or your friends?

2 Describe the last souvenir you bought or were given.

3 What souvenirs are typical of your country/city/region?

Long turn (Part 2)
speculating (2)

▶ **EXAM** FOCUS p.204

1 Work in pairs. Look at the pictures and decide what they have in common and in what way they are different.

2 What do you think the instruction for this task might be?

3 ▶ 29 Listen to the examiner's instructions and see if you were right.

4 ▶ 30 Listen to a candidate doing the task and tick (✓) the things she speculates about.

1 what is being sold

2 where the pictures were taken

3 whether these items were presents

4 what kind of souvenirs most tourists are interested in

5 why the people are shopping for these items

5 Complete the phrases for speculating. Then listen again and check.

1 I .... imagine that most people who travel to a new country …

2 I .... whether most tourists actually check to see …

3 I'm .... certain that the people in both photographs are making impulse purchases.

4 I .... say if they're buying presents or not.

5 In all .... , the Russian dolls will be put on a shelf somewhere …

6 I'd .... if the woman buying the handmade bracelet wanted it as a reminder of her trip.

EXAM TIP

Try to use a variety of phrases for speculating, comparing and contrasting – don't keep repeating the same ones.

---

6 Work in pairs. Turn to page 155 and do Task 1. Then turn to page 159 and do Task 2.

7 Work in pairs. Turn to page 166 and do the activity.

Cross-text multiple matching (Part 6)
identifying attitude and opinion

▶ **EXAM** FOCUS p.200

1 **Work in pairs and answer the questions.**

1 What do you think the difference is between an expat and an immigrant?

2 How much of a problem are these things for people living abroad? Which would be the most difficult thing to cope with?

A • being cut off from your roots
A • finding a sense of belonging
B • maintaining a sense of cultural identity
C • overcoming the language barrier
A • experiencing culture shock

2 **Work in pairs and read extracts from articles about expats in New York. Which of the issues in Activity 1 are mentioned by writers A–D?**

3 **Look at the underlined words and phrases in Text A (1–4). Match them with descriptions A–D below.**

A an opinion about something stated as fact 3
B an adverb of attitude 1
C an expression for giving opinions 2
D an impersonal phrase for making a recommendation 4

4 **Find three examples of adverbs of attitude and two impersonal phrases for making recommendations in extracts B–D.**

EXAM TIP

You need to identify different ways in which writers express their attitude and opinions. Opinions are not only expressed through expressions such as *to my mind* or *in my experience*. To discover the writer's attitude, you also need to look for opinions stated as facts, adverbs of attitude and impersonal phrases for making recommendations.

5 **Read the extracts again. For questions 1–4, choose from extracts A–D. The extracts may be chosen more than once.**

Which writer

1 has a different attitude to writer D on the impact of superficial relationships on the expat worker in New York? 1 B Av

2 disagrees with writer C about the way to deal with problems caused by language differences? 2 B✓

3 shares writer D's view about the difficulty for expats of achieving a sense of belonging in New York? 3 C✓

4 has a similar opinion to writer A about how well prepared most newcomers are for life in New York? 4 C✓

6 **Work in pairs. Find the words and phrases in italics in the extracts and answer the questions.**

1 Do you think relationships with friends need to be *nurtured*? (Text A)

2 What kind of expectations do you have to *live up to*? (Text B)

3 What other changes in life may seem like a *daunting prospect*? (Text B)

4 How important is it to try and *blend in* when you're in a new situation? (Text C)

Speaking

7 **Work in pairs. How far do you agree with the statements from the extracts?**

1 Technology has made it possible to maintain ties with friends and family across time zones.

2 The best thing about leaving your old life behind is that you are free to reinvent yourself.

Expats in New York

Four journalists reflect on the experience of being an expat in New York.

A

Adjusting to life in New York can seem overwhelming for newly arrived expats. There's the initial culture shock to contend with, the language barrier, loneliness and, worst of all, the realisation that the average New Yorker is entirely indifferent to the challenges they face. Yet their situation is (1) unquestionably better than those who have decided to migrate on a permanent basis. For, unlike immigrants, expats do not expect to make New York their home long term. They already have a home and a homeland to return to. (2) To my mind, there isn't the same need to *nurture* new relationships. The polite detachment of New Yorkers (3) is of no consequence because technology has made it possible to maintain ties with friends and family across oceans and time zones. (4) It's worth making the effort to do this because then it will be possible to slip effortlessly back into your old life when the time comes.

B

Adapting to life in a new city, country and culture needn't be such a *daunting prospect*. Many expats find the experience liberating. Back in your home country you may be defined by your job title, your family background and the area you come from. But in a place as dynamic and diverse as New York, these, thankfully, become insignificant details. There is no longer the pressure to *live up to* the expectations of your family. The best thing about leaving your old life behind is that you are free to reinvent yourself because New Yorkers won't judge you. But one thing you will have to put up with is your new identity as a foreigner. New Yorkers will treat you as an object of curiosity for the way you speak, regardless of what you have to say. It can't be avoided, so it's best to embrace and even celebrate your 'charming' or 'cute' manner of speaking.

C

Many expats from English-speaking countries arriving to work in New York mistakenly assume that fitting in will be easy. They don't really count themselves as foreigners. After all, they speak the language and they're already familiar with the culture (even if that's only through a diet of American TV series such as *Friends*). This over-confidence can prompt something of an identity crisis at first, once it becomes clear that many New Yorkers regard them in the same light as any other expat. The language barrier is as great a divide for them as it is for those who are learning English for the first time. The only way to overcome this is to try and *blend in* by picking up an American accent, vocabulary and expressions. This will probably happen naturally over time. But those who resolutely refuse to change will find their accent becomes a topic of conversation wherever they go.

D

Most expats in New York lose the sense of being a stranger quite quickly. After only a few months in the city, they find themselves acting and even speaking like a native New Yorker. Life becomes routine, yet at the back of their minds they'll always be conscious that this existence is transient and that one day they'll return home. New Yorkers sense this and, understandably, don't want to invest too much in a friendship that is ultimately going nowhere. In my experience, far from forming lifelong bonds, socialising for most expats is reduced to a series of disappointing casual encounters, compounding a sense of loneliness and isolation. It takes people a little while before it eventually dawns on them that true acceptance by New Yorkers will have to be earned over a minimum of five years – way too long for someone on a two-year contract.

Describing trends

1 **Work in pairs and check you understand the meaning of the underlined words/phrases.**

1   The population of New York City <u>reached a peak</u> in the year 2000.

2   The number of people living in New York <u>remained relatively stable</u> from 1900 to 1950.

3   The number of people moving out of New York <u>overtook</u> those moving to the city during the 1950s.

4   New York experienced a <u>brief dip</u> in its population during the 1950s.

5   The <u>decrease</u> in the number of people leaving New York for the suburbs continued until 1980.

6   There is expected to be a <u>steep fall</u> in the population of New York between 2020–2030.

2 ▶ **31** **Listen to part of a radio programme with an economist and decide if the statements in Actvity 1 are true (T) or false (F).**

3 **Which words in the recording match meanings 1–4?**

1   a lot (two words)

2   a little (one word)

3   go up (three words)

4   go down (two words)

4 **Work in pairs. How do you think the population trends in New York City compare to where you live? What do you think it would be like to emigrate? What would you miss about home?**

5 **Complete the text with the words in the box.**

decline	dropping	overtaken	peak
risen	sudden		

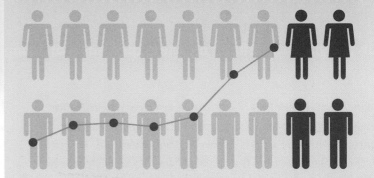

Population survey

A recent survey has revealed that the city's population has **(1)** .... unexpectedly. After a period of slow population **(2)** .... , with increasingly larger numbers of young people leaving to find jobs in the bigger metropolitan areas, the number of people settling in the city has **(3)** .... those leaving for the first time in six years. Over 7,000 more people arrived in the city last year than left, which brings the total population to just under 319,000.

This **(4)** .... rise is welcome news for some local schools where pupil numbers had been **(5)** .... The trend is likely to continue but researchers don't expect the population to reach its former **(6)** .... of 350,000.

Speaking

6 **Work in pairs. Make some predictions about future trends where you live. Then compare your predictions with another pair. Think about**

- population growth.
- immigration.
- emigration.

7 **How do you think the predicted trends for your country compare with worldwide trends?**

Verb patterns with reporting verbs

▶ **GRAMMAR** REFERENCE p.179

1 **Which of the verbs in the box can be used to complete each of the reported statements based on the quote?**

advise	recommend	suggest	urge

'There are lots of opportunities here; you should emigrate too', Louis told his brother.

1 Louis .... his brother to emigrate.

2 Louis .... that his brother should emigrate.

3 Louis .... emigrating to his brother.

4 Louis .... that his brother emigrate.

2 **Complete each of the reported statements with as many verbs from the box as possible. Sometimes only one verb can be used.**

accused	admitted	announced
blamed	claimed	doubted
invited	objected	permitted
persuaded	regretted	warned

1 The president .... that the economy would recover.

2 The police officer .... people not to panic.

3 The doctor .... having to leave his country to find work.

4 The student .... that he wanted to get work experience abroad.

5 The immigration officer .... the man to enter the country.

6 The lawyer .... the witness of not being entirely truthful.

7 The unemployed man .... the government for not providing enough jobs.

8 The politician .... to being accused of doing too little to ease unemployment.

3 **Which of the verbs in Activity 2 are followed by**

1 *that* + clause?

2 *-ing*?

3 object + infinitive?

4 object + preposition + *-ing*?

5 *to* + *-ing*?

4 ▶ **32** **What did the speakers actually say? Change the sentences into direct speech. Then listen and compare.**

1 Orla admitted that there was no alternative to her emigrating.

2 Una reassured her mother that she was fine.

3 Sean regretted leaving home to set up a business abroad.

4 Conor blamed the government for not creating enough employment.

5 Ryan's dad encouraged him to stay in Australia.

6 Keira claimed that emigrating was the best decision she'd ever made.

LANGUAGE TIP

Remember you only need to give a summary of the advice. You don't need to report exactly what was said.

Impersonal reporting verbs

5 **Which of the sentences sounds more formal and official? In which type of text would you be likely to find it?**

1 Everyone believes that there aren't enough opportunities for young people.

2 It is believed that there aren't enough opportunities for young people.

6 **Tick (✓) the statements you agree with and discuss with a partner. Then rewrite the underlined words using an impersonal reporting form and the verb in brackets.**

1 Everyone is sure that the number of young people moving abroad to work will increase. (*accepted*)

2 Recent studies seem to show that young migrant workers find culture shock more difficult to deal with than the language barrier. (*suggested*)

3 People think that having access to social networking sites makes it easy to stay in touch with friends and family. (*claimed*)

4 Most people believe that young people with good qualifications will be able to find well-paid work abroad. (*expected*)

5 Most young people used to think they would have the same standard of living as their parents. (*assumed*)

6 Some people have been saying that it's better to have qualifications from a university abroad. (*argued*)

7 **Work in pairs and think of some facts about language learning. Present them to the class using impersonal reporting verbs.**

Proposal (Part 2)
using an appropriate style
▶ **WRITING** REFERENCE p.192

1 **Look at the exam task and think about what information you need to include in the proposal, why you are writing it and who it is for.**

> Your college has been invited to participate in an exchange programme with colleges in other countries. You see this notice in the library.
>
> *The college would like to find out whether students would be interested in participating in an exchange programme with colleges in other countries. Students are invited to send in a proposal outlining the possible benefits of the exchange programme and suggesting ways it could be promoted.*
>
> *The proposal will help the college to decide whether to accept the invitation to join the exchange programme.*
>
> Write your **proposal** in **220–260** words in an appropriate style.

2 **Organise your ideas under the headings.**

1 Introduction
2 Benefits of the exchange programme
3 Ways to promote the exchange programme
4 Recommendations

3 **Which of the recommendations are written in an appropriate style for a proposal?**

✗1 I think it would be a great idea if people who've already been on an exchange programme could give a talk to other students about it.

✓2 It is recommended that the college should hold an open day to give information about the exchange programme to students and their parents.

3 The college should certainly accept the invitation to join the exchange programme as it would provide a great opportunity for students to gain valuable skills and experience.

4 It is hoped that the college would be able to offer students a place on an exchange programme as early as next year.

✗5 You'd think students would grab this chance but a lot of them are too lazy.

6 It is doubtful whether there would be sufficient funding available to sponsor all students interested in participating in the college and it is suggested that the college would only be able to offer some funding to the most disadvantaged students.

4 **Which of the below would be suitable to use in a proposal?**

1 use of the pronouns *I* and *you* ✗   4 passive forms
✗2 impersonal reporting verbs   5 reporting verbs
✗3 phrases for speculating   6 contractions

5 **Write your proposal for the exam task in Activity 1 OR for the task below.**

> Your college currently doesn't provide enough support for students planning to spend time studying in another country. You see this notice in the library.
>
> *The college is planning to introduce a special course for students planning to spend time studying in another country. The college principal invites students to send a proposal outlining any problems students may face when studying abroad and suggesting ways in which the course could address these problems. A decision can then be made about what to include on the course.*
>
> Write your **proposal** in **220–260** words in an appropriate style.

6 **Work in pairs. Read your partner's proposal and make suggestions on ways it could be improved.**

1 Choose the correct option to complete the sentences.

1 My boss .... me to apply for a promotion.
   A recommended B advised   C suggested

2 The applicants were .... to arrive early.
   A warned   B recommended   C encouraged

3 The tourist .... to missing out the museum.
   A claimed   B objected   C insisted

4 The student .... that he hadn't finished his essay on time.
   A admitted   B blamed   C accused

5 The teacher .... the student not to be late.
   A warned   B objected   C recommended

6 The journalist .... the politician of not being honest.
   A blamed   B regretted   C accused

7 The hotel manager .... that there would be more jobs available in the summer.
   A urged   B doubted   C encouraged

8 My aunt .... on paying for our trip to Paris.
   A admitted   B announced   C insisted

2 Complete the second sentence so that it has a similar meaning to the first sentence, using the word given. Do not change the word given. You must use between three and six words, including the word given.

1 'I think it would be best for Sam to travel by bus,' said Mia.   **RECOMMENDED**
   Mia .... by bus.

2 It is predicted that the population will not fluctuate in the short term.   **STABLE**
   It is predicted that the population .... in the short term.

3 The number of visitors to the museum was at its highest point in June.   **PEAK**
   The number of visitors to the museum .... June.

4 The demand for luxury travel fell last year.   **DROP**
   There .... for luxury travel last year.

5 People claim that the government hasn't built enough new homes for migrant workers.   **ACCUSED**
   The government .... enough new homes for migrant workers.

6 You have to have such a good knowledge of the city to be a tour guide.   **KNOWLEDGEABLE**
   You .... the city to be a tour guide.

3 Complete the article with the words in the box.

drop	expected	growth	increasing
lower	overtaken	rise	steadily

Tourism trends

One **(1)** .... trend in tourism is the 'digital detox', hotel packages which offer gadget-free holidays. This trend has been rising **(2)** .... in popularity over the last few years. It indicates a significant **(3)** .... in demand for quality family time. Another expected area of **(4)** .... is the luxury shopping package, which has seen large numbers of Asian tourists flock to Europe to take advantage of the **(5)** .... taxes and favourable exchange rates. Demand for luxury shopping trips has **(6)** .... demand for cultural tourism in the large European cities, with tourists citing shopping as their main purpose for travelling. It is **(7)** .... that the luxury shopping market will continue to grow as there is no sign of a(n) **(8)** .... in demand for these products.

4 Choose the correct alternative in each sentence.

1 Many people whose grandparents emigrated from the countryside to the city are cut *off/out* from their roots.

2 It can be very hard for immigrant communities to *manipulate/maintain* a sense of cultural identity.

3 I experienced culture *stress/shock* when I moved from a small village in Scotland to Hong Kong.

4 It's important for everyone to find a sense of *belonging/background* in the community where they live.

5 Once you overcome the language *bridge/barrier*, it's so much easier to make friends.

6 Some people don't want to *assimilate/accept* into the host culture.

Reading the mind

Open cloze (Part 2)

▶ **EXAM** FOCUS p.198

1 **Answer the questions. Then discuss your answers with other students.**

1   Which do you think has more impact on intelligence: nature or nurture?
2   Do you think babies are born knowing certain things (e.g. about language) or are their brains more like the hard drive of a new computer?

2 **Read the article about what babies know. Why did researchers in the 1980s think babies understood the laws of physics?**

3 **Read the article again. For questions 1–8, think of the word which best fits each gap. Use only one word for each gap.**

EXAM TIP

Before you decide on how to fill a gap, check that the word isn't being used in combination with other words in a way you may not have expected.

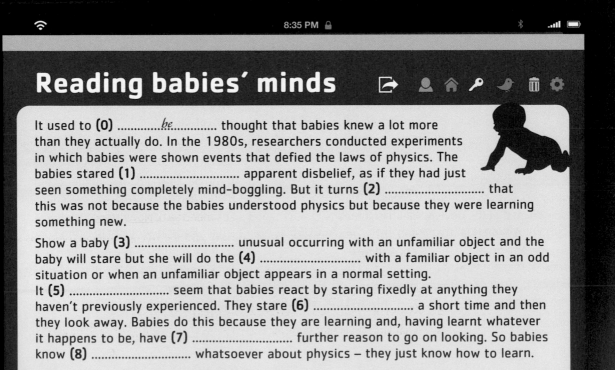

Reading babies' minds

It used to **(0)** ....*be*.......... thought that babies knew a lot more than they actually do. In the 1980s, researchers conducted experiments in which babies were shown events that defied the laws of physics. The babies stared **(1)** .... apparent disbelief, as if they had just seen something completely mind-boggling. But it turns **(2)** .... that this was not because the babies understood physics but because they were learning something new.

Show a baby **(3)** .... unusual occurring with an unfamiliar object and the baby will stare but she will do the **(4)** .... with a familiar object in an odd situation or when an unfamiliar object appears in a normal setting.

It **(5)** .... seem that babies react by staring fixedly at anything they haven't previously experienced. They stare **(6)** .... a short time and then they look away. Babies do this because they are learning and, having learnt whatever it happens to be, have **(7)** .... further reason to go on looking. So babies know **(8)** .... whatsoever about physics – they just know how to learn.

Speaking

4 ▶ **33** **Work in pairs. Put the developmental milestones in the order that a child learns to do them. Then listen to the extract from a radio programme and check.**

- recognise familiar faces
- learn to put on her own clothes
- know her own name and respond to it
- enjoy hiding games
- try to be a help
- return a smile

5 **Listen again and note down the phrases the speaker uses for each of the milestones in Activity 1.**

Example: return a smile – smile back

Expressions with *brain* and *mind*

6 **Look at the words in the box and answer the questions.**

boggling	child	damage	drain	reader	scan	storm
teaser	wash	wave				

1 Which words can be used in compound nouns, verbs or adjectives with *brain*?
2 Which words can be used with *mind* to complete sentences A and B?
   A I always found maths completely .... when I was at school.
   B You must be a .... ! How did you know I was going to say that?

7 **Complete the sentences with compound nouns or verbs from Activity 6.**

1 The current lack of research funding is leading to a .... , with some of our country's best scientists being forced to go abroad to continue their work.
2 The design for the new centre was the .... of Stephanie Wilson but it was finally built several years after she retired.
3 Initially, the doctors feared she had suffered permanent .... but, if anything, she seemed more intelligent after the accident.
4 Why don't we try and .... some ideas for the new TV series?
5 I didn't think we would be able to go to the party but then I had a .... and realised I could invite everyone to our house.
6 I love doing .... like cryptic crosswords and Sudoku.
7 The group have been accused of .... members and persuading them to donate all their money.
8 She was having such terrible migraines that the doctor suggested she had a .... to find out what was wrong.

8 **Work in pairs and discuss the questions.**

1 What might have happened to you if a friend said, 'Never mind!'?
2 If you give a friend some advice and she says she will bear that in mind, has she accepted your advice?
3 If you offer someone a drink and they say, 'I wouldn't mind,' do they want one or not?
4 Why might someone say, 'Mind your language!'?
5 Why might you begin a sentence with, 'Mind you, …'?
6 What kind of question might you begin with, 'If you don't mind my asking, …'?

Reading

1 Work with a partner and think of activities that might help develop team spirit in a group or organisation.

2 Read the first part of an extract from a blog. Were any of the activities you and your partner mentioned similar to the activity described?

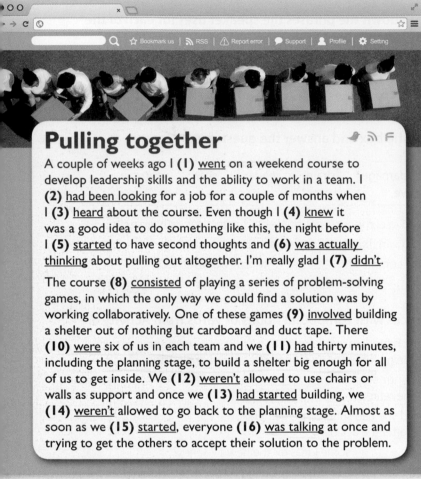

Pulling together

A couple of weeks ago I **(1)** <u>went</u> on a weekend course to develop leadership skills and the ability to work in a team. I **(2)** <u>had been looking</u> for a job for a couple of months when I **(3)** <u>heard</u> about the course. Even though I **(4)** <u>knew</u> it was a good idea to do something like this, the night before I **(5)** <u>started</u> to have second thoughts and **(6)** <u>was actually thinking</u> about pulling out altogether. I'm really glad I **(7)** <u>didn't</u>.

The course **(8)** <u>consisted</u> of playing a series of problem-solving games, in which the only way we could find a solution was by working collaboratively. One of these games **(9)** <u>involved</u> building a shelter out of nothing but cardboard and duct tape. There **(10)** <u>were</u> six of us in each team and we **(11)** <u>had</u> thirty minutes, including the planning stage, to build a shelter big enough for all of us to get inside. We **(12)** <u>weren't</u> allowed to use chairs or walls as support and once we **(13)** <u>had started</u> building, we **(14)** <u>weren't</u> allowed to go back to the planning stage. Almost as soon as we **(15)** <u>started</u>, everyone **(16)** <u>was talking</u> at once and trying to get the others to accept their solution to the problem.

Review of narrative tenses

▶ **GRAMMAR** REFERENCE p. 181

3 Look at the underlined verbs (1–16) in the extract in Activity 2 and find examples of

1 the past continuous to say that something was in progress at a particular time or when an event occurred.

2 the past perfect to show that something happened before something else.

3 the past simple with expressions that refer to a completed period of time.

4 the past perfect continuous to show that one long event happened before another in the past.

5 the past simple for describing past actions or states.

4 Complete the second part of the blog entry with the correct form of the verbs in brackets. Where there is more than one possible form, what is the difference in meaning (if any)?

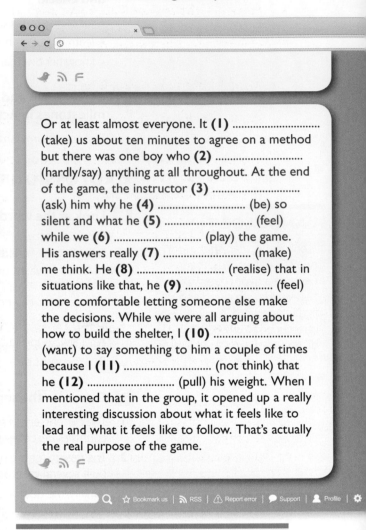

Or at least almost everyone. It **(1)** .... (take) us about ten minutes to agree on a method but there was one boy who **(2)** .... (hardly/say) anything at all throughout. At the end of the game, the instructor **(3)** .... (ask) him why he **(4)** .... (be) so silent and what he **(5)** .... (feel) while we **(6)** .... (play) the game. His answers really **(7)** .... (make) me think. He **(8)** .... (realise) that in situations like that, he **(9)** .... (feel) more comfortable letting someone else make the decisions. While we were all arguing about how to build the shelter, I **(10)** .... (want) to say something to him a couple of times because I **(11)** .... (not think) that he **(12)** .... (pull) his weight. When I mentioned that in the group, it opened up a really interesting discussion about what it feels like to lead and what it feels like to follow. That's actually the real purpose of the game.

LANGUAGE TIP

If a time adverbial is used in a sentence about two actions or events that happened in sequence, it is not absolutely necessary to use the past perfect to indicate the earlier of the two actions.

*After I **spoke** to Victoria, I **wrote** an email summarising what we had said.*

5 Work in pairs and discuss the questions.

1 Would you have enjoyed playing a game like this? Why/Why not?

2 Tell a partner about an experience you have had that you thought would turn out badly but ended up being beneficial in some way.

Long turn (Part 2)

paraphrasing

▶ **EXAM** FOCUS p.204

1 Work in pairs and look at the pictures. How often, if ever, do you play a game, go to the cinema or eat in a restaurant alone?

2 ▶ 34 Listen to an examiner giving candidates instructions about the pictures. What does he ask the first candidate to do?

3 Work in pairs. Take it in turns to choose two of the pictures and talk about them, following the examiner's instructions.

4 ▶ 35 Listen to a candidate talking about two of the pictures. Does she compare the same pictures as you did? Does she follow the examiner's instructions?

5 Listen again and complete the sentences with words and expressions which have a similar meaning to *on their own*.

1 There is a young woman .... watching a film in a cinema.

2 ... whatever it is she is watching and perfectly happy to be there ....

3 She's got a huge container of popcorn ....

4 In the second picture, a woman is having a(n) .... meal in a restaurant.

5 ... she's feeling a bit self-conscious about being a .... diner.

6 ... other cinema-goers probably wouldn't even notice that she is ....

6 ▶ 36 Listen to the question the examiner asks the other candidate and the candidate's response. What does the examiner ask? Does the candidate respond effectively?

7 Work in pairs. Turn to page 155 and do Task 1. Then turn to page 156 and do Task 2.

EXAM TIP

Try to paraphrase any vocabulary the examiner uses in the instructions rather than repeating their actual words.

Gapped text (Part 7)

▶ **EXAM** FOCUS p.200

1 What can you remember about your first day at primary school and your first teacher? Compare your answers with a partner.

2 Here are some comments people made about things they found difficult in primary school. Did you find any of these things particularly easy or difficult?

- It took me ages to be able to tell the time.
- We had to memorise loads of stuff. That was really hard.
- I couldn't tie my shoelaces properly myself.
- I don't know why but I sometimes couldn't understand what I read or what the teacher explained to us.
- I hated reading aloud. I used to hide behind my friend so the teacher wouldn't pick me.

3 You are going to read an article about a woman who had learning difficulties in primary school. Read the text and the missing paragraphs quickly. Which of the difficulties you discussed in Activity 2 are mentioned?

4 Read the article again. Six paragraphs have been removed from the article. Choose from the paragraphs A–G the one which fits each gap (1–6). There is one extra paragraph which you do not need to use.

EXAM TIP

Read the whole text before trying to answer the questions so that you have an understanding of its meaning and structure.

Vocabulary

working out meaning from context

5 Complete the sentences with the correct form of the underlined words and phrases in the article and missing paragraphs.

1 The government's attempts to deal with the problem of youth unemployment have been a .... failure.

2 Scientists have made a major .... in the treatment of cancer.

3 She has .... a method for quicker communication between the offices.

4 I don't think she .... that joke I told.

5 The legal system rests on the .... that a person is innocent until proven guilty.

6 The project was eventually .... as a non-starter after over six months' work.

6 Tell a partner about something you had difficulty learning. Why do you think you experienced this difficulty? Did you overcome it?

A
She started devising exercises for herself to work the parts of her brain that weren't functioning. She drew 100 two-handed clock faces on cards and wrote the time each told on the back. Then she started trying to tell the time from each. She did this eight to ten hours a day, gradually becoming faster and more accurate.

B
On the one hand, she was brilliant with near-total auditory and visual memory. 'I could memorise whole books.' On the other hand, she was a dolt. 'I didn't understand anything,' she says. 'Meaning just never crystallised. Everything was fragmented, disconnected.'

C
She occasionally came across a boy she knew during these study vigils but if he had any of the problems Arrowsmith-Young experienced, they certainly weren't of the same order. He, in fact, went on to get top marks in all his subjects.

D
She developed more exercises, for different parts of her brain, and found they worked too. Now almost thirty, she was finally beginning to function normally.

E
Faced with little receptivity for her ideas, Arrowsmith-Young decided to found her own school in Toronto in 1980; she now has thirty-five such schools. Thousands of children dismissed as impossible to teach have attended Arrowsmith schools and gone on to academic and professional success.

F
The breakthrough came when she was twenty-six. A fellow student gave her a book by a Russian neuropsychologist, Aleksandr Luria. The book contained his research on the writings of a highly intelligent Russian soldier, Lyova Zazetsky, who had been shot in the brain during a battle and recorded in great detail his subsequent disabilities.

G
The bullet had lodged in a part of the brain where information from sight, sound, language and touch is synthesised, analysed and made sense of. Arrowsmith-Young began to realise that, in all probability, this was the region of her own brain that had been malfunctioning since she was born.

How to rebuild your own brain

It's not the kind of thing you would ever forget. When Barbara Arrowsmith-Young started school in Canada in the early 1950s, her teacher told her mother – in her presence – that she would never be able to learn. Having helped over 4,000 children overcome exactly the same diagnosis, she can laugh at it. But she didn't at the time. Today Arrowsmith-Young holds a master's degree in psychology and has published a groundbreaking book called *The Woman Who Changed Her Brain*. But until she was in her mid-twenties, she was desperate, tormented and often depressed. She didn't know what was wrong.

1 In exams, she sometimes got 100 percent but whenever the task involved reasoning and interpretation, she would fail <u>dismally</u>. 'The teachers didn't understand,' she says. 'They thought I wasn't trying and I was often punished.' To help her, her mother <u>devised</u> a series of flashcards with numbers and letters and, after much hard work, she achieved literacy and numeracy of a sort, even getting into university, where she disguised her learning disabilities by working twenty hours a day. 'I used to hide when the security guards came to close the library at night, then come back out and carry on.'

2 For the first time, Arrowsmith-Young says, 'I recognised somebody describing exactly what I experienced. His expressions were the same: living life in a fog. His difficulties were the same: he couldn't tell the time from a clock, he couldn't tell the difference between the sentences *the boy chases the dog* and *the dog chases the boy*. I began to see that maybe an area of my brain wasn't working.'

3 Then she read about the work of Mark Rosenzweig, an American researcher who found that laboratory rats given a rich and stimulating environment developed larger brains. Rosenzweig concluded that the brain continues developing rather than being fixed at birth – a concept known as 'neuroplasticity'. Arrowsmith-Young decided that if rats could grow bigger and better brains, so could she.

4 'I was experiencing mental exhaustion like I had never known,' she says, 'so I figured something was happening. After three or four months of this, it really felt like something had fundamentally changed in my brain. I watched an edition of a news programme and I <u>got</u> it. I read pages from ten books and understood every single one. It was like stepping from darkness into light.'

5 It was revolutionary work, and not just for her. 'At that time,' she says, 'all the work around learning disabilities involved compensating for what learners couldn't do. It all started from the <u>premise</u> that they were unchangeable.'

6 'So much human suffering is caused by cognitive mismatches with the demands of the task,' says Arrowsmith-Young. 'So many wrong diagnoses get made, so many children get <u>written off</u>, so many people take wrong decisions and end up in lives and careers they did not choose for themselves but were chosen for them by cognitive limitations that can be identified and strengthened. There is hope for these people.'

Speaking

1 Work in pairs. Look at the comments about forgetfulness. Which ones apply to you?

> Without reminders in my mobile, I think I'd forget half the things I have to do. I've got a memory like a sieve.

> I never forget a face. Names? Well, that's another matter.

> If I'm very busy, I can be quite absent-minded. I leave my keys at home and things like that.

> I remember what I choose to remember and forget the rest.

Multiple matching (Part 4)

▶ **EXAM** FOCUS p.203

EXAM TIP

Read the options carefully to understand how they are different and what to listen for.

2 Work in pairs. Look at Task 1 below. Discuss how the consequences of being forgetful might arise and how the problem might be overcome.

3 Look at Task 2 and the strategies people use to overcome forgetfulness. Are they good strategies? Can you improve on them?

4 ▶ 37 You will hear five short extracts in which people are talking about being forgetful. While you listen, you must complete both tasks.

Task 1

For questions 1–5, choose from the list (A–H) what the consequences of being forgetful were for each speaker.

A hurting someone's feelings
B having to pay a lot of money
C feeling foolish
D not being understood
E losing a friendship
F failing to achieve something
G making someone angry
H experiencing anxiety

Speaker 1	**1**	
Speaker 2	**2**	
Speaker 3	**3**	
Speaker 4	**4**	
Speaker 5	**5**	

Task 2

For questions 6–10, choose from the list (A–H) the way each speaker says they could overcome the problem.

A making notes in a diary or notebook
B doing a memory improvement course
C using a special technique
D learning to pay more attention to the surroundings
E recalling how the information was learnt
F translating into another language
G making use of technology
H leaving reminders

Speaker 1	**6**	
Speaker 2	**7**	
Speaker 3	**8**	
Speaker 4	**9**	
Speaker 5	**10**	

5 Work in pairs.

Student A turn to page 164.

Student B turn to page 169.

6 Work in pairs. Tell your partner about something you forgot, what happened as a result and how you would avoid forgetting something like that again.

Emphasis

cleft sentences with *what*

▶ **GRAMMAR** REFERENCE p.175

1 Read the extract from a review of a book about neuroscience. Explain to a partner why we are 'unreliable witnesses'.

reviews

Unreliable witnesses

In their book *Welcome to Your Brain: Why You Lose Your Car Keys but Never Forget How to Drive and Other Puzzles of Everyday Life*, Sandra Aamodt and Sam Wang explain that when you call up a memory, you are capable of – and prone to – rewriting that memory in some form. **(1)** <u>What this means is that we're effectively changing our stories all the time without knowing it</u>. Consider how often we mix up events that are very similar but not the same. Let's say you've eaten at the same restaurant ten times in the last three months. You will probably find it very difficult to say on which of the ten occasions a certain conversation took place, especially without other distinguishing details such as something particularly disastrous that happened. It seems that the brain tries to condense all these similar events into one so that when you recall something, you may be rewriting the story in the light of new information. **(2)** <u>What is more worrying is the change we make to our mental model of the event</u>. But it's more than a change. **(3)** <u>What we're actually doing is replacing it altogether with a newer, expanded version</u>. As a result, we are all rather unreliable witnesses, something that lawyers have always exploited when cross-examining in the law courts.

2 Look at the underlined sentences in the extract. What is being emphasised in each of the sentences? Which words are used to introduce it?

3 Which of the sentences in the extract emphasises

1 a whole sentence?
2 the verb or event?
3 the object?

LANGUAGE TIP

Cleft sentences with *what* are used to emphasise a particular part of the sentence. They are often used with verbs that show the writer or speaker's emotional response (e.g. *like, loathe, find worrying, want, prefer*).

---

4 Complete the second sentence so that it has a similar meaning to the first sentence, using the word given. Do not change the word given. You must use between three and six words, including the word given.

1 I'd like to go to the cinema tonight. **DO**
   What I'd like .... to the cinema tonight.

2 He decided to drop out of university, which surprised me. **THAT**
   What .... he decided to drop out of university.

3 I really need a good night's sleep. **WHAT**
   A good night's sleep .... really need.

4 We had chicken when we went to that new Thai restaurant. **WAS**
   What .... when we went to that new Thai restaurant.

5 He was really motivated because he had had such an unhappy childhood. **FACT**
   What made him so .... he had had such an unhappy childhood.

6 I dislike the way she never tells me when she's going out. **ABOUT**
   What .... the way she never tells me when she's going out.

5 Complete the sentences with your own ideas. Then tell a partner about them.

1 What the world needs now …
2 What would almost certainly help me improve my English …
3 What makes our generation different from previous generations …
4 What I will probably be doing in five years' time …
5 What makes my town such a great place to live …
6 What people in this class will remember me for …

Reading

1 Read the blog entry about a woman's experience of learning Spanish. What advice in the blog do you agree or disagree with?

How I (almost) taught myself Spanish

I just can't live without books. It was hard to get hold of English books in Spain, so what I did was to teach myself to read. I used to listen to the news on the BBC in the morning and then buy *El País* and read the same news again in Spanish. I also started re-reading some novels I'd read years before in English. I resisted the temptation to look up every word I didn't recognise and tried to work out what the unfamiliar words meant in the context. I tried to remember them and to use them as soon as I could in a conversation to test out whether they really did mean what I thought they meant. Sometimes I got it wrong, though. I was reading a novel set in Peru and I kept using this very colloquial Peruvian vocabulary from the novel. People thought it was hilarious, especially with my very English accent. But my total immersion approach was only getting me so far. I decided to enrol in a language course. It was a great way of meeting people, though we did end up speaking English a lot of the time outside class.

Email (Part 2)

adopting the right tone

▶ **WRITING** REFERENCE p.190

2 Read the blog again. Do you think the style is formal or informal? Why?

3 Read the pieces of advice and decide if they are formal (F) or informal (I).

1 You would be well advised to invest in a good dictionary.

2 Get yourself a Spanish boyfriend!

3 If I were intending to learn another language, in all likelihood, I would enrol in a course.

4 I would suggest reading as widely as possible.

5 Spending a week living with a Spanish family is worth a try.

6 Something that I found really useful was joining a club where I had to speak to people.

7 I would not recommend trying to learn the language entirely on your own.

8 What seems to work for a lot of people is learning pop songs.

4 Do you agree with the advice in Activity 3? Rewrite the formal items in a less formal tone.

5 Look at the exam task and the points a student has written for her answer. The points are not in a logical order. Put them in the right order to make a coherent plan for a six-paragraph email message.

Read part of an email from a friend who is planning to come and live in your country.

Of course, I'd really need to learn the language. I know you've been learning English for years, so you've had loads of experience. Are there any tricks of the trade that might help me pick up your language a bit more quickly?

Reply to the email message offering your friend some advice. Write your **email** in **220–260** words in an appropriate style.

Points for inclusion:
- Express the hope of having been of some assistance.
- Make a series of suggestions about learning my language drawing on my own and others' experience.
- Express pleasure about friend's plans to relocate and reiterate the question in the email.
- Conclude with the wish to receive a reply and the usual salutation.
- Comment briefly on my experience of learning English.
- Acknowledge receipt of the message and apologise for not writing before.

6 The student has used very formal language in the list of points. Use the points to help you write a draft of your email message but make sure you use an informal tone.

7 Show your answer to other students and see if they can suggest any improvements.

1 Cross out the verb forms that are not possible.

Bright as a button

Heidi Hankins, aged four, sat an IQ test after staff at her nursery (1) *said/were saying/had said/had been saying* she was so intelligent they (2) *struggled/were struggling/had struggled/had been struggling* to find activities to challenge her. The average score for an adult is 100 and a 'gifted' individual 130 but the exceptional youngster (3) *impressed/was impressing/had impressed/had been impressing* examiners with a staggering 159. Heidi, who can already add, subtract, draw figures and write in sentences, (4) *read/was reading/had read/had been reading* books for seven-year-olds when she was just two. Heidi's dad hopes she can now skip a school year to ensure she is challenged. Her parents (5) *always thought/were always thinking/had always thought/had always been thinking* their little girl was clever because she (6) *learnt/was learning/had learnt/had been learning* to read early and (7) *tried/was trying/had tried/had been trying* to talk almost immediately after she was born. She now speaks very well for a child of her age. When her father (8) *gave/was giving/had given/had been giving* her something rather boring and very easy to cook for dinner, her response was, 'That's impressive,' so it seems she has a sense of humour too.

2 Cross out the alternative that is not possible in each sentence.

1 Advertising seems to be *brainwashing/brainstorming* people into thinking they have to be thin.

2 None of the doctors could work out why he had lost his eyesight, so they sent him for a brain *scan/wave*.

3 I found the explanation of the new mathematical theory completely *mind/brain* boggling.

4 *Brainchild/Brainteaser* of legendary rock producer Eddie Bond, The Mitfords new album is everything fans were hoping for.

5 You must be a *mind/brain* reader. Vegetarian lasagne was exactly what I was thinking of cooking for dinner and you've bought all the ingredients.

6 Now the former minister for science wants not only to keep local talent at home but to reverse the brain *drain/damage*.

3 Complete the second sentence so that it has a similar meaning to the first sentence, using the word given. Do not change the word given. You must use between three and six words, including the word given.

1 I think governments need to spend more money on creating jobs.
   DO
   What I think governments .... more money on creating jobs.

2 If I spent a year in an English-speaking country, it would almost certainly help me improve my English.
   WHAT
   Spending a year in an English speaking country .... almost certainly help me improve my English.

3 We will spend much longer in the education system, which makes our generation different from previous generations.
   FACT
   What makes our generation different from previous generations .... we will spend much longer in the education system.

4 I hope to be living in another country and working in the music industry in five years' time.
   DOING
   What I hope to be .... living in another country and working in the music industry.

5 My town is such a great place to live because of the people and the climate.
   ARE
   The people and the climate .... my town such a great place to live.

6 I have a very quirky sense of humour and people in this class will remember me for that.
   IS
   My quirky sense of humour .... will remember me for.

7 Travelling to Australia is difficult because of the huge time difference with Europe.
   MAKES
   What .... the huge time difference with Europe.

8 I love the view from the bedroom window better than anything else about the house.
   MOST
   The thing .... is the view from the bedroom window.

Things to come

10

Speaking

1 Work in pairs. Think of definitions for *idealist*, *realist*, *optimist* and *pessimist*. Which kind of person do you think it is best to be?

Past participles + dependent prepositions

2 Choose the correct alternative in each sentence. Do you think the statements were made by an optimist, an idealist, a pessimist or a realist?

1 I am concerned *of/about* the future of the planet.
2 I am inspired *on/by* people who believe they can change the world.
3 I am dedicated *in/to* making the world a better place.
4 I am terrified *of/on* what might happen in the future.
5 I am easily discouraged *on/by* bad news.
6 I am focused *in/on* making a positive contribution to society.
7 I am influenced *by/for* people who are enthusiastic and positive.
8 I am frustrated *on/with* people's lack of ability to make sensible choices.
9 I am motivated *by/for* people who have a can-do attitude to life.
10 I am opposed *with/to* the idea of relying on intuition to make decisions.

3 Decide which statements in Activity 2 are true about you and which you would like to be true. Compare your ideas with a partner.

4 Complete the sentences with prepositions. Which past participles can be followed by more than one preposition?

1 I am confused .... all the decisions I have to make about my future.
2 I am satisfied .... what I have achieved so far.
3 Older people are generally respected .... their wisdom.
4 I feel disappointed .... myself if I don't go for a run every day.
5 My teacher is committed .... helping everyone achieve their potential.
6 Many people are worried .... what will happen in the future.

Multiple-choice cloze (Part 1)

▶ **EXAM** FOCUS p.197

5 Work in pairs. How different will your future self be from the person you are now? Do you think your future self might be critical of some of the decisions you have made?

6 Work in pairs. Read the article and describe the writer's attitude to his future self.

7 Read the article again. For questions 1–8, decide which answer (A, B, C or D) best fits each gap.

0   **A** spending   **B** devoting
      C occupying   **D** offering

1   **A** focusing   **B** looking
      C aiming   **D** trying

2   **A** dedicated   **B** motivated
      C interested   **D** committed

3   **A** admire   **B** favour
      C praise   **D** approve

4   **A** draw   **B** give
      C clean   **D** take

5   **A** bring   **B** let
      C make   **D** do

6   **A** struggle   **B** energy
      C effort   **D** trouble

7   **A** purposes   **B** objectives
      C motives   **D** intentions

8   **A** lead   **B** reach
      C arrive   **D** jump

EXAM TIP

Some very strong verb/noun collocations are known as fixed phrases because the noun only collocates with one or perhaps two verbs, e.g. *make a sacrifice*. These are sometimes tested in this part of the exam.

8 Work in pairs and discuss the questions. Give personal examples where relevant.

1 How much do you think about your future?

2 What kind of sacrifices should people make for their future selves?

3 Do you think it's a good idea for young people to have a life plan?

YOU | *Be happy*

Failing to please our future selves

We are more concerned about the happiness of the person we think we will be in the future than of who we are now, **(0)** ....*B devoting*........ most of our waking hours to constructing a future that we imagine they will be content with. Rather than **(1)** .... on what makes us happy in the present, we are more **(2)** .... by what we think our future selves will **(3)** .... of. We are encouraged to **(4)** .... up large amounts of our monthly salaries in order to save for the future so that they can enjoy the benefits in their retirement. We **(5)** .... sacrifices thinking that we are taking wise decisions, only to wonder at some future date why we ever bothered to buy that house or start that business. It seems our future selves will never be satisfied with the **(6)** .... we have made on their behalf. They may appreciate our good **(7)** .... and come to accept that we did the best we could but with the benefit of hindsight, they will almost certainly **(8)** .... the conclusion that our best just wasn't good enough.

Listening

1 ▶ 38 **Read the article and say what Chris should do to achieve his goals. Then listen and compare with the advice a life coach gives.**

workrest**play**

CHRIS STUBBS, 30

commercial executive

'I tend to take each day as it comes and I've never really worried about the future that much. There's a couple I know who have their future all mapped out. They've decided they'll start a family within the next year or so and they even know how they'll finance their future children's education. They're moving to a bigger house soon. In their early fifties they think they'll have enough money to travel around the world for a year.

I think it's very important to plan for the future, but neither my wife nor I are that great at doing it. We're going to start a family at some point but it never seems to be the right time.

Every so often I think about long-term goals but it's fleeting. Two years from now, I hope I'll have been promoted or found another job. But I need to start thinking about how I'm going to achieve that. I'm worried that I'll be doing exactly the same job in five years' time if I don't start planning ahead. Perhaps I'll start doing that tomorrow!'

2 **Work in pairs. How useful would it be to have a life coach?**

Future forms

▶ **GRAMMAR** REFERENCE p.182

3 **Read the article in Activity 1 again and find an example of**

1 the present continuous for future plans.
2 *going to* for intentions.
3 *will* for predictions.
4 *will* for spontaneous decisions.
5 the future perfect.
6 the future continuous.

4 **Cross out the verb forms that are not possible.**

BLOG

So tomorrow is the day I've decided
(1) *I'm going to start/I'll start/I'm starting* planning my future. The first thing **(2)** *I'll do/I'm doing/I'm going to do* is to make a wish list of all the things I hope **(3)** *I'll achieve/I'm achieving/I'm going to achieve*. I need to try and imagine what **(4)** *I do/I'll be doing/I'm going to do* in five years' time. Then **(5)** *I'll be spending/I'm going to spend/ I'll have spent* the rest of the morning looking at job websites. **(6)** *I see/I'll see/I'm going to see* what kind of jobs are available. Ideally, **(7)** *I'll stay/I'll be staying/I'll have stayed* with my current employer but if I don't get promoted, I really hope **(8)** *I'll have found/I'm finding/I'll find* another job within two years.

5 **Complete the sentences with the correct form of the verb in brackets.**

1 Two years from now I hope I .... (*do*) my dream job.
2 By the time I'm twenty-five, I expect I .... (*leave*) home.
3 By this time next year, it's likely that I .... (*find*) a new job.
4 Within the next six months, I .... (*pass*) my driving test.
5 It's only a matter of time before I .... (*meet*) the right man.
6 It won't be long until I .... (*find*) the perfect apartment.
7 For the time being I .... (*live*) at home while I save money for my own apartment.
8 I'm sure I .... (*learn*) Arabic in no time.
9 It's about time I .... (*get*) some more up-to-date qualifications.
10 In twenty years I .... (*be*) glad that I took the decision to find my dream job.

LANGUAGE TIP

Some expressions which refer to the future are followed by the present simple/past simple (e.g. *it's only a matter of time before* + present simple, *it's about time* + past simple).

6 **Work in pairs. Use the time expressions in Activity 5 to talk about your own plans and predictions for the future.**

Speaking

1 Look at this advice from a magazine. How useful do you think it is?

Why put off until tomorrow what you can do today?

Make SMART goals!

S PECIFIC: Identify what exactly you want to achieve and by when.

M EASURABLE: Make your targets something you can tick off on a graph or table.

A CHIEVABLE: Don't be too ambitious – choose something you know you can comfortably achieve.

R EALISTIC: Reassess your goals if necessary and be prepared to be flexible as circumstances may change.

T ARGETS: Set monthly targets and stick to them.

2 Work in pairs. Make the goals *SMART* using the advice in Activity 1.

1 I'm planning to build my own dream house.
2 I will start my own business after I leave college.

3 Work in pairs. Ask your partner to help you identify some *SMART* goals of your own.

Collaborative task (Part 3)
reaching a decision

▶ **EXAM** FOCUS p.205

4 ▶ 39 Work in pairs. Listen to the examiner's instructions and do the first part of the task.

EXAM TIP

You may be able to discuss all the options but don't worry if you run out of time without talking about each one.

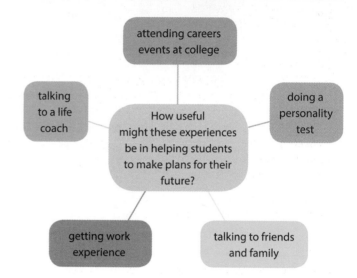

attending careers events at college

talking to a life coach

doing a personality test

How useful might these experiences be in helping students to make plans for their future?

getting work experience

talking to friends and family

5 ▶ 40 Listen to the second part of the task. Which things do you need to do in order to complete this part successfully?

1 Find out your partner's opinion.
2 Agree with your partner quickly.
3 Evaluate more than one option.
4 Give reasons for your decision.
5 Choose the right answer.

6 Look at the strategies for reaching a decision and add a second useful phrase for each one.

1 Narrow down the options: *For me it would be between X and Y.*
2 Reject one or more options: *Would you agree that we can rule out X?*
3 Summarise your partner's opinion: *So, basically, you're saying that … .*
4 Be willing to compromise: *Well as you feel so strongly about X, I don't mind going for that.*

7 Work in pairs. Listen again and do the second part of the task.

Multiple matching (Part 8)

▶ **EXAM** FOCUS p.201

1 Work in pairs. How interested are you in where or how the food you eat is produced? Is there anything that you would refuse to eat?

2 Work in pairs. Read the article quickly and put the developments in food science in order of importance.

3 Read the article again. For questions 1–10, choose your answers from the sections A–D. You may choose any of the sections more than once.

Which person

gives an opinion about why the produce may be unappealing?	**1**
thinks that this type of cultivation will have positive implications for other produce?	**2**
highlights the negative view of some critics who doubt the produce could be commercially successful?	**3**
predicts that people could be unaware they are consuming this product?	**4**
identifies a surprisingly unexpected place for the cultivation of this food source?	**5**
admits that he could be mistaken about something?	**6**
is sure that a solution to an increased need for food has been discovered?	**7**
states that one advantage of this food source is that it grows more quickly than alternative options?	**8**
describes how a particular farming problem has been resolved?	**9**
doubts that demand from local people for the produce will grow significantly?	**10**

4 Work in pairs and discuss the questions.

1 Would you be prepared to eat synthetic meat?
2 How likely do you think it is that people will eat less meat in the future?
3 How do you think your diet may change as you get older?

Vocabulary
working out meaning from context

5 Look at the underlined words in the article and use the context to help you choose the correct meaning, A or B.

1	texture	**A**	taste	**B**	feel
2	staple	**A**	basic	**B**	balanced
3	insatiable	**A**	possible to satisfy	**B**	impossible to satisfy
4	viable	**A**	possible	**B**	impossible
5	outcome	**A**	disadvantage	**B**	result
6	yields	**A**	profits	**B**	amount produced
7	prone	**A**	likely to get	**B**	unlikely to get
8	maturity	**A**	perfection	**B**	adulthood

How a new generation of radical farmers and food producers are trying to balance the needs of the environment with the need for increased productivity.

Future food

A Seaweed farmer

Seamus O'Higgins

Although Seamus has been harvesting red seaweed called dillisk on the West coast of Ireland for decades to make a traditional snack, large-scale seaweed farming is a new venture. 'It has huge potential,' says Seamus. 'It's both plentiful and fast-growing – an ideal crop.' Although seaweed is an established food product in many parts of the world, it hasn't taken off to the same extent in northern Europe. 'That's probably because people are familiar with its texture, smell and colour and are put off by this, although I have to say it certainly tastes better than it looks!' Seamus admits. 'While we're not anticipating it becoming a staple part of the local diet, I can see it becoming widely used as a supplement. Seaweed has a strong salty taste but, ironically, is actually low in salt, so it's more than likely that salt could be replaced by seaweed granules in many supermarket ready-meals, for example, and people wouldn't even notice the difference.'

B Tissue engineer

Dr Mark Post

Animal farming consumes about one-third of the planet's land area. It may take much more to satisfy the world's insatiable appetite for meat. A radical solution is required: synthetic meat. Dr Mark Post is at the forefront of this revolution. 'A few years ago it felt like science fiction to suggest that this would be viable but we've proved that meat can be reared from stem cells in a Petri dish rather than on a farm. Bio-engineered meat could be used in processed meat products like hamburgers, sausages and meatballs. We are working under the assumption, which might be naive, that if you let the cells grow under conditions that are very similar to those in an animal, then they will recreate the taste of the original animal. Whether that's true, we'll find out,' Mark confesses. But the outcome is far from clear. 'There are other people who say you will never be able to make it taste exactly the same as meat. So there are lots of sceptics'.

C Plant breeder

Dr Jauhar Ali

The Green Super Rice (GSR) project is aiming to produce varieties of rice that are resistant to drought, floods, pests and do not require chemical fertilisers. At the same time researchers are identifying varieties which produce higher yields, without resorting to genetic modification. 'We have already had some success,' explains Dr Jauhar Ali from the International Rice Research Institute. 'One example is a weed-tolerant GSR variety, which establishes itself much faster than weeds. This means the chemicals aren't needed to control the weeds, which makes it both cheaper to produce and less harmful for the environment. We've also identified five GSR varieties that have performed well under severe drought conditions in several sub-Saharan African countries. Rice production must double in this region in order to support a rapidly rising population and we believe GSR technology is the answer. But the production method is perhaps even more important than the rice itself. That is because it can be applied to other crops, such as wheat, that feed millions of people.'

D Professor of aquaculture

Dr Paul Melville

With stocks of other fish species in severe decline, the popularity of fish like cobia is growing so rapidly that it's difficult to keep up with demand. Cobia have been successfully farmed in other parts of the world but where they are kept in cages in the sea, it causes pollution. Dr Paul Melville believes aquaculture systems are best operated in big empty spaces away from coastal areas. One possible location might be the desert, which, although not usually associated with either fish or water, is actually ideal, because marine food production doesn't require freshwater as a resource. 'Increasingly, I'm sure we will see fish farms operating inland far from the sea. I believe cobia is preferable to salmon for fish farmers because it isn't as prone to disease and reaches maturity in half the time. It can reach a weight of six to ten kilograms in the first year compared with up to two kilograms for salmon.'

Speaking

1 Work in pairs and discuss the questions.

1 How have attitudes to behaviour such as recycling and smoking changed in the last decade?

2 What do you think is the most successful way to change people's behaviour? Think of examples for the following and put them in order of effectiveness.

- a financial reward
- peer pressure
- government regulation
- setting an example

Sentence completion (Part 2)

▶ **EXAM** FOCUS p.202

2 Look at the exam task below. Try to predict what kind of information is missing. Can you predict any possible answers?

A nudge in the right direction

Some things we do every day out of (1) .... habit .... are harmful to the environment.

Marcus says it should be easy to persuade people turn (2) .... off the lights .... because it saves them money.

Marcus thinks we're less likely to change our behaviour if we know there will only be a(n) (3) .... long-term .... impact.

Marcus says studying people's attitudes often reveals a(n) (4) .... gap .... between their actions and their beliefs.

The Copenhagen study found that putting (5) .. green footsteps ... on the ground to encourage people to throw sweet wrappers in litter bins was very successful.

Marcus supports the idea of using creative ways to encourage good behaviour, rather than giving people (6) .... fines .... for littering.

Some governments are using the idea of 'nudging' instead of (7) .. regulation .. to change people's behaviour.

Marcus disagrees with some environmentalists who claim a real change in attitudes to (8) .. recycling .. and buying cars hasn't been achieved by nudging.

3 ▶ 41 Listen to part of a radio report by a behavourial psychologist called Marcus King, talking about how to encourage people to change their behaviour towards the environment. For questions 1–8, complete the sentences.

EXAM TIP

Complete the sentences with the most obvious answers if you are not sure. There is a chance you could be right.

4 Work in pairs and discuss the questions.

1 Can you think of any ways you could be 'nudged' into changing your behaviour?

2 How effective are measures to reduce traffic, increase recycling and reduce energy consumption where you live?

3 What other measures could your college/place of work introduce to improve the environment?

5 Complete the phrases with the verbs in the box.

act	cause	cut	follow
lead	move		

1 .... energy consumption
2 .... serious harm to the environment
3 .... in the right direction
4 .... to a reduction in …
5 .... in our own interests
6 .... a good example

6 Work in pairs. Turn to page 165 and do the activity.

Conjunctions

▶ **GRAMMAR** REFERENCE p.174

1 **Work in pairs.**

1 Read the article and summarise the concept of collaborative consumption. Do you agree that it is an attractive idea?

2 Try to work out what the statements are referring to and then decide how far you agree with them.
  • Big fences make good neighbours.
  • the days of keeping up with the Joneses are numbered.
  • There is a world of difference between sharing and hand-me-down.

TheReporter

Blog feed 🔊 All feeds

OME   NEWS   WORLD   SPORT   FINANCE   **COMMENT**   BLOGS   CULTURE

The power of collaborative consumption

The market in sharing goods and services is now estimated to be worth £310 billion. The classic examples are enterprises such as Zipcar and Whipcar. Instead of paying upfront to purchase their own car, people are tapping into online networks that enable them to rent or share a car for trips to the supermarket, etc. **(1)** <u>Nor</u> is this a fringe craze. On a planet with finite resources, collaborative consumption is considered to be the sign of things to come. As yet, transport and travel are the significant sharing sectors but the movement's advocates see little reason why the idea won't keep spreading. **(2)** <u>As long as</u> people need goods and services, the opportunities are endless. **(3)** <u>Whereas</u> sharing, renting and swapping used to take place in market squares, these days smart phones are used to make electronic transactions.

The popularity of sharing suggests something deeper could be going on within society as a whole. 'This generation is starting to question **(4)** <u>whether</u> big fences make good neighbours,' argues Rachel Botsman, author of What's Mine is Yours. She believes the days of keeping up with the Joneses are numbered. Instead, we'll be sharing cars and lawn mowers with them. This seems a reasonable prediction, **(5)** <u>provided</u> the majority of consumers can be convinced there is a world of a difference between sharing and hand-me-down.

---

2 **Match the underlined conjunctions (1–5) in the article with their functions.**

1 making a contrast
2 giving a condition
3 adding information

LANGUAGE TIP

Be careful to use the correct word order with *nor*. It is followed by a verb and then the subject. *As* is also used in this way.

I wasn't happy, **nor was I** *sad.*

Buying a car is expensive, **as is insurance**.

---

3 **Choose the correct alternative in each sentence.**

1 Forgetting to switch the lights off, on the other hand, has a personal cost, *as/nor* does driving a gas-guzzling car.

2 But some environmentalists argue that the congestion charge hasn't led to a change in attitude to car ownership, *as yet/nor* does increased recycling at work necessarily lead to changed behaviour at home.

3 *As yet/As long as* no restrictions on water use have been introduced, despite the lower than average rainfall.

4 In the city door-to-door recycling collections are made weekly, *whether/whereas* in the country people have to take their own rubbish to recycling centres.

5 People must try to cut down on their use of water. *Provided/Whereas* they do this, a serious shortage will be avoided.

6 Despite the pollution caused by cars, many people will refuse to walk or cycle, *nor/as long as* petrol remains an affordable option.

---

4 **Match the underlined phrases with *as* in the sentences to the meanings in the box.**

current	regarding	since	starting on
until now	while		

1 <u>As</u> time begins to run out, the need to take action is increasingly urgent.

2 <u>As for</u> people who deny climate change against all scientific evidence, they should not be given such prominent publicity.

3 The government <u>as yet</u> has not managed to reach any of its recycling targets.

4 The situation <u>as it is</u>, seems alarming but there is cause for optimism.

5 <u>As</u> the government has failed to solve the problem, it's up to local communities to take action.

6 <u>As from</u> next Monday, anyone caught littering will be given an automatic fine.

Formal letter (Part 2)
using an appropriate range of language
▶ **WRITING** REFERENCE p.188

1 **Read the letter. Do you agree with the writer's opinion?**

LETTER PAGE

Letters to the editor

Dear Sir/Madam,

Thank you for once again bringing to the public's attention the shameless use and wasteful disposal of plastic shopping bags that are polluting our cities, countryside and beaches.

Retailers need a strong government lead to discourage them from giving shoppers free plastic bags and until that lead is given, bags will continue to be manufactured and handed out in shops for just one use. It is unacceptable that bags are so thoughtlessly discarded when it is clear that they cause a hazard to wildlife.

If we accept the need for drastically reducing the amount of waste being sent to landfill, the government has got to do more than simply nudge changes in consumer behaviour. It is about time a charge was introduced for single-use plastic bags. Countries which have already introduced plastic bag charges have seen their consumption drop by up to ninety percent, yet the government continues to ignore this evidence. It is hoped the government soon realises there is little to be gained by waiting any longer and much to be lost.

Yours faithfully,

Penelope Moss

2 **Find a more 'advanced' word in the second and third paragraphs of the letter to match meanings 1–6.**

1 stop	4 danger
2 produced	5 amount used
3 thrown away	6 but

3 **Find one or more examples in the third paragraph of**

1 an impersonal reporting verb.
2 a passive form.
3 a conditional form.
4 a participle clause.
5 a relative clause.
6 a conjunction.

4 **What is being done to reduce the use of plastic bags where you live?**

5 **Look at the exam task and plan your answer. Then write your letter.**

EXAM TIP

To do well in the Writing paper, you must demonstrate you can use a range of complex language accurately. This includes vocabulary and structures, as well as using a variety of conjunctions, linking words, etc.

Your college needs to cut down the amount of plastic water bottles thrown away by students in order to meet stricter government regulations. Students have been asked for their suggestions on how the college can achieve this. Your letter should explain

• how you think the college can cut down the use of plastic bottles.
• the advantages of your idea.
• ways to make sure students co-operate.

Write your **letter** in **220–260** words in an appropriate style.

6 **Check your work using the checklist on page 185.**

7 **Work in pairs. Check your partner's letter. How many of the advanced language features in Activity 3 has he/she included?**

1 Read the article and think of the word which best fits each gap. Use only one word for each gap.

▶ Recruitment

thestandard

☁ 16°C 8°C

News | Sport | Comment | Culture | Business | Money | Life & style | Travel

News | UK | World | Development | US | Politics | Media | Education | Law

Planning ahead

Sally Keating, who runs an online recruitment service, admits she often worries (1) .... the future. 'My biggest concern for my future is that my company (2) .... not be the success that I hope for as I'm depending on that to make all my dreams come true.' But when Sally starts worrying about the future, she isn't just thinking about the immediate needs of her business. By the time her online business (3) .... successful, she also wants to (4) .... bought a flat and got married. She is also uncertain how she (5) .... be able to save for her retirement.

This is the advice life coach Paddy Carson had to offer Sally: '(6) .... it's a good idea to think about your goals in life, Sally's problem is that she's identified too many. Instead, Sally needs to focus on her priorities. First, she needs to focus on making her business a success. She should get some advice from someone who understands the recruitment business and set some realistic targets. She should not delay doing this. (7) .... should she allow herself to wonder (8) .... her business will be successful. She should only picture what it will be like when she's achieved her goals.'

2 Match the first half of the sentences (1–6) with the second (A–F).

1 Ten years from now the government
2 By the time I'm twenty-five
3 Within the next six months
4 It's only a matter of time
5 For the time being
6 It's about time

A I'll have started my own business.
B you faced reality and got a job.
C before everyone starts sharing cars.
D the government isn't going to raise taxes on petrol.
E we anticipate that the restaurant will start using artificial meat.
F expects there'll be fewer cars on the roads.

3 Choose the correct option to complete the sentences.

1 The book was inspired .... his mother, who had been a huge influence.
   A on   B by   C for
2 I admire people who are dedicated .... finding solutions to environmental problems.
   A for   B in   C to
3 Don't let yourself be discouraged .... negative comments.
   A from   B on   C by
4 I am focused .... achieving my goals by the time I'm thirty.
   A in   B on   C to
5 Sarah is easily influenced .... people who are confident and self-assured.
   A from   B by   C for
6 It's easy to get frustrated .... yourself when things go wrong.
   A on   B with   C by
7 Not everyone would be motivated .... having a life coach.
   A by   B for   C on
8 Many people are opposed .... eating meat.
   A from   B by   C to

4 Complete the sentences with the conjunctions in the box.

as   as from   as long as   as yet   nor   since   whether   while

1 I am not sure .... we will still be living here this time next year.
2 My boss is committed to making this company successful, ... are all the team.
3 .... I've been sent no information, despite my repeated requests.
4 I feel well and positive .... I take some exercise every day.
5 .... I can't afford to run a car, I am going to buy a bicycle.
6 Many people doubt that the Green Party will win the next election, ... do they think this is a serious problem.
7 .... next month we won't be able to drive in the city centre.
8 .... he is determined to get a promotion within the next six months, he clearly doesn't want to take on more responsibility.

PROGRESS TEST 2

Multiple-choice cloze (Part 1)

5 For questions 1–8, read the text below and decide which answer (A, B, C or D) best fits each gap. There is an example at the beginning (0).

Srinivasa Ramajunan

Srinivasa Ramajunan, possibly the (0) ....*A...greatest*...... mathematical genius of the last century, was born in

Tamil Nadu, India. He came from a poor family and did not go to university but he developed his own individual way of writing formulae and even (1) .... to publish some of his work in an Indian mathematics journal. Ramajunan believed that his results were (2) .... to him by a Hindu goddess and so he did not show how he had arrived at his conclusions. Because of this, his work (3) .... largely ignored until he sent letters to prominent international mathematicians, (4) .... them the British mathematician G. H. Hardy. As Hardy read Ramajunan's letter, his amazement steadily (5) .... He recognised that the young Indian had (6) .... at several results in pure mathematics that were already (7) .... but had used completely new techniques. Even more astounding was the fact that there were some entirely new results quoted without proofs. Hardy immediately invited Ramajunan to work with him. Ramajunan made the journey to Cambridge in April 1914 and began a very productive (8) .... with Hardy.

0	A	greatest	B	best	C	highest	D strongest
1	A	accepted	B	achieved	C	managed	D succeeded
2	A	communicated	B	provided	C	distributed	D shared
3	A	maintained	B	remained	C	kept	D continued
4	A	among	B	within	C	inside	D between
5	A	multiplied	B	increased	C	boosted	D expanded
6	A	gained	B	acquired	C	landed	D arrived
7	A	noticed	B	discovered	C	realised	D known
8	A	teamwork	B	collaboration	C	co-operation	D participation

Open cloze (Part 2)

6 For questions 1–8, read the text below and think of the word which best fits each gap. Use only one word for each gap. There is an example at the beginning (0).

Language across borders

Sali Tagliamonte, a language researcher specialising (0) ....*in*............ young people's speech, had noticed that Canadian young people telling stories and reporting their (1) .... and others' actual words had started to use *be like* instead of *said*. As this trend had begun in the US, Tagliamonte's assumption (2) .... that the Canadians had picked it (3) .... from Americans they had actually spoken to. Tagliamonte, (4) .... with other linguists, believed that people only change their speech if they interact with others who have already adopted the change. But she wanted to test her hypothesis by recording some British students as (5) .... She thought they would use *like* to quote far (6) .... frequently than the Canadians since they had only limited and sporadic contact with Americans. When she analysed the recordings, she found, (7) .... her astonishment, that the British teens were using *like* to quote even more than their Canadian counterparts. Her results showed that for the first time a language change was spreading (8) .... means of movies and TV rather than interaction.

Word formation (Part 3)

7 For questions 1–8, read the text below. Use the word given in capitals at the end of some of the lines to form a word that fits in the gap in the same line. There is an example at the beginning (0).

Hospitable career opportunities

Travel and **(0)** ...*tourism*... provide more jobs than any other industry, accounting for 255 million jobs worldwide. Given the high levels of youth **(1)** .... in large parts of the developed world and a severe **(2)** .... of jobs in developing countries, you might think the industry should have no difficulty filling those vacancies. But the hospitality sector has to contend with negative **(3)** .... among **(4)** .... employees of low wages, unsociable hours and a lack of career opportunities. These **(5)** .... are false, according to Suzy Jackson of the Hospitality Guild, which was set up in 2011 to improve **(6)** .... She makes the point that there are many career **(7)** .... for young people in the industry at entry level, and that they can rise through the ranks to become chief executive or managing director. This may only happen in **(8)** .... circumstances but because the hospitality industry takes so many young people with minimal formal qualifications, it devotes time and money to training. This makes it a very good choice for young people considering a long-term career.

TOUR	
EMPLOY	
SHORT	
PERCEIVE	
PROSPECT	
ASSUME	
RECRUIT	
OPEN	
EXCEPT	

Key word transformations (Part 4)

8 For questions 1–6, complete the second sentence so that it has a similar meaning to the first sentence, using the word given. Do not change the word given. You must use between three and six words, including the word given.

1 Waiting another day to book my ticket would have meant paying a lot more.

IF

I would have had to pay a lot more .... another day to book my ticket.

2 If there's any chance of your passing the post office, could you get me some stamps?

HAPPEN

If .... the post office, could you get me some stamps?

3 There is no possibility whatsoever of my attending the meeting.

QUITE

It's .... the meeting.

4 'Have any of you stayed in the Hotel Belmondo?' asked Kim.

IF

Kim asked .... stayed in the Hotel Belmondo.

5 'I wish I hadn't told Angela about the row with Miriam,' said Carla.

REGRETTED

Carla .... about the row with Miriam.

6 I'll stay and look after my sister until I'm not needed anymore.

AS

I'll stay and look after my sister .... necessary.

A perfect match

Expressions for describing compatibility

1 Work in pairs. Is compatibility the most important thing for you in a friendship?

2 Complete the questions. Then ask and answer them with a partner.

1 What kinds of people are you usually compatible .... ?

2 Do you enjoy spending time with people whose opinions differ .... yours but are in some ways complementary?

3 Are all your friends .... exactly the same wavelength as you?

4 Do you have any friends who are .... different .... chalk and cheese, yet still get on like a house .... fire?

5 Do the ads that come up when you are online correspond .... your interests or are you offered products and services that have nothing to do .... your needs at all?

3 Work in pairs. Write a short conversation using at least five of the expressions in Activity 2 and other expressions to talk about compatibility.

4 Complete the sentences with *match*, *fit* or *suit*.

1 Your socks .... your tie exactly.

2 That colour doesn't .... you at all.

3 These jeans don't .... me anymore. I can barely do up the zip.

4 The personal details you enter on the booking form must .... those in your passport or other ID exactly.

5 Few cities in Europe can .... the cultural richness of Berlin.

6 The government promised to .... any private donations to the earthquake fund dollar for dollar.

5 Work in pairs. Use the words in Activity 4 to talk about the clothes you usually wear, the clothes you are wearing today and current fashions.

LANGUAGE TIP

We also use *suit* to mean 'be convenient for'.

*Would it **suit** you to join us for dinner that evening or would lunch be more convenient?*

Reading

6 Answer the questions. Then compare your answers with a partner.

1 What information do you include in your profile on social networking sites? Is there anything you tend to leave out? Why?

2 Have you ever done a search with your own details to see what information is available about you online? Did you find anything that surprised you?

7 Read the article about profiling on a well-known search engine. How does the writer feel about her profile?

Who does Google think I am?

You might think that Google has no idea who you are, or perhaps you're like me and have discovered they sometimes think you're somebody else!

(1) <u>Whenever I did an internet search, I noticed that ads for products I wouldn't have dreamt of buying kept popping up.</u> **(2)** <u>Google was matching whoever they thought I was to the products they thought</u> I should like, but why? The problem was the profile Google had generated for me. Firstly, they'd obviously noticed me searching nerdy topics like cybernetics and assumed I was male. I started going grey when I was a teenager and occasionally search hair products for people who share my condition, so they think I'm in my sixties but I'm only twenty-nine!

But sometimes Google does get it right. Last month I was looking for images of ballet classes in the early 1990s and typed the description into my browser. The first photo that came up was of me as a small girl in a ballet class over twenty years ago. **(3)** <u>Amazed, I tested it out on both my laptop and work computer but whichever computer I happened to use, there I was again.</u> I began to think I might be rather famous. When I told friends to search with the same terms, they got me, too. It turns out I'm not famous though. Google does know who I am and it knows who my friends are, too. **(4)** <u>Whatever they happen to search, if Google has a picture of me that somehow fits that description, that</u> will be one of the images my friends get to see. ◆

whoever, whatever, etc.

▶ **GRAMMAR** REFERENCE p.184

8 Look at the underlined sentences in the article in Activity 7 and rewrite them without using -*ever* words. What do the -*ever* words mean? What part of speech are they (object, pronoun, adverb)?

9 Complete the sentences with *however, whoever, whatever, whichever, wherever* or *whenever*.

1 .... she wears, she always looks great.

2 .... hard I try, I always forget the number.

3 I don't have anything planned, so we can meet up .... it suits you.

4 I like both shirts – .... one you buy will look good on you.

5 He's willing to move .... he can find work.

6 You need to send the report to .... is in charge of international sales.

10 Rewrite the advice on social networking sites using -*ever* words.

1 It doesn't matter how well you know and trust the person – never share your log-in details.

2 Set your notifications to tell you every time someone tags you in a photo.

3 Regardless of how much you like an image, think carefully before you post it on your wall.

4 It doesn't matter where you're going on holiday – don't put the details up on your wall. You might not want everyone to know you're away.

11 Work in pairs. Discuss whether you agree with the advice in Activity 10. Then write two more pieces of advice of your own.

> **LANGUAGE TIP**
>
> *Whatever* can be used as a short response meaning 'I don't mind'. It can sound impatient or rude.
>
> A: *Would you rather have tea or coffee?*
>
> B: *Whatever.*
>
> To make it more polite, add *you like/prefer*.

12 Work in pairs. Take turns to make suggestions about things to do at the weekend and respond using *whatever*.

Speaking

1 Work in pairs and discuss the statement.

Online services that match people to compatible friends, romantic partners or professional contacts do a better job than real people who try to match-make their friends.

2 Read the article about online dating services and choose the best title.

1 Reasons why online dating may not always work
2 A history of online dating services
3 Couple finds true love through online dating

Multiple choice (Part 5)

▶ **EXAM** FOCUS p.199

3 Look at the underlined word in the first paragraph of the article. What do you think it means? Use the information that comes later in the paragraph to help you.

EXAM TIP

Don't be put off by vocabulary you don't know. Keep reading and the meaning may become clear.

4 Read the article again. For questions 1–6, choose the answer (A, B, C or D) which you think fits best according to the text.

1 Why, according to the writer, did Peter Lake feel the need to sign up to Operation Match?

  A He knew he would not be able to afford more expensive services.

  B There were very few girls in the degree course he was taking.

  C He was too shy to go out and meet girls in the normal way.

  D He and the girls he met at university didn't seem to be compatible.

2 What is the writer's attitude to the modern versions of computer dating?

  A He is impressed by the sophistication of their approach.

  B He thinks the simpler methods of the past were just as effective.

  C He is not entirely convinced that they always fulfil their claims.

  D He dislikes the way they restrict access to their database.

3 What prompted the psychologists to write a journal article about the dating services?

  A They objected to the fact that the services were out to make money.

  B They believed the method the services used should be checked by independent scientists.

  C They thought the services should employ professional scientists.

  D They had evidence which undermined the validity of the tests.

4 How does the writer explain the apparent success of the services?

  A It is easy to find partners for people who have a lot of money.

  B Unsuitable people are excluded from subscribing.

  C Many subscribers lie when they complete the questionnaires.

  D Subscribers to services like these all share a number of characteristics.

5 What does Professor Eastwick consider the services do effectively?

  A match subscribers to people they get on quite well with

  B convince subscribers that the methods used actually work

  C eliminate people who are unlikely to find partners

  D make people feel better about their chances of finding a partner

6 Why does the writer return to Peter Lake's story in the last paragraph?

  A to demonstrate that online dating services have major limitations

  B to make readers feel sorry for Lake

  C to persuade readers that it may be worth giving online dating services a try

  D to suggest that other methods of finding a partner may be more effective

5 Replace the underlined verbs with phrasal verbs from the article. You may need to change the form of the verbs.

1 I'm thinking of <u>registering</u> to do a yoga course.
2 He asked her out but she <u>refused him</u>.
3 Education spending cannot be <u>reduced</u> any further.
4 There's no evidence to <u>support</u> his claims.
5 He spent the whole evening <u>talking seductively to</u> my best friend.
6 Personality tests sometimes help human resources staff <u>eliminate</u> unsuitable candidates.

9:48 67%

News   Voices   Technology   Politics   Travel   Finance

Online dating: the way to find Mr or Mrs Right?

Staff Reporter

In Autumn 1965, Peter Lake filled out a survey that changed the course of his life. He signed up to Operation Match, a computer dating service. 'It was such a good deal you couldn't turn it down,' Lake says. 'For three dollars they would guarantee to match you with at least three compatible people or they would give you your money back.' But there was more to Lake's decision than the fact that it made good economic sense. Although he had met lots of girls during his first semester at college, he just hadn't clicked with any of them. He mailed the survey back and was matched with a <u>dozen</u> women. With the exception of one who lived too far away, he met all of them. 'The eleventh was a student at Wellesley College. She and I talked on the phone and then we met for coffee and I just fell in love with her right there and then. We started dating immediately and married a year later.' Computer dating was simple way back then.

Fast forward almost fifty years and it has graduated from paper-based surveys directed at lonely students to become a multi-billion dollar global industry, generating income from both subscriptions and advertising. While many dating sites allow their subscribers to freely roam through lists of potential mates, niche services promise to match you with that special someone. The punch card technology that united Peter Lake with his future wife has been replaced by patented online personality tests, devised by psychologists and anthropologists. One site, for example, uses a questionnaire with more than 400 items – cut back to 100 if you're using the mobile app – supposedly designed to match clients with the man or woman of their dreams. But can they?

The dating service claim that their product is backed up by rigorous research into the characteristics of couples in committed, long-term relationships and that they have managed to identify the shared personality characteristics and values that best predict successful matches. Not everyone is sold on the science, however. In a recent issue of a major psychology journal, psychologists sought to pour cold water on the scientific claims of this and other similar sites, noting that none have ever subjected their algorithms – their secret sauce that matches couples – to peer scrutiny.

In fact, a 'selection bias' – a statistical bias that occurs when your sample population is different from the norm – may be at work. People using matching sites are, after all, different from the average Joe or Jill. For starters, they're likely to have a higher disposable income and, given that they sit

through a 400-question survey, more highly motivated than the average dater. In my opinion, the claimed success of matching sites may have more to do with narrowing the pool of eligible daters than psychological tests or computer science.

Associate Professor of Psychology Paul Eastwick says that another problem is that the sites claim to do much more than weed out Mr or Ms Wrong. 'They promise to find you someone who is especially compatible with you – your soul mate. That's a very different promise that they cannot fulfil,' says Eastwick. He argues, for example, that there may be a placebo effect at work. Just as placebos work because of the aura of authority around the person prescribing the 'drug', rather than its inherent medicinal value, so online matching services may work because the couple believe their coupling has been validated by relationship experts using complex computer science.

But can the digital Cupids guarantee living happily ever after? Peter Lake and his wife, two of computer matching's first success stories, divorced after eleven years of marriage. Lake has returned to computer dating but the barrier to finding true love has turned out to be more geographical than technological. 'I met a really nice dentist but she lived too far away,' says Lake. 'Eventually, I realised unless they live down the street, I'm really not interested.' He has abandoned algorithm-assisted online dating in favour of online chat rooms and forums. 'Now, if I want to meet somebody, I just go online, find them and chat them up.' Matching software, it seems, is no match for a good chat up line.

Open cloze (Part 2)

▶ **EXAM** FOCUS p.198

1 Work in pairs and discuss the questions.

1 What makes it easy or difficult to meet people where you live?

2 What would be the best way for someone who is new in town to meet people and make friends?

3 Have you heard of speed dating? What would it be like in a professional situation?

2 Read the title and the article quickly. Do you think it is about professional or personal contexts?

Business Daily

Speed networking

Speed dating events were originally set **(0)**............*up*............ to help young people from the same background meet and make connections. Although speed daters only talk to **(1)** .... another for a few minutes, that's plenty of time to decide if they want to take the relationship any **(2)** .... In fact, people know whether they do or they don't in a matter **(3)** .... seconds, only rarely changing their minds.

Nowadays, speed dating is increasingly finding its **(4)** .... into the boardroom and the scientific conference, not **(5)** .... a means for business people and scientists to find their soul mates but as an efficient and fun way of generating ideas and sharing information. Rather than spending valuable time listening to only a **(6)** .... other people, everyone gets to talk and everyone gets to listen. Just as in romantically-oriented speed dating events, participants put a tick **(7)** .... to the names of the people they would like to see again. They say it's all **(8)** .... networking and information but I bet there's the occasional romance too.

3 Choose the correct alternative in each sentence. Why is the other alternative not possible?

1 They married a *matter/few* weeks after they met.

2 I'd like to be someone who really *makes/does* something for other people.

3 He set *up/out* to make as many friends as he possibly could.

4 She put a cross *against/next* to the names of all the students who were absent from her class.

5 Someone offered me a job in the US but I decided not to take them *up/out* on it.

6 She wasted *all/some* her time in the exam trying to remember an answer she had memorised.

4 Read the article again. For questions 1–8, think of the word which best fits each gap. Use only one word for each gap.

> **EXAM TIP**
>
> Rather than focussing on individual phrases, make sure you have understood the meaning of the whole sentence, paragraph and text before you decide on your answer.

Speaking

5 Answer the questions. Then compare your answers with a partner.

1 What advantages does speed dating have over other ways of meeting new people?

2 What are the disadvantages?

3 Would you be more (or less) interested in attending a speed dating event if you knew it was an opportunity to network with people in your profession or with those who study similar things to you?

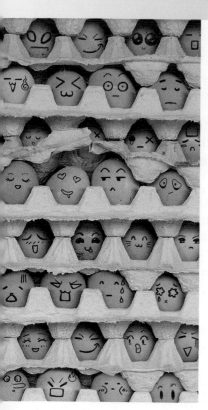

Multiple matching (Part 4)

▶ **EXAM** FOCUS p.203

1 Look at the two exam tasks in Activity 3. Have you ever done a personality test for any of the reasons listed in Task 1? Have you ever reacted to the results in any of the ways mentioned in Task 2?

EXAM TIP

You can answer either of the two questions about each speaker (one in Task 1 and one in Task 2) in any order. Sometimes the answer to the question in Task 2 actually comes first.

---

2 ▶ 42 You will hear five short extracts in which people are talking about personality tests. Listen to the first extract. Does the information come in the same order as the two tasks?

3 ▶ 43 Listen to all five extracts. While you listen, you must complete both tasks.

Task 1

For questions 1–5, choose from the list (A–H) what prompted each speaker to do the test.

A wanting to learn more about personality testing

B making a spontaneous decision

C having no other option

D wanting someone else's opinion about a problem

E having confidence in the accuracy of the test

F being easily tempted by questionnaires

G believing it would help their career prospects

H hoping to impress a friend with the test results

Speaker 1 [1]
Speaker 2 [2]
Speaker 3 [3]
Speaker 4 [4]
Speaker 5 [5]

Task 2

For questions 6–10, choose from the list (A–H) how each speaker felt about the test results.

A uncertain about their implications

B upset because they were worse than expected

C amazed at their accuracy

D indignant because they seemed to be unjustified

E unhappy about the way they were obtained

F concerned because they revealed a mismatch

G curious about what they might really mean

H suspicious because the results were similar to someone else's

Speaker 1 [6]
Speaker 2 [7]
Speaker 3 [8]
Speaker 4 [9]
Speaker 5 [10]

Speaking

4 **Discuss the questions with other students.**

1 How would you feel if you were asked to do a personality test for a job?

2 When do you think personality testing can be helpful?

3 If you see a personality quiz in a magazine or online, are you tempted to do it? How much faith do you have in the results of tests like these?

4 Would you ever lie or bend the truth in a personality test?

Reading

1 What would be the positive and negative aspects of working as a stylist, choosing clothes and accessories for celebrities or in the fashion or film industry?

2 Read the article written by a stylist. Does she mention any of the aspects you thought about?

Making sure it all *matches*

(1) Having studied fashion at college, I knew there were only two real career paths open to me: being a fashion designer and being a stylist. I chose the latter.

My work is all about matching; I match clothes to clients and accessories to clothes. **(2)** Celebrities, hoping to improve a tarnished image or simply trying to make the most of their assets, often hire stylists to help them out. This can be challenging but even more demanding is work on fashion shows. The wardrobe stylist, holding responsibility for pulling all the elements of the show together, often ends up working round the clock checking that everything is there on the day and ready to be worn. Editorial stylists face some of the same challenges in their work on fashion shoots for magazines. I've done that too and it's also great fun because you get to travel. The fashion houses chosen by the magazine provide the clothes they want featured but it's the stylist's job to make sure they're shown in the best possible light. That means finding accessories to set them off, making decisions about the models' hair and make-up, and even ironing the clothes or checking that they hang properly. Having worked in these areas for several years, I decided to turn my hand to film work. I simply love it. Working in close collaboration with costume and set designers has given me a range of new skills, including learning to do research. ◆

Participle clauses

▶ **GRAMMAR** REFERENCE p.177

3 Look at the underlined sentences with participle clauses (clauses that begin with a present or past participle) in Activity 2 and answer the questions.

1 Which clause expresses a reason or condition?
2 Which clause talks about something that took place just before the action in the main clause?

4 Find four more sentences in the article with participle clauses.

5 Match the first half of the sentences (1–6) with the second (A–F). Then rewrite the sentences using participle clauses.

Example: Tim had told everyone it was his birthday, so he received lots of messages and cards.

Having told everyone it was his birthday, Tim received lots of messages and cards.

1 I realised I was going to be late,
2 I hadn't slept a wink the night before
3 I was worried about finding myself in another tense situation with Andrea
4 I didn't want to have to be responsible for running the meeting,
5 Since I was convinced everyone knew about the situation with Andrea,
6 I was feeling very nervous as I walked into the room,

A so I tried not to look anybody in the eye.
B since I hadn't actually spoken to her since our last disastrous encounter.
C I decided it was pointless to behave as if nothing had happened.
D so I tried to find a taxi.
E and as a result, I was really tired.
F so I asked Victoria if she would chair it for me.

LANGUAGE TIP

Check that the subject of the participle clause and the main clause are the same. If they are not, many people will consider the sentence incorrect.

***Picking up the phone**, an unfamiliar voice greeted me.* (This sounds as if the unfamiliar voice picked up the phone.)

---

6 Work in pairs.

Student A: turn to page 164.
Student B: turn to page 166.

Collaborative task and discussion (Parts 3 and 4)

negotiating and co-operating

▶ EXAM FOCUS p.205

1 ▶ 44 **Look at the Part 3 task and the questions for Part 4. Listen to two candidates, Nadia and Anton, doing the Part 3 task. Do they talk about all the methods?**

Part 3

Part 4

• What is the most important quality for a stylist to have?

• Some people prefer to have someone choose their clothes and accessories for them. Why do you think this is?

• Many people don't actually enjoy shopping. Why do you think this is?

• Is there too much emphasis on personal style and appearance?

• Some people say that we can change our style and appearance but not our basic character. What do you think?

• Do you think fashion and style are the same thing?

EXAM TIP

Even though it is better not to be too hesitant in your discussion with the other candidate, it is also important not to be so direct and forthright that you sound rude.

2 **Listen again and complete the extracts with the phrases Nadia (N) and Anton (A) use to negotiate and co-operate.**

N: A well-designed personality test would be likely to give you that information. **(1)** .... ?

A: I would, **(2)** .... I mean, personality testing might be the best approach in some circumstances, but not with something like this.

N: I suppose it would, now that you mention it. So, **(3)** .... some kind of interview? Do you think that would be useful?

A: Possibly, but I think **(4)** .... get a clear picture of their skills by looking at their portfolio.

N: We could also learn a lot by observing them at work. That would tell us about how they communicate with colleagues. I still think that's really important, too.

A: Maybe, but I **(5)** .... practical that would be.

A: Yes, as well as seeing their portfolio. That would be important too. Don't you agree?

N: Yes, **(6)** .... conducting an interview and seeing their portfolio would work best.

3 **Work in pairs. Turn to page 154 and do the activity.**

4 ▶ 45 **Listen to the candidates discussing the Part 4 questions in Activity 1. Which of the questions does the examiner ask?**

5 **Listen again and tick the phrases you hear the students use to negotiate and co-operate.**

1 Isn't it sometimes the case that … ?
2 That may well be so, but I wonder if …
3 I would think that this is unlikely to hold true in all cases, but …
4 Might it not be the case that … ?
5 It's impossible to be categorical about something like this, but …
6 I'm not entirely convinced that that would be true.
7 How far would you regard that as feasible?
8 … it's difficult to give a *yes* or *no* answer, but …
9 I have no hard and fast view on this, really, but …
10 Have you considered the possibility that … ?

6 **Put phrases 1–10 in Activity 5 under headings A–C.**

A politely answering a question
B politely introducing a point
C politely challenging a partner's point

7 **Work in pairs. Turn to page 158 and discuss the Part 4 questions. Use phrases for negotiating and co-operating.**

Formal letter (Part 2)
including relevant information

▶ **WRITING** REFERENCE p.188

1 Work in pairs. Look at the exam task and the list of points a student made for inclusion in the letter. Decide which of the points you would and would not include.

> Your school or college is going to participate in an online service matching students to educational courses. You have been asked by the school director to write a letter to the person in charge of the website explaining why your school should be included. You should explain:
>
> • what your school or college specialises in.
> • what strengths your school or college has.
> • what kinds of students would enjoy or benefit from coming to study at your school or college.
>
> Write your **letter** in **220–260** words in an appropriate style.

- what kinds of students currently study at the school
- your opinion about these students
- what is not taught at the school
- other subjects you would like to see introduced
- why you can't offer some courses at the moment
- something your school is particularly proud of
- teachers' skills and qualifications
- what skills and qualifications students can expect to gain
- what you've heard people say about your school
- how your school compares to other schools

2 Look at the answer a student wrote for the task in Activity 1. Each of the three main paragraphs contains some irrelevant information. Find the information and discuss why it should not be included with a partner.

EXAM TIP

Don't go over the word limit. If you write too much, it is very likely that you will include irrelevant information.

Dear Sir or Madam,

I am writing to you on behalf of the Fenwick School. As you know, we hope to include an entry on our school on your website.

The Fenwick School offers language courses at all levels of proficiency. Although English as a foreign language teaching is an important part of our work, we also provide courses in other European languages, among them French, Italian, Spanish, Portuguese and Russian. Apparently, there is some discussion about offering Chinese at some time in the future but it is not currently available. In addition, we have courses in German for foreigners. One of the school's particular strengths is preparation for the official examinations in each of the languages we teach. Students have obtained excellent results in these examinations this year.

Standards of teaching at the school are very high. All the teachers are fully qualified and they also attend regular in-service training programmes. In addition to the teaching staff, there is a student welfare officer who helps students find accommodation. It can be very difficult to find accommodation here, so it is a good thing that the school provides such a service. Another excellent service the school offers is a complete social programme. This term alone we have had three trips to the theatre, two weekend excursions to nearby beauty spots and a party to celebrate the school's twenty-fifth anniversary.

I feel sure that anyone seeking to improve their level in any of the languages the Fenwick School offers would be delighted with the school. Although most students are in their early to mid-twenties, there are also older and younger people currently enrolled. The oldest student we've ever had was seventy-eight years old. In terms of nationalities, there is a very wide mix, though students from European and Latin American countries predominate.

We feel sure that you will want to include our school in the database for your educational matching service and look forward to hearing from you.

Yours faithfully,

K. Niemeyer

Klaus Niemeyer
Student Services Co-ordinator
The Fenwick School

3 Work in pairs. Turn to page 165 and do the activity.

1

Complete the second sentence so that it has a similar meaning to the first sentence, using the word given. Do not change the word given. You must use between three and six words, including the word given.

1 Whatever she wears, she always manages to look amazing. **MATTER**

It .... she wears, she always manages to look amazing.

2 However hard I try, I always seem to forget Charlie's birthday. **DIFFERENCE**

It .... hard I try, I always seem to forget Charlie's birthday.

3 I made sure to take my umbrella as I had heard it was going to rain. **HAVING**

I made sure to take my umbrella .... to rain.

4 I bought you some of those Belgian chocolates because I know how much you like them. **HOW**

Knowing .... , I bought you some of those Belgian chocolates.

5 She seems to take offence whatever you say. **REGARDLESS**

She seems to take offence .... you say.

6 I always make sure I have a good relationship with my neighbours irrespective of where I happen to be living. **WHEREVER**

I always make sure I have a good relationship with my neighbours .... to be living.

7 Whatever we have for supper will be fine with me. **MIND**

I .... have for supper.

8 You can come around whenever you like. **WOULD**

Any time .... is fine with us.

2

Complete the sentences with one or two words.

1 I think they broke up because they were just not compatible .... one another.

2 Her views on all sorts of topics differ radically .... mine, but we're still good friends.

3 Nigel and Laura get on like a house ....

4 Tom and I used to be close, but we're just not .... the same wavelength any more.

5 The new policy corresponds best .... the interests of families living in rural areas.

6 She's always making comments that have absolutely nothing to .... what we were saying.

3

Read the blog entry below and decide which answer (A, B, C or D) best fits each gap.

It was a set-up!

Just over four years ago I was set up on my first ever and only (1) .... date. My friend Simon had met a writer while doing a reading of his latest book in a local library. Convinced that his friend and I would be a perfect (2) .... , Simon passed on my email details and then came back and told me all about him.

The next (3) .... I knew, Simon and I were on Google, typing in his new friend's full name to see if any (4) .... of wives, girlfriends or long-term relationships appeared in any of his profiles. Having satisfied ourselves that the man in (5) .... was available, I sent him an email and we arranged to meet for coffee the following Sunday. We got (6) .... like a house on fire and though we're as different as (7) .... and cheese in all sorts of ways, we are essentially on exactly the same (8) .... Four years on, we now share our lives. And when anyone asks how we met, I say, quite proudly, 'We were set up.'

	A	**B**	**C**	**D**
1	surprise	secret	blind	unknown
2	fit	suit	partner	match
3	thing	time	moment	minute
4	information	idea	mention	rumour
5	interest	question	issue	mind
6	up	on	over	off
7	cream	butter	chalk	ham
8	wavelength	bandwidth	frequency	modulation

Soundtracks

12

Word formation (Part 3)

EXAM FOCUS p.198

1 Work in pairs. Find out which sounds your partner loves and hates.

2 Read the article. Which sound was voted the most popular?

Our favourite sounds

Is there anything more **(0)** ....*reassuring*.... than the sound of rain lashing against the windows? Or more **(1)** .... than a baby's laugh? According to some new research, these are some of our favourite sounds. But as you may have guessed, **(2)** .... , there is nothing we love more than the **(3)** .... sound of waves crashing against rocks. Fireworks, walking on snow and cheerful screams from people on a rollercoaster were also high in the **(4)** .... The reason for the popularity of many of these sounds is that they are associated with happy memories or the **(5)** .... of something good to come. The sounds around us create atmosphere and emotion as **(6)** .... as any other sense and that shared sense of exhilaration that comes from going to a football match or theme park can be **(7)** .... to any memorable experience. The survey also revealed the sounds that we loathe. **(8)** .... , the noise that makes us shudder the most is the sound of nails being scraped down a chalkboard.

REASURE
RESIST
SURPRISE
SOOTHE

RANK
ANTICIPATE
POWER

CENTRE
PREDICT

3 Work in pairs. Look at the words in capitals in Activity 2 and list as many forms of each word as you can. Then decide which of the missing words are adjectives, adverbs or nouns.

4 Read the article again. For questions 1–8, use the word given in capitals at the end of some of the lines to form a word that fits in the gap in the same line.

5 Work in pairs. Try to predict five more unpopular sounds that you think were listed on the survey. Then turn to page 167 and check your ideas.

Future in the past

▶ **GRAMMAR** REFERENCE p.180

6 Read the article and find two uses of the Mosquito.

◁ ▷   ▷ Sales

Weird sounds

The 'Mosquito' is an electronic device which operates at a frequency that can only be heard by people under the age of about twenty. Most people lose the ability to hear this sound once they reach their early twenties.

The sound was originally developed in 2005 as a type of alarm by a British inventor, Howard Stapleton, who **(1)** <u>was aiming</u> to repel teenagers from loitering around shops near his home in Wales. The idea behind it was that teenagers **(2)** <u>would be put off</u> by the noise and leave before they could cause any trouble. And older shoppers **(3)** <u>would be able to</u> get on with their shopping undisturbed by either groups of teenagers or the sound that, in theory, **(4)** <u>would drive</u> them away.

It **(5)** <u>would have been</u> impossible to imagine that this teenage deterrent would actually be used by the very teenagers it was supposed to deter, who quickly understood the Mosquito's potential as a ringtone undetectable by parents or teachers. Or that the Mosquito, or Teen-buzz, as it is also known, **(6)** <u>was going to become</u> such a commercial success. ∎

7 Work in pairs. Have you noticed a difference in your hearing to that of other age groups? Do you think there's anything unethical about using the Mosquito as a sonic weapon against teenagers?

8 Look at the underlined verbs in the article. Are they referring to a future plan or a prediction about the future that was made in the past?

9 Rewrite the second paragraph of the article as if it were 2005. What changes do you need to make?

Example: The sound has just been developed as a type of alarm by a British inventor, Howard Stapleton, who …

LANGUAGE TIP

The future in the past is often used to talk about a change of plan or to make excuses for things you haven't done.

I **was planning to go/would have gone/was going to go** to the party but I wasn't feeling well.

---

10 Choose the correct alternative in each sentence.

1 The government *was considering/would consider* banning the use of the Mosquito alarm but has decided not to.

2 I was sure my mum *was going to be/would have been* angry when I lost my phone but she was OK about it.

3 I never dreamt that I *was winning/would win* the lottery. I still can't believe it.

4 We *would hope/were hoping* to get tickets but they've all just sold out.

5 The lesson *would have been/would be* cancelled but too many students had already arrived.

6 When I set off for work this morning, I had no idea it *was going to take/was taking* three hours to get there.

Speaking

11 Work in pairs.

Student A: turn to page 163.
Student B: turn to page 164.

Speaking

1 Tick (✓) the statements you agree with. Then compare your responses with a partner.

1 I find silence awkward and I always try to fill the gaps in a conversation.

2 I need silence to be able to concentrate properly.

3 I would rather shops and airports were silent than have to listen to bland, canned music.

4 The idea of going to a retreat and spending several hours a day in silence fills me with horror.

Multiple matching (Part 8)

▶ **EXAM** FOCUS p.201

EXAM TIP

Don't assume that because a word appears in both the question and a section of the text, it is the correct answer. Focus on matching the meaning and looking for paraphrases of key words.

2 You are going to read an article about silence. For questions 1–10, choose from the sections of the article (A–D). The sections may be chosen more than once.

In which section are the following mentioned?

an explanation of how silence is really a lack of mechanical sound **1**

the contradictory and sometimes disturbing nature of silence **2**

a missed opportunity for some to pay close attention to accidental and uncontrollable sounds **3**

an opinion on where it may still be possible to experience silence **4**

a description of the sounds made in a familiar setting that we become aware of during quiet periods **5**

an unpredicted realisation following an attempt to experience true silence **6**

how an unexpected loss of familiar background sounds can cause a change of mood **7**

a comment about how our perception of a sound depends on the environment in which it is heard **8**

how the experience of hearing something different to what was expected in a particular environment provoked a strong reaction **9**

a contrast between the physical and emotional effect sounds can have, depending on their source **10**

Speaking

3 Work in pairs and discuss the questions.

1 Do you agree with the definitions of silence in the text?

2 How would you have reacted to John Cage's *4'33"*?

3 Can you think of any endangered sounds that need to be preserved?

4 What's the quietest place you've ever been to? Could you hear anything? How did it make you feel?

Vocabulary

working out meaning from context

4 Answer the questions. Then compare your answers with a partner.

1 In section A, find a word which means *non-stop* and *huge size*.

2 In section C, find a noun which means *lacking control or planning* and a noun which means *becoming louder*.

3 In section D, underline four words which describe feelings of anger.

5 Look at the underlined words and phrases and choose the correct meaning.

1 You'll have to speak up. He's a bit hard of hearing.
   A is a little deaf
   B doesn't listen to people

2 A teenager who doesn't like loud music? That's unheard of!
   A very unusual   **B** unbelievable

3 I overheard the bus driver saying there'll be a bus strike next week.
   A was given an explanation
   B listened to someone's conversation

4 Please turn the music down. I can't hear myself think.
   A can't concentrate   **B** have a headache

5 I won't hear of you getting the bus to the hospital. I'll drive you.
   A won't let you
   B wasn't thinking about

6 Most people would benefit from a hearing aid over the age of seventy-five.
   A hearing test   **B** hearing device

Culture

Sounds of silence

A

It was 10.37 p.m. on a bitterly cold midwinter's night when an ice storm hit, cutting off our electricity for days. Suddenly, the incessant humming, buzzing and chattering of TVs, microwave ovens, radios, computers, digital clocks, lamps and the refrigerator were gone and with it, my sense of tranquillity. Other than the occasional snapping and popping of a perky fireplace fire, the house was doused in the sudden immensity of silence.

Silence unsettles us. Silence both widens our attention and focuses it at the same time. Not because of what we can't hear but because of what we suddenly can. At 2 a.m. a silent house can be an unsettling house. It creaks. It clicks. It shuffles. It's not that we hear nothing – we hear everything. Each and every unintended noise draws our attention. A silent house jumps to life.

B

The composer John Cage once entered a soundproof chamber at Harvard University with the intention of listening to absolute silence. 'I literally expected to hear nothing,' he said. Instead of nothing, he heard the whooshing and gurgling of his nervous system and circulating blood. When he emerged, he declared that silence does not exist.

What we think of as silence is actually the absence of man-made noise. Kathleen Moore, in her article *In Search of Silence*, wrote: 'It's not easy to find silence in the modern world. If a quiet place is one where you can listen for fifteen minutes in daylight hours without hearing a human-created sound, there are no quiet places left in Europe. In the USA, a country with huge wide open spaces, there are none in the east. And in the American West? Maybe twelve.'

C

Natural sound has a different quality and texture to man-made sound. There's randomness. It's stripped of intention. Think of the difference between the sound of a river or the continuous roaring and splashing of a waterfall to that of shopping centre music, a nearby freeway or even white noise machines. Man-made noise dulls us. Thought narrows. Sitting by a river or waterfall, or on a secluded stretch of beach, our thoughts become expansive. Our nervous system slows and soothes. We all become philosophers; we see and hear life's bigger picture with clarity.

Gordon Hempton, an acoustic ecologist, on a mission to preserve the natural sounds of the wilderness, noted that in a dense moss-covered forest it is possible to be aware of something as delicate as the sound of a falling rain drop – undetectable in any city. 'A drop of rain may hit twenty times before it reaches the ground and each impact – against the bough of a tree, a leaf or a rock – makes its own sound.' And you will hear each drip with deafening precision. It's not the sound itself but the silence surrounding it. Silence is not the absence of sound but the amplification of sound.

D

In 1952 John Cage's experimental work *4′33″* was performed by the young pianist David Tudor. The concert hall was ideal for Cage's *4′33″* because the back of the hall was open to the surrounding forest. The piece was four minutes and thirty-three seconds of the pianist sitting at the keyboard without playing a single note. Four minutes and thirty-three seconds of listening not to music but to silence. During the first movement only the wind in the trees outside the auditorium was audible. The second movement brought rain drops pattering the roof. The third whispers and mutterings from a confused and frustrated audience. The piece was a requiem to unintended sound.

Cage said, 'People began whispering to one another and some people began to walk out. They didn't laugh – they were just irritated when they realised nothing was going to happen and they haven't forgotten it thirty years later; they're still annoyed.' When Tudor finished, raising the keyboard lid and himself from the piano, the audience burst into an uproar – 'infuriated and dismayed,' according to the reports.

But Cage's work wasn't silent at all. It's not that nothing happened. For those who actually widened their awareness and listened carefully, they would have heard a world of unintended sound. ■

Review (Part 2)
making recommendations
▶ **WRITING** REFERENCE p.194

1 Work in pairs. Read the review and answer the questions.

1 Does the review make you want to listen to this album?
2 Who do you think the target reader is?
3 Where would you expect to find this review?

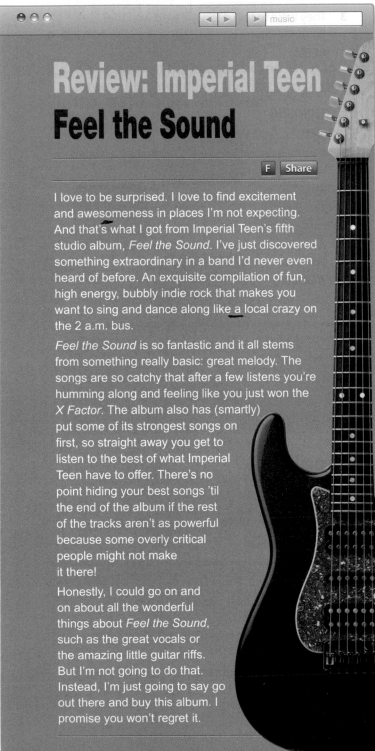

Review: Imperial Teen

Feel the Sound

F | Share

I love to be surprised. I love to find excitement and awesomeness in places I'm not expecting. And that's what I got from Imperial Teen's fifth studio album, *Feel the Sound*. I've just discovered something extraordinary in a band I'd never even heard of before. An exquisite compilation of fun, high energy, bubbly indie rock that makes you want to sing and dance along like a local crazy on the 2 a.m. bus.

Feel the Sound is so fantastic and it all stems from something really basic: great melody. The songs are so catchy that after a few listens you're humming along and feeling like you just won the *X Factor*. The album also has (smartly) put some of its strongest songs on first, so straight away you get to listen to the best of what Imperial Teen have to offer. There's no point hiding your best songs 'til the end of the album if the rest of the tracks aren't as powerful because some overly critical people might not make it there!

Honestly, I could go on and on about all the wonderful things about *Feel the Sound*, such as the great vocals or the amazing little guitar riffs. But I'm not going to do that. Instead, I'm just going to say go out there and buy this album. I promise you won't regret it.

2 Read the review again and find examples of

1 colourful, lively language.
2 a simile (using comparison to describe something).
3 specialised topic vocabulary.

3 Match the first half of the sentences (1–5) with the second (A–E). Then decide if they are formal (F) or informal (I).

1 I promise you won't regret
2 You definitely wouldn't want
3 I would have no hesitation
4 If you're looking for something different,
5 I can't see how anyone could

A to miss this exhibition.
B in recommending this show.
C dislike this album.
D buying this book.
E then this is the band for you.

✗ Look at the exam task and write your review.

You see the following advertisement in a music magazine.

> **Ever fancied yourself as a music journalist? Now's your chance.**
>
> We're looking for enthusiastic music lovers to write a review of their favourite album of all time. We want to know why you love it and why you think everyone should listen to it. It doesn't matter who the artist is or how old or new the music is. Send in a review of your favourite album of all time giving reasons for your choice.

Write your **review** in **220–260** words in an appropriate style.

EXAM TIP

Try to make your review interesting by using a wide range of vocabulary. This is necessary in order to do well in the Writing test.

5 Work in pairs. Use the checklist on page 185 to check each other's work. Make any necessary changes or improvements.

1 Read the conversation and choose the correct alternatives.

A: Hi, Angie – have you managed to get tickets for the festival yet?

B: I **(1)** *was planning/would be planning* to get them today but the computer system crashed because so many people were trying to book tickets.

A: So who are you going with?

B: Well, Belinda **(2)** *was meant to be coming/ was about to come* with me but she says she can't afford it now, so I **(3)** *was due ask to/was going to ask* around and see if anyone else **(4)** *would have been/would be* interested.

A: Well, I'd be interested.

B: Would you? I thought you **(5)** *were to work/ were working* this weekend.

A: I **(6)** *was supposed to/was about to* but then my boss said he could manage without me.

B: Great! Well, I'll try and get tickets again later.

A: I heard that Summer **(7)** *would have played/ were due to play*.

B: No, I don't think so. That was just a rumour. There **(8)** *would have been/was going to be* something about it on the website by now.

2 Complete the sentences with the correct form of the words in the box.

buzz	croak	hoot	hum	roar
shuffle	snap	whoosh		

1 There was a .... of delight when the election results were announced.

2 'I've lost my voice,' I .... to the doctor.

3 She .... with laughter when she realised what she'd done.

4 The old man .... along in his slippers.

5 What's that .... noise? It sounds like the wind.

6 I think these headphones are broken – they're making a loud .... sound like an angry insect.

7 Don't keep .... that tune – it's very annoying.

8 I have to buy new glasses – the frame just .... in two.

3 Read the text below. Use the word given in capitals at the end of some of the lines to form a word that fits in the gap in the same line.

The Museum of Endangered Sounds

Can you imagine hearing the hissing of a dial-up modem or the sound of a cassette rewinding? Things change so quickly that little things that were once part of our daily routine have become instantly **(1)** ....   **FORGET**
For those of us who do feel a certain **(2)** .... to the sounds   **ATTACH**
of our youth, it's of some **(3)** .... to know   **COMFORTABLE**
that we can hear them at The Museum of Endangered Sounds, a website **(4)** .... to   **DEDICATE**
preserving the noises we thought we'd never hear again. The museum's **(5)** .... came up with   **FOUND**
the idea on a car journey. As the car pulled up at a traffic light, the only sound that could be heard was the repeated **(6)** ....   **CLICK**
sound of someone texting on a mobile phone. Someone else was texting on a touch screen phone but that didn't make a peep. They realised that a lot of our technologies were getting quieter. Even some automobile engines are barely **(7)** ....   **AUDIO**
nowadays. Who knows – within a few decades you could even be feeling **(8)** .... about the   **NOSTALGIA**
deafening roar of motorbikes zooming down the road.

Face value

13

Speaking

1 Work in pairs and decide if the statements are true (T) or false (F). Then turn to page 167 and check your answers.

1 Babies are born with the ability to smile.
2 Smiling uses more muscles than frowning.
3 There are ten different types of smile.
4 Smiling is a universal sign of happiness.
5 People who smile frequently live longer.
6 Smiling is a good way to relieve stress.
7 Men smile more than women.
8 Pretending to smile can increase stress.

Words to describe emotions

2 What is the adjective form of the words in the box?

amusement	astonishment	bitterness	confusion
contentment	delight	embarrassment	exhilaration	frustration
hysteria	indifference	nervousness	relief	shame

3 Work in pairs and discuss the questions.

1 Which of the emotions in Activity 2 might you experience when
  • receiving a letter of rejection from a potential employer?
  • trying to communicate with someone whose English is difficult to understand?
  • celebrating getting your degree?
  • failing to understand a joke?
  • opening the exam results you'd been dreading to discover you'd actually done well?
  • copying your boss in to a personal email by mistake?
  • doing a sky dive?
  • discovering just in time that you hadn't really lost your train ticket?
2 How likely are people to smile when experiencing these emotions?

Open cloze (Part 2)

▶ **EXAM** FOCUS p.198

4 **Discuss the questions in pairs.**

1 How easy do you think it is to read people's emotions accurately?

2 Are you good at hiding your emotions or are they written all over your face?

3 How similar do you think an expression of frustration might be to an expression of delight?

5 **Read the article and summarise the research findings. Then look at the pictures and see if you can tell which smile is of frustration and which expresses delight.**

6 **Read the article again. For questions 1–8, think of the word which best fits each gap. Use only one word for each gap.**

EXAM TIP

Sometimes you may need to choose between words with opposite meanings which both fit grammatically (e.g. *much* and *little*), so you need to check that the word you have chosen fits the meaning of the whole text as well as fitting grammatically in a particular sentence.

7 **Work in pairs. Compare your answers to Activity 6. Then check your answers to questions 6 and 8 by answering the questions.**

1 In question 6, do you need a word which means *a lot of* or *hardly any*?

2 In question 8, do you need a word which means *in addition to* or *in contrast to*?

Speaking

8 **Discuss the questions in pairs.**

1 In what situations might you smile at a stranger or smile to yourself?

2 Do you agree that 'when you're smiling, the whole world smiles with you'?

Smiles of
FRUSTRATION

How can you tell if **(0)** ....*someone*........ is feeling frustrated? Most people are convinced smiling is not a typical reaction to frustration but a new study has proved this to be a misconception. What's **(1)** .... , it turns out that computers programmed with the latest information from this research **(2)** .... a better job of differentiating smiles of delight and frustration than human observers.

(3) .... part of the experiment, participants were asked to act out feelings of frustration. Many of them stamped their feet or frowned deeply but they didn't smile. But **(4)** .... given a task that caused genuine frustration, ninety percent of participants reacted instinctively **(5)** .... smiling. Interestingly, the recorded images showed very **(6)** .... difference between these frustrated smiles and the smiles showing delight at the video of a cute baby. **(7)** .... closer inspection, however, video analysis showed that the progression of both kinds of smile was quite noticeable: **(8)** .... the happy smiles built up gradually, frustrated smiles appeared quickly but faded fast.

Speaking

1 **Work in pairs. In what situations do you laugh?**

Example:
- *finding something someone's said funny*
- *wanting to make the other person feel good*

Multiple choice (Part 3)

▶ **EXAM** FOCUS p.203

2 ▶ 50 **Listen to a radio discussion between two authors called Mark Shaw and Diana Abel about a book on laughter by Robert Provine. For questions 1–6, choose the answer (A, B, C or D) which fits best according to what you hear.**

> **EXAM TIP**
>
> Ignore a question you can't answer the first time you listen and move on to the next question. You will have another chance to answer any questions you've missed or aren't sure of during the second listening.

1 According to Mark Shaw, the idea that the main motivation for laughter is not humour

  A is hard for people to understand.

  B needs further investigation.

  C is now widely accepted.

  D contradicts findings in other studies.

2 What surprised Diana Abel about differences in laughter between men and women?

  A the greater frequency of women's laughter

  B the changing role of laughter in relationships between the sexes

  C the difficulties faced by female comedians

  D the value women place on laughter

3 What recommendation for increasing laughter does Diana find attractive?

  A Spend more time with friends.

  B Watch more comedy on TV.

  C Practise laughing.

  D Stop taking life too seriously.

4 How has both speakers' attitude to laughter changed after reading the book?

  A They find themselves more inclined to laugh.

  B They are more conscious of their own laughter.

  C They are more aware of people's reasons for laughing.

  D They find other people's laughter strange.

5 Mark and Diana would both have liked more information on

  A different kinds of humour.

  B the origins of laughter.

  C the negative aspects of laughter.

  D the physical effects of laughter.

6 Why does Mark think the book will appeal to a non-academic audience?

  A It is written in a lively, conversational style.

  B It will teach people about relationships.

  C It contains fascinating stories.

  D It can be used as a self-help guide.

3 **Work in pairs and discuss the questions.**

1 Do you think you laugh often enough?

2 How important do you think a good sense of humour is?

3 Do you ever laugh at jokes that you don't find funny?

4 When did you last have a fit of uncontrollable laughter?

4 ▶ 51 **Choose the correct alternative in each sentence. Then listen and check your answers.**

1 He's not *admitting/advocating* attending laughter workshops or laughter yoga.

2 Provine thinks laughter is important for maintaining relationships, but doesn't necessarily support the idea that laughter improves health or *longevity/quality of life*.

3 The effect it had on me was to monitor my own *impulses/reactions* to laugh – it made me less spontaneous, in a way.

4 But you can just skip those bits and move on to some of the lovely *anecdotes/reports* about the research.

5 Some of the accounts of the *contagious/dangerous* nature of laughter are really amazing. In some places, people couldn't stop laughing for days.

Speaking

1 Work in pairs and discuss the questions.

1 How easy do you think it is to tell the difference between an original painting and a fake?

2 Would you be prepared to pay a lot of money for a copy of an original painting?

3 Why do you think people often prefer to have copies of famous paintings on their walls rather than original paintings by unknown artists?

Passive forms

▶ **GRAMMAR** REFERENCE p.177

2 Match the examples of the passive (A–D) with the reasons for using it (1–4).

A Some of Picasso's best works of art are to be displayed in a new exhibition in Madrid.

B Discoveries of new drawings by well-known artists have to be authenticated by experts.

C Many famous works of art have been stolen from galleries around the world.

D Picasso is considered to have been the greatest artist of the twentieth century.

1 The agent (person doing the action) is not known or unimportant.

2 The focus of the sentence is on the action.

3 The sentence is describing a process or rules.

4 Generally held opinions are being given.

3 Look at the active form of the sentences in Activity 2 and answer the questions.

A A new exhibition in Madrid will display some of Picasso's best works of art.

B Experts have to authenticate discoveries of new drawings by well-known artists.

C Thieves have stolen many famous works of art from galleries around the world.

D Many people think Picasso was the greatest artist of the twentieth century.

1 Do you think the sentences sound less or more objective?

2 Are they less or more personal?

3 Are they less or more official?

4 Read the article. What point is the writer trying to make?

thestandard

☀ 19°C 12°C

News | Sport | Comment | Culture | Business | Money | Life & style | Travel

The genuine article?

Imagine, if you will, that you have found a Picasso in your attic. You make arrangements to auction it and then get a thrill as the bids escalate ever upwards. But then the dream (1) *is/ has been* shattered. The multi-million-dollar painting turns out to (2) *be/have been* done by your uncle rather than Picasso. True, it is brilliantly done and the experts agreed (before finding it to be a fake) that it was better than all of Picasso's other works. But since it (3) *would be/has been* painted by Uncle Ted and not Picasso, it is only worth about ten dollars.

In a strange turn of events, you find what seems to be a duplicate of the painting in your attic, which (4) *is/are* confirmed by experts to be a genuine Picasso, who happened to have copied Uncle Ted's painting just for fun. This painting sells for millions, since it (5) *is/can be* thought to be a genuine Picasso. As a small joke, you donate Uncle Ted's painting to the museum that buys Picasso's painting and ask them to display them side by side. When no one is watching, you switch the labels and (6) *are/are being* amused to see how people react.

In this scenario, what makes the difference between the two works is nothing about the works but rather about who created the work. As such, what (7) *is being/was to be* sold is not so much a work of art but the artist who created the work. The work itself, it (8) *can be/is to be* argued, is not particularly relevant.

5 Read the article again and choose the correct alternatives.

LANGUAGE TIP

The past passive infinitive is often used after certain verbs (*think, consider, hope, want, need,* etc.).

*The painting **was thought to have been sold** for over £10,000,000.*

6 Work in pairs. Turn to page 167 and do the activity.

Speaking

1 **Work in pairs and discuss the questions.**

1 What do you think the portraits reveal about the people in the photos?

2 What skills do you think you need to be a professional photographer?

3 How do you usually feel about having your photograph taken?

4 Why do you think posting photos of yourself has become so popular?

Cross-text multiple matching (Part 6)

▶ **EXAM** FOCUS p.200

2 **Read the reviews of a photography exhibition quickly and decide if they are mainly positive or negative. Would they encourage you to visit the exhibition? What would it be like to be the subject of one of Penn's portraits?**

3 **Look at question 1 in Activity 4 and answer the questions.**

1 What is Reviewer C's opinion of Penn's influence as a photographer? Underline the section of the review which refers to this.

2 Look at the other reviews and underline what they have to say about Penn's influence. Which reviewer has the same opinion as reviewer C?

3 Do any of the reviewers have a different opinion to reviewer C about Penn's influence?

4 **Read the reviews again. For questions 1–4, choose from the reviewers (A–D). The reviewers may be chosen more than once.**

Which reviewer

1 shares Reviewer C's view of Penn's influence as a photographer? **1** ☐

2 disagrees with Reviewer A about Penn's consistency over the years? **2** ☐

3 agrees with Reviewer B about the effect of the background in Penn's portraits? **3** ☐

4 has a different opinion to the other reviewers regarding how well the portraits on display have been selected? **4** ☐

EXAM TIP

One question may ask which writer has a different opinion to the others on a particular issue. You need to identify whether each reviewer has a negative or positive opinion about the issue and choose the one that is the odd one out.

5 **Work in pairs and discuss the questions.**

How far do you agree that

1 a person's face can reveal their character?

2 people are judged too often on their appearance?

3 celebrities are too conscious of their image?

4 fashion photography is of little relevance to most people?

Behind the façade

Four reviewers comment on an exhibition of the works of portrait photographer Irving Penn.

A What is most apparent from this exhibition of Irving Penn's portraits, which covers the photographer's entire career, is his commitment to quality and style. From the 1940s until his last work in 2007, he remained constant in his approach, never failing to deliver anything less than utter perfection. As his career progressed, Penn moved from classic fashion shots to focus more on portraits, investigating how far a person's character can be portrayed on their face. He managed to shine a light on the inner qualities of his subjects by exaggerating an expression or gesture. The simplicity of the sets he used in all his portraits cleverly leaves his subjects nowhere to hide, exposing the individual behind the icon. The result is, for some, awkward but for others it is liberating and only serves to magnify their status. The collection offers a fascinating insight into the true nature of some of the most significant cultural figures of the twentieth century.

B Irving Penn once wrote that 'very often what lies behind the façade is rare and more wonderful than the subject knows or dares to believe'. The exhibition displays portraits of some of the most celebrated figures of the last century, including John F. Kennedy, Pablo Picasso and Truman Capote. The less obvious points of his subjects' personalities are unashamedly portrayed by the photographer in characterless, bare surroundings. In showing the sitters without any of the trappings of celebrity, Penn successfully reveals qualities not seen in other portraits of such superstars. The development in style that takes place over Penn's fifty-year career is clearly shown, from his full-body images of the forties, to more intimate close-up portraits of later years. These all demonstrate that Penn's technical mastery is without equal. He undoubtedly created a style that later generations of photographers have found impossible not to imitate.

C *Irving Penn Portraits* at the National Portrait Gallery follows the progress of the American photographer's studio portraits from 1947–2007, emphasising the continuity of his vision, sensitivity to his subject and technical skill. It celebrates his interest in the power of photography (and its limitations) as a means of depicting the inner life of sitters and to discover, as Penn states, 'what lies behind the façade'. Penn's success lies in the importance of precision, attention to detail and meticulously planned composition. Penn is and will continue to be a giant in the world of photographic portraiture. But while he transformed the style of studio portraiture, his relevance also endures as a fashion photographer and the omission from this exhibition of some of his most iconic images for *Vogue* results in an incomplete portrayal of his achievements.

D As Penn's reputation inevitably begins to fade, those unfamiliar with his work might at first see only a collection of slightly out-of-date black and white portraits. But a closer inspection will reveal how Penn turns the face into a landscape to be explored and discovered. Every feature is highlighted in a manner that most photographers appear incapable of capturing today.

The exhibition spans some fifty years of his work and one clearly sees a development in his confidence and style. The majority of these portraits were taken in his studio using a plain background and very few props. This helps to create a mood which, together with his expert use of light and shadow, make his images never less than exhilarating. Only in the last decade of his life does his work lose some of its magic: he experiments more with modern trends in lighting and appears to have been persuaded by celebrity publicists and fashion stylists to flatter his famous subjects.

6 **Choose the correct alternative in each sentence.**

1 The film *portrays/displays* the lives of two artists.
2 At the end of the story the family's secrets are *exposed/depicted*.
3 The paintings are *displayed/highlighted* in chronological order.
4 The portrait *highlights/exposes* the man's delight.
5 In his autobiography, the writer *reveals/portrays* the inspiration for his main character.
6 The paintings *depict/display* life in the early part of the nineteenth century.

7 **What is the noun form of the verbs in Activity 6?**

8 **Work in pairs and discuss the questions.**

1 Can you describe anything which has been revealed or exposed recently in the news?
2 How do you feel about people who display a lot of emotion?
3 What do you think your clothes reveal about you?
4 Which actor do you think would portray you in a film about your life?

Speaking

1 Work in pairs and discuss the questions.

1 What ideas and themes link the three pictures?

2 In what ways are they different?

3 What questions could an examiner ask about these pictures?

Long turn (Part 2)

expressing certainty and uncertainty

▶ **EXAM** FOCUS p.204

2 ▶ **52 Listen to the examiner's instructions and see if your predictions were correct.**

3 Which of the pictures do you think the statements are referring to? Underline the phrases which express certainty or uncertainty.

1 There's no denying the fact that people are so obsessed with celebrity that they find models of their idols appealing.

2 I'm convinced that tricks like this are actually quite easy to pull off.

3 It's doubtful that people will be fooled by this trick.

4 There's no doubt at all that anyone who can reproduce a work of art is an extremely gifted artist.

5 There's no doubt that everyone is fascinated by magic.

6 I think I can say with confidence that I'd never pay to go to a waxworks museum.

4 Which of the statements in Activity 3 do you agree with?

5 ▶ **53 Listen to a candidate answering the follow-up question. Do you agree with her?**

6 Listen again. What phrase does the candidate use to

1 give herself thinking time?

2 give a speculative opinion?

3 avoid repeating words in the examiner's question?

EXAM TIP

Don't just give a one- or two-word answer in response to your partner's picture.

7 Work in pairs. Practise doing the task in Activity 2 using one of the pictures that the candidate didn't talk about. Try to use some of the phrases in Activity 3.

8 Work in pairs. Turn to page 157 and do Task 1. Then turn to page 160 and do Task 2.

Speaking

1 **Work in pairs and discuss the questions.**

1 On what occasions might you wear a suit?
2 How does wearing a suit make you feel?
3 Would you prefer a job where you could dress casually?
4 Why do you think many company dress codes are becoming less formal?

2 **Work in pairs. Read the text below quickly and discuss the questions.**

1 What type of person do you think would be interested in this text?
2 Where do you think this text was taken from?

   A a business magazine
   B a website for an expensive shop selling suits
   C a fashion blog

3 What advantages of wearing a suit are mentioned? Do you agree with the writer's analysis?
4 Do you agree that most people judge on appearances and rely on first impressions when meeting someone for the first time?

3 **Is the text written in a formal or informal style? Find some evidence to justify your answer.**

Linking adverbials

▶ **GRAMMAR** REFERENCE p.170

4 **Read the text again and cross out the linking adverbials that are not possible.**

	A	B	C
1	In view of	Apart from	Given
2	Additionally	Moreover	Alternatively
3	Furthermore	What's more	In contrast
4	Besides this	As well as this	Despite this
5	Even so	On the other hand	Alternatively
6	For this reason	On the contrary	Consequently

LANGUAGE TIP

Linking adverbials connect one sentence in a logical way to another. They usually appear at the beginning of a sentence and are followed by a comma. They help to make writing more cohesive.

5 **Which of the linking adverbials in Activity 4 are used to**

1 give extra information?
2 give a reason or result?
3 make a contrast?

6 **Work in pairs. Think of three reasons why employees in a company should not have to wear a suit to work. Use linking adverbials to explain your reasons.**

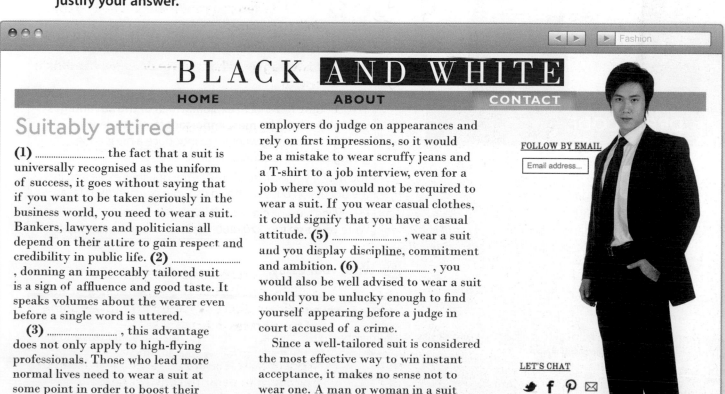

BLACK AND WHITE

HOME   ABOUT   CONTACT

Suitably attired

(1) .... the fact that a suit is universally recognised as the uniform of success, it goes without saying that if you want to be taken seriously in the business world, you need to wear a suit. Bankers, lawyers and politicians all depend on their attire to gain respect and credibility in public life. (2) ...., donning an impeccably tailored suit is a sign of affluence and good taste. It speaks volumes about the wearer even before a single word is uttered.

(3) .... , this advantage does not only apply to high-flying professionals. Those who lead more normal lives need to wear a suit at some point in order to boost their career chances. (4) .... most

employers do judge on appearances and rely on first impressions, so it would be a mistake to wear scruffy jeans and a T-shirt to a job interview, even for a job where you would not be required to wear a suit. If you wear casual clothes, it could signify that you have a casual attitude. (5) .... , wear a suit and you display discipline, commitment and ambition. (6) .... , you would also be well advised to wear a suit should you be unlucky enough to find yourself appearing before a judge in court accused of a crime.

Since a well-tailored suit is considered the most effective way to win instant acceptance, it makes no sense not to wear one. A man or woman in a suit means business.

FOLLOW BY EMAIL

Email address...

LET'S CHAT

Speaking

1 **Work in pairs and discuss the questions.**

1 Do you think the dress code for students at the business school in the poster below is reasonable?

2 Should pierced noses and tattoos be acceptable in college?

3 Should the dress code where you work or study be changed?

4 Is it acceptable for employers to tell employees how to style their hair?

ACE BUSINESS SCHOOL

DRESS CODE

MEN

• must wear: formal suits in a dark colour, leather shoes

• mustn't wear: jeans or hoodies, sandals, flip flops or trainers

• optional: a tie

WOMEN

• must wear: formal skirts/trousers

• mustn't wear: mini skirts, shorts, very high heels, large earrings

Essay (Part 1)

planning your essay

▶ **WRITING** REFERENCE p.186

2 **Look at the exam task and write a plan including points 1–4.**

1 In the introduction, briefly describe the current situation and say why the college is considering introducing a dress code.

2 Choose which two advantages you are going to discuss and decide on the main point for each paragraph.

3 Think of some examples/evidence to support the main point in each paragraph.

4 Decide what arguments to use in your conclusion to support the idea of introducing a dress code.

> Your class has been involved in a discussion on whether a dress code should be introduced at the college where you are studying. You have made the notes below.
>
> > Advantages of proposed dress code
> > • image of college
> > • health and safety
> > • discipline
>
> > Some opinions expressed in the discussion:
> > 'Wearing more formal clothes will prepare students for the workplace'.
> > 'College isn't work or school, so students should be free to wear what they want.'
> > 'Students are turning up to college in inappropriate clothes more frequently, so it's time for a dress code.'
>
> Write an essay for your tutor discussing **two** of the advantages in your notes. You should **explain which of the advantages you think would be most important** for the college to consider in deciding whether to introduce a dress code, **giving reasons** to support your opinion.
>
> You may, if you wish, make use of the opinions expressed in the discussion but you should use your own words as far as possible.
>
> Write your **essay** in **220–260** words in an appropriate style.

3 **Write your essay.**

EXAM TIP

Remember to use linking adverbials to organise your ideas and to make it easy for the reader to follow your argument.

4 **Check your work using the checklist on page 185. Then swap with a partner. Check if they have used a range of linking adverbials and passive forms.**

1 Read the article and think of the word which best fits each gap. Use only one word for each gap.

◄ ► ► Mirror

Mirror, mirror on the wall

What can mirrors tell us about our self-image? Researchers have discovered that being aware of a mirror on the wall can influence the way we behave and if this research **(1)** .... to be believed, always **(2)** .... the better.

The results of the research show that when there is a mirror present, people are more likely to work harder, be more co-operative and are less likely to cheat. In one experiment, participants **(3)** .... given a series of exercises to do and their performance was compared with a control group who did the same activities **(4)** .... a mirror present.

One possible explanation for the improved behaviour could be that mirrors make us more self-aware, which may lead us to give more consideration to our own behaviour and to think **(5)** .... we act, rather than acting on impulse. **(6)** .... greater level of self-awareness would seem, therefore, to have a positive impact on behaviour, if **(7)** .... because we like to have a positive self-image and prefer to see **(8)** .... in a favourable light.

2 Complete the sentences with the correct form of the word in brackets.

1 She reacted as if she were completely .... (*differ*) to the news. I don't think she cares at all.

2 Some people will always be .... (*content*), no matter how lucky they are.

3 The feeling of .... (*astonish*) was overwhelming – I just couldn't believe I'd won.

4 Trying to explain yourself in another language can be extremely .... (*frustrate*).

5 I was so .... (*relief*) when my magic trick actually worked – I really wasn't sure that it would.

6 Many people suffer from .... (*nervous*) before a job interview.

7 It's a .... (*delight*), if not very original painting. It cheers you up just looking at it.

8 The audience didn't find the joke at all .... (*amuse*) – I think some of them were quite offended.

3 Complete the second sentence so that it has a similar meaning to the first sentence, using the word given. Do not change the word given. You must use between three and six words, including the word given.

1 The original idea was to ban the wearing of jeans by the start of last term.
HAVE
Originally, the wearing of jeans .... by the start of last term.

2 Experts are convinced the painting was completed in the 16th century.
CONSIDERED
The painting .... completed in the 16th century.

3 Everyone had thought the painting was worth over £100,000,000.
BEEN
The painting .... worth over £100,000,000.

4 No one can do anything about students having tattoos if they want them.
DONE
There .... about students having tattoos if they want them.

5 People want others to notice that they are doing the right thing.
SEEN
People .... doing the right thing.

6 The audience were confused by the magician's trick.
CONFUSION
The magician's trick .... the audience.

4 Read the text and choose the correct alternatives.

🏠 **Contact Us** 👤

Slaves to fashion

(1) *Given / As well as* the fact that fashions change so frequently, it makes no sense to buy expensive clothes. **(2)** *Consequently/Even so*, many people, men included, spend far more than they can afford on designer clothes. **(3)** *Besides/Despite* this, some really dedicated followers of fashion are prepared to go so far as to get into serious debt in order to keep up with the latest trends. **(4)** *What's more/For this reason*, slavishly following the latest trends means not only that you have no individuality or personal style but also that you are likely to be broke.

All parts

improving your performance

▶ **EXAM** FOCUS p.204

1 ▶ 55 **Listen to two candidates doing Part 1 of the Speaking test. One of the candidates does not perform as well as the other. Which candidate is this, Gustave or Maria? How could they improve?**

2 ▶ 56 **Listen to Maria talking about the pictures in Part 2 and look at the strategy for Part 2 on page 204. Is there anything that she should do but doesn't, or does do but shouldn't? Is Gustave's answer to the examiner's question long enough?**

3 **Work in pairs.**

Turn to page 157 and do Task 1.
Then turn to page 160 and do Task 2.

4 ▶ 57 **Listen to Gustave and Maria doing Part 3 and look at the strategy for Part 3 on page 205. Is there anything mentioned in the strategy that either of the candidates doesn't do well?**

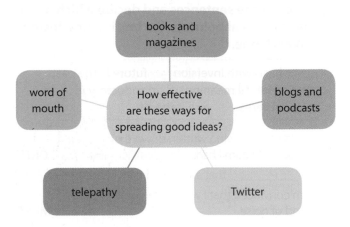

5 **Which of the candidates do you agree with? Compare your answer with a partner.**

6 **Work in pairs. Turn to page 154 and do the activity. Then look at the General marking guidelines on page 207 to help you evaluate your own performance.**

7 ▶ 58 **Listen to Gustave, Maria and the examiner discussing some of the questions below. Which of the two candidates performs well? How could the other candidate have done better?**

- How important is it for people to learn about the history of science at school?
- Some people say they don't see the point of scientific research. Why do you think this is?
- Whose responsibility should it be to inform people about science – scientists or the media? Why?
- Science departments at universities often get more government funding than departments devoted to humanities subjects like history, languages and literature. Do you think this is right? Why/Why not?
- Which do you think is more important for success in a scientific career – talent or hard work?

8 **Work in groups of three.**

Students A and B: you are the candidates. Discuss one of the questions in Activity 7 the examiner didn't ask.

Student C: you are the examiner. Listen and make a note of what the candidates do well and anything they could improve.

Grammar quiz

1 **Work in pairs.**

Student A: look at the test and follow the instructions. Then compare your answers with Student B.

Student B: turn to page 168 and do the activity.

2 Look back over your written work and find some mistakes you made. Write a quiz like the one below with your mistakes. Show your quiz to some other students and see if they can correct your mistakes and tell you how to avoid them in future.

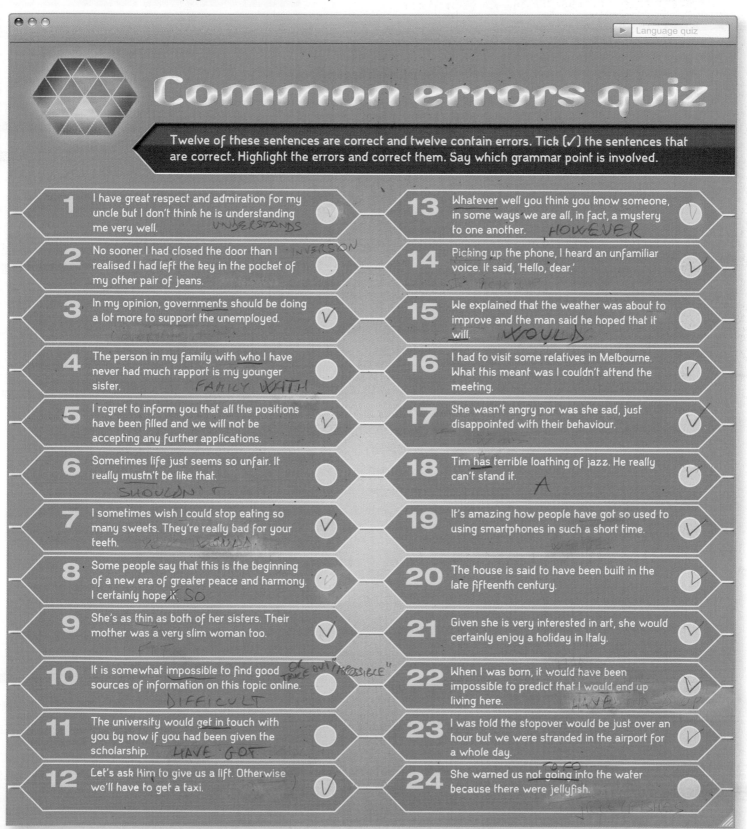

Common errors quiz

Twelve of these sentences are correct and twelve contain errors. Tick (✓) the sentences that are correct. Highlight the errors and correct them. Say which grammar point is involved.

1 I have great respect and admiration for my uncle but I don't think he is understanding me very well. *UNDERSTANDS*

2 No sooner I had closed the door than I realised I had left the key in the pocket of my other pair of jeans. *INVERSION*

3 In my opinion, governments should be doing a lot more to support the unemployed. ✓

4 The person in my family with who I have never had much rapport is my younger sister. *FAMILY WITH*

5 I regret to inform you that all the positions have been filled and we will not be accepting any further applications. ✓

6 Sometimes life just seems so unfair. It really mustn't be like that. *SHOULDN'T*

7 I sometimes wish I could stop eating so many sweets. They're really bad for your teeth. ✓

8 Some people say that this is the beginning of a new era of greater peace and harmony. I certainly hope it *SO* ✓

9 She's as thin as both of her sisters. Their mother was a very slim woman too. ✓

10 It is somewhat impossible to find good sources of information on this topic online. *TAKE OUT "IMPOSSIBLE" DIFFICULT*

11 The university would get in touch with you by now if you had been given the scholarship. *HAVE GOT*

12 Let's ask him to give us a lift. Otherwise we'll have to get a taxi. ✓

13 Whatever well you think you know someone, in some ways we are all, in fact, a mystery to one another. *HOWEVER* ✓

14 Picking up the phone, I heard an unfamiliar voice. It said, 'Hello, dear.' ✓

15 We explained that the weather was about to improve and the man said he hoped that it will. *WOULD*

16 I had to visit some relatives in Melbourne. What this meant was I couldn't attend the meeting. ✓

17 She wasn't angry nor was she sad, just disappointed with their behaviour. ✓

18 Tim has terrible loathing of jazz. He really can't stand it. *A*

19 It's amazing how people have got so used to using smartphones in such a short time. ✓

20 The house is said to have been built in the late fifteenth century. ✓

21 Given she is very interested in art, she would certainly enjoy a holiday in Italy. ✓

22 When I was born, it would have been impossible to predict that I would end up living here. *HAVE END UP* ✓

23 I was told the stopover would be just over an hour but we were stranded in the airport for a whole day. ✓

24 She warned us not going into the water because there were jellyfish. *TO GO JELLYFISHES*

Speaking

1 Turn to page 169 and do the quiz. Compare your answers with a partner. How many questions did you answer?

Gapped text (Part 7)

▶ **EXAM** FOCUS p.200

2 Read the article about Nikola Tesla. How many of the quiz questions in Activity 1 can you answer as a result of reading the article?

3 Read the article again. Six paragraphs have been removed from the article. Choose from the paragraphs A–G the one which fits each gap (1–6). There is one extra paragraph which you do not need to use.

> **EXAM TIP**
>
> When you have chosen an option (A–G) for each gap, read the whole text through with your chosen paragraphs in place to double-check that it makes sense.

4 Has there ever been a situation where you were not given credit for something you did? How did you feel?

5 Look at the underlined words and phrases in the article and the paragraphs and choose the correct meaning.

1	pip him at the post	A accuse him of something	B	narrowly beat him
2	edging	A gradually advancing	B	cutting
3	eulogising	A criticising	B	praising
4	panned	A evaluated negatively	B	described fully
5	pleas	A requests	B	declarations
6	got wind of	A discovered	B	preferred

Vocabulary

expressions with matter

6 Choose the correct alternative in each sentence.

1 Astrophysicists are still trying to solve the puzzle of *grey/dark* matter in the universe.

2 As a matter of *truth/fact*, I'd never heard of Tesla until you told me about him.

3 She couldn't take the money. It was a matter of *principle/honour*.

4 As a matter of *enquiry/interest*, where was Tesla born?

5 It can only be a matter of *time/waiting* before someone is seriously injured.

6 Can't it wait? It's hardly a matter of *life and death/living or dying*.

A
It was not the first time Tesla had seen a rival <u>pip him at the post</u>, nor was it to be the last. If his contemporary fans are to be believed, he was responsible for any number of inventions and discoveries from X-rays to radar to dark matter in the universe, and, most controversially of all, the electric light bulb.

B
Donors purchased all kinds of Tesla merchandise, ranging from glossy photos at twenty dollars through to guest passes to something called a 'Tesla event' at a thousand. It seems their generosity and devotion to the Serbian genius knew no bounds.

C
Tesla fans often demonise his great rival, casting their hero as innocent victim. They also tend to exaggerate Tesla's inventive genius and attribute to him alone discoveries that were the result of generations of hard working scientists and engineers <u>edging</u> towards solutions to problems.

D
If, like me, you have never seen one of these, I should tell you that it's the same machine that electrifies the monster and brings him to life in Frankenstein movies. It was in fact an expensive project involving a giant version of the device that was Tesla's undoing.

E
Conflicts like this occurred throughout his life perhaps because he was in some ways the quintessential mad scientist. He slept only two to three hours a night and had obsessions such as a loathing for round objects, human hair, jewellery and numbers not divisible by three.

F
We also have Tesla to thank for the fact that enough electricity comes out of sockets to power our appliances. But to achieve this goal he had first to win what is sometimes called 'the war of the currents' against the man who gave him a job but was later his most vehement detractor.

G
It would seem that Tesla's hugely loyal fan-base is largely made up of geeky young people who play real-time strategy games. To publicise their hero they have developed literally hundreds of sites devoted to <u>eulogising</u> his work. There are biographies and articles and a film, largely <u>panned</u> by the critics, starring the singer David Bowie. There is even a car called the Tesla.

NIKOLA TESLA: the ultimate geek?

Frances Mulrennan tells us what she learnt about an extraordinary man.

I had actually never heard of Nikola Tesla until I happened to read that his fans had responded to <u>pleas</u> to fund a Tesla museum by pledging donations of $900,000 only a couple of days after the appeal was launched. The group promoting the project now have even more than they thought they needed. But who were the people who so rapidly answered the call?

	1

Given his notoriety, I now wonder how it was possible for Tesla to have escaped my attention. But that he did, even though he was once very famous and is still in the news. When you consider that many children know about him because of something called the Tesla coil, often used in science demonstrations, my ignorance is more surprising still.

	2

It was to be the key element in a plan to transmit energy to the entire world and to create a transatlantic wireless telecommunications system. Potential profits from the scheme meant that Tesla was able to attract investment, to the tune of almost the same amount as the current funding for the museum. But when shareholders <u>got wind of</u> the fact that a competitor of Tesla's, the Italian inventor Marconi, had successfully transmitted a long-distance radio signal, they lost faith in the project and refused to fund it further.

	3

Of course, Thomas Edison usually gets the credit for this, the most ubiquitous of twentieth century inventions. But Tesla, who was employed by Edison, played a major role in turning it into a workable device that could be sold to consumers.

	4

Why they had such intense antipathy towards one another remains unclear. Whatever the motives, Edison became a passionate defender of direct current, or DC – the sort that comes out of an ordinary battery and is still used in cars – believing it to be the way forward for electrical power generation and distribution. To his great irritation, Tesla was eventually able to show that alternating current (AC) was far more efficient.

	5

It is true, though, that Tesla was a man of exceptional talents. Yet even as a young man, he was extremely volatile, challenging the opinions of one of his professors at a prestigious Austrian technical university. The professor refused to back down and soon after, Tesla dropped out of the course.

	6

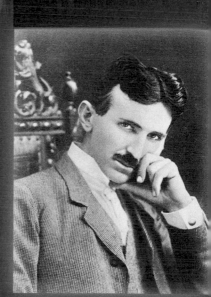

Even so, and despite these strange habits, for the work on electricity alone he deserves our gratitude. I for one am certainly glad I came to learn a little more about this quite remarkably gifted man.

Essay (Part 1)

using linking words and phrases

▶ **WRITING** REFERENCE p.186

1 **Complete the advice for writing essays with *Do* or *Don't*. Then compare your answers with a partner.**

1 .... give your own opinion immediately.

2 .... have a balanced approach.

3 .... give your own opinion at the end.

4 .... use connectors to link your ideas together.

5 .... use ideas from the task input to support your arguments but change the wording.

6 .... involve the reader by using rhetorical questions.

7 .... use a formal register and present your ideas in a clear, objective way.

8 .... use bullet points.

2 **Look at the exam task and a candidate's essay. Find examples in the essay of each of the good pieces of advice in Activity 1.**

> Your class has attended a panel discussion on what methods the government should use to encourage an appreciation of scientific research. You have made the notes below.
>
> **Methods governments could use to encourage an interest in science**
> - media coverage
> - adult education
> - greater financial investment
>
> **Some opinions expressed in the discussion**
>
> 'Science reporting in the media often emphasises less useful research.'
>
> 'Some older adults didn't enjoy their science classes at school, so they won't want to go to science classes now.'
>
> 'The problem is that politicians don't understand the importance of science.'
>
> Write an essay for your tutor discussing **two** of the methods in your notes. You should **explain which method you think is more important** for governments to consider, **giving reasons** to support your opinion.
>
> You may, if you wish, make use of the opinions expressed in the discussion but you should use your own words as far as possible.
>
> Write your answer in **220–260** words in an appropriate style.

Methods to encourage an interest in science

Nowadays we frequently hear people complaining about government spending on scientific research. This lack of appreciation is the result of insufficient information about scientists and the work they do. Closer connections between the scientific community and the general public need to be forged to overcome this problem. But how might this be achieved?

One possible approach would be to increase media coverage. The government could insist that journalists emphasise scientific findings the public see as necessary and of benefit to them. While this would almost certainly give scientific research a more positive image, it implies placing restrictions on the freedom and autonomy of the press. Generally speaking, people seek to avoid this.

A second tactic the government might take is to extend the excellent science teaching in our secondary schools to the adult education sector. A potential difficulty here is that some adults might feel uncomfortable about returning to formal education because of bad memories of their school days. Nevertheless, any resistance might be overcome by holding free lectures on science at science museums and exhibitions, and possibly even in bars and cafés rather than in classrooms and lecture theatres.

In my view, the second of these two approaches should be implemented. If this were done, members of the public would have closer informal contact with scientists and thus a change in attitude would almost certainly come about. Rather than demanding cutbacks, we may even find that members of the public start to ask why more money is not being spent.

3 **Find four linking words or phrases in the essay. Which one introduces**

1 the first idea?   **3** an opinion?

2 a contrasting idea?   **4** a result?

EXAM TIP

In the exam, allow yourself time to check your grammar, spelling and punctuation thoroughly.

4 **Turn to page 167 and do the exam task. Read your work through carefully and make sure you have followed all the advice in the checklist on page 185.**

1 Complete the multi-part verbs in the sentences.

1 They .... out a study of how people interpret facial expressions.

2 The theory she put .... was not taken seriously till many years later.

3 They .... issue with some of the things he had said during the meeting.

4 He tried to take all the different factors .... account.

5 It took her several months to arrive .... a good design for the new light fitting.

6 I don't care what he does, he'll never get her to back ....

2 Choose the correct option to complete the sentences.

1 Our study .... that lack of sleep contributes to weight gain.

   A determined   B found out   C realised

2 If you have paid close attention to a cat drinking, you will have .... that they use their tongues as straws.

   A watched   B observed   C witnessed

3 Our .... hypothesis was that a low carbohydrate diet would have a detrimental effect on children's health.

   A beginning   B initial   C early

4 Our .... show that people who give money or gifts to others in need are happier than those who spend only on themselves.

   A discoveries   B understandings   C findings

5 The hypothesis was modified because it was not .... by the results of our study.

   A shown   B validated   C justified

6 The amount of stress people experience when moving house .... considerably according to their age at the time.

   A differs   B diverges   C varies

3 Read the story and think of the word which best fits each gap. Use only one word for each gap.

All's well that ends well

Carla introduced David to the people she had met in France. (1) .... was sure (2) .... would get on like a house on fire. She suggested they all go out for dinner together and (3) .... couples agreed to meet that evening at 8.30. Carla offered to book a table in a restaurant. (4) .... there were several dozen good restaurants in town, (5) .... of them had a table for five that night at 8.30. One of the head waiters suggested that Carla should call back at 8.00 to see if there had been any cancellations and, as luck would have it, there was (6) .... Carla asked the head waiter to reserve the table in her name and he promised he (7) .... When they got to the restaurant, however, there was no record of Carla's booking at all. Her friends thought she should make a formal complaint but she decided not (8) .... They found a very good place two doors down the street, (9) .... their evening was certainly not ruined. In fact, it was one of the most enjoyable evenings any of them had ever (10) ....

149

Multiple-choice cloze (Part 1)

4 For questions 1–8, read the text below and decide which answer (A, B, C or D) best fits each gap. There is an example at the beginning (0).

Classic comedy: When Harry met Sally

Since its **(0)** ....*release*............ in 1989, *When Harry met Sally* has **(1)** .... a lasting place in the affections of audiences around the world. Director Rob Reiner could never have predicted that the film's central question, 'Can men and women really be friends?' would have such wide **(2)** .... It won the **(3)** .... of audiences and critics alike, with Nora Ephron **(4)** .... a nomination for best screenplay at the Academy Awards. The film **(5)** .... the relationship of the two main characters, Harry (Billy Crystal) and Sally (Meg Ryan), over the course of twelve years. At first it seems they are completely **(6)** .... to each other; she's a romantic optimist, while he's cynical and **(7)** .... in commitment. Unlike the characters, however, audiences will not be deceived by their seeming incompatibility, aware that the laws of romantic comedy dictate that love **(8)** .... prevails.

0	A	release	B	rise	C	emergence	D	origin
1	A	remained	B	gained	C	continued	D	reached
2	A	appeal	B	charm	C	fame	D	popularity
3	A	celebration	B	success	C	approval	D	recognition
4	A	holding	B	collecting	C	taking	D	receiving
5	A	portrays	B	displays	C	reveals	D	demonstrates
6	A	inappropriate	B	unsuited	C	unfit	D	inadequate
7	A	lacking	B	faulty	C	missing	D	insufficient
8	A	absolutely	B	exactly	C	inevitably	D	truly

Open cloze (Part 2)

5 For questions 1–8, read the text below and think of the word which best fits each gap. Use only one word for each gap. There is an example at the beginning (0).

Designed to inspire

The Melbourne Brain Centre is one example of a new trend **(0)** ....*in*............ science building design emerging in universities **(1)** .... the world. Instead of the isolating partitions and cubicles intended to promote competition, the architects who designed the Brain Centre set **(2)** .... to promote openness and collectivity. Both are qualities which, **(3)** .... to historian of innovation Steven Johnson, have **(4)** .... a far greater contribution to scientific advancement. Johnson's analysis of innovative thinking highlighted the importance of creating an environment in **(5)** .... ideas can develop. In the case of the Brain Centre, **(6)** .... includes cafés and lounges throughout the building and laboratories, which are open spaces **(7)** .... equipment and conversation can be shared. The walls of lounges are covered in a markable surface so that two researchers talking about their work can jot their thoughts down **(8)** .... having to interrupt the flow to look for pen and paper. In short, the Brain Centre is an environment designed to inspire.

Word formation (Part 3)

6 For questions 1–8, read the text below. Use the word given in capitals at the end of some of the lines to form a word that fits in the gap in the same line.

Just testing

It is not actually possible to fail a

(0) ....*personality*........ test but many people

react **(1)** .... if they feel the results   INDIGNATION

don't match their own ideas of their strengths

and **(2)** .... What is simply an   ABLE

interpretation of the results is sometimes

understood as a **(3)** .... or even an   CRITICISE

outright attack. Those who find themselves

repeatedly turned down for jobs on the basis

of test results may start to feel that the tests

are simply too **(4)** .... and may   DEMAND

even decide to try and cheat on the next test

they do. This is harder to do than you might

think. Someone analysing test results would

immediately become

(5) .... if they were to notice that   SUSPECT

a candidate had answered inconsistently.

Finding a series of **(6)** .... between a   MATCH

candidate's answers will make it obvious that

the person taking the test is **(7)** ....   TRUST

The best advice, then, is to make your

(8) .... as authentic as you can.   RESPOND

Key word transformations (Part 4)

7 For questions 1–6, complete the second sentence so that it has a similar meaning to the first sentence, using the word given. Do not change the word given. You must use between three and six words, including the word given.

1 It would be a good idea for you to talk to the careers advisor first.

SUGGEST

I .... to the careers advisor first.

2 Do you realise we might lose our funding for the project?

DANGER

Are you aware that we .... our funding for the project?

3 They sometimes tell the people who arrive late that they can't enter the theatre.

PREVENTED

People arriving late .... the theatre.

4 Although the painting is worth much more, it was recently sold for only £10,000.

BEING

The painting was recently sold for only £10,000, ... much more.

5 The museum intends to put the collection on show from September.

IS

The collection .... at the museum from September.

6 People think that Edison invented the light bulb.

THOUGHT

Edison .... the light bulb.

Support for Speaking tasks

Unit 1, Speaking and Use of English focus, Activity 5

Take turns to take the role of examiner and candidate. Ask and answer the questions.

1 **Choose one or two questions from the list.**

- Where are you from?
- What do you do there?
- How long have you been studying English?
- What do you enjoy most about studying English?

2 **Choose one or more questions from the list.**

- What has been your most interesting travel experience so far?
- What did you like most about the area where you grew up?
- Who has more influence on your life – your friends or your family?
- Do you prefer to get the news from newspapers, television or the internet?
- Do you ever wish you were rich and famous?

Unit 2, Speaking and Use of English focus, Activity 7

Task 1

Student A: Here are your pictures. They show people putting up messages. I'd like you to compare two of the pictures and say why the people might be putting up the messages and what sort of reaction they might get.

Student B: Do you think putting up messages is a good way to help people remember things?

- **Why are the people putting up the messages?**
- **What sort of reaction might they get?**

Unit 4, Speaking focus, Activity 6

Part 3

Talk about something together for about two minutes. Here are some factors which affect young people's ability to do well at a sport and a question for you to discuss.

Talk to each other about how these factors influence a young person's ability to excel at playing a sport.

Part 4

- How easy do you think it is to recognise talent in a child?
- What risks might there be if young people are pushed too hard to excel at something?
- Should parents always have high expectations of their children?
- Do you think schools should encourage competition among children?

access to training

good facilities

How might these factors influence a young person's ability to excel at playing a sport?

natural ability

encouragement from family

expectations of teachers

Unit 5, Speaking focus, Activity 8

Task 1

Student A: Here are your pictures. They show people doing things in unusual places. I'd like you to compare two of the pictures and say what might be difficult about doing these activities in places like these.

Student B: Which of these activities would surprise other people most? Why?

> **What might be difficult about doing these activities in places like these?**

Unit 6, Speaking focus, Activity 7

Task 1

Student A: Here are your pictures. They show people using different types of memory aids. I'd like you to compare two of the pictures and say what kind of information these things can help people remember and how effective they might be.

Student B: Which sort of memory aid do you think is most useful for students? Why?

> • **What kind of information can these things help people remember?**
> • **How effective might they be?**

Unit 7, Speaking focus, Activity 9

Work in groups of three.

Student A: You are the examiner. Choose a question to ask. Then listen to the candidates' answers, thinking about the points on the checklist.

Students B and C: You are the candidates. Follow Student A's instructions.

Examiner's questions

- Do you think there should be more careful regulation of advertising?
- Were people able to make up their own minds about products and services before there was so much advertising?
- How have the internet and social networking changed the way products are marketed and advertised?
- Do you agree with bans on advertising aimed at certain groups, e.g. young children or products, e.g. cigarettes?
- Do you think marketing and advertising are appropriate ways to use psychology and linguistics research?

Examiner's checklist

Did the candidate

1 say enough?
2 avoid basic errors like lack of agreement between subject and verb, double negation, etc.?
3 use clear, intelligible pronunciation?
4 respond naturally to what the other candidate said?
5 use expressions for justifying an opinion?
6 use expressions for agreeing and disagreeing?

Unit 11, Speaking focus, Activity 3

Part 3

Talk about something together for two minutes. Here are some methods which people might use to try to make new friends and business contacts and a question for you to discuss.

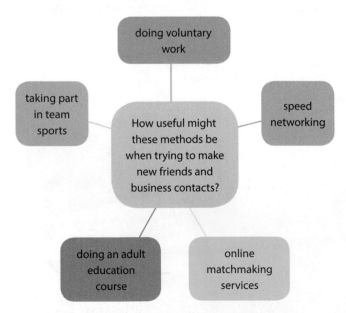

doing voluntary work

taking part in team sports

speed networking

How useful might these methods be when trying to make new friends and business contacts?

doing an adult education course

online matchmaking services

Talk to each other about how useful these methods might be when trying to make new friends and business contacts.

Unit 14, Speaking focus, Activity 6

Talk to each other about something for about two minutes. Here are some kinds of scientific research that people do. Talk to each other about how important these kinds of research are for contemporary society.

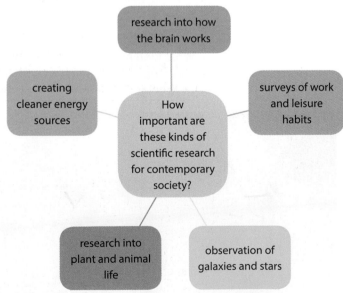

research into how the brain works

creating cleaner energy sources

surveys of work and leisure habits

How important are these kinds of scientific research for contemporary society?

research into plant and animal life

observation of galaxies and stars

Now you have about a minute to decide which kind of research would have the greatest long-term benefit.

Unit 8, Speaking focus, Activity 6

Task 1

Student A: Here are your pictures. They show people arriving at an airport. I'd like you to compare two of the pictures and say what the purpose of the people's trip might be and how they might be feeling about their trip.

Student B: Give your partner feedback on his/her performance using the general marking guidelines on page 207.

> - **What might the purpose of the people's trip be?**
> - **How might they be feeling about their trip?**

Unit 9, Speaking focus, Activity 7

Task 1

Student A: Here are your pictures. They show people doing things that are usually learnt from a teacher. I'd like you to compare two of the pictures and say why people might prefer to learn these things on their own and what difficulties they might have.

Student B: Who do you think looks the most confident? Why?

> - **Why might people prefer to learn these things on their own?**
> - **What difficulties might they have?**

Unit 9, Speaking focus, Activity 7

Task 2

Student B: Here are your pictures. They show people doing activities to help them learn to work as a team. I'd like you to compare two of the pictures and say why these activities might help people learn to work as a team and what difficulties they might have.

Student A: Which group do you think are enjoying the activities most? Why?

> • **Why might these activities help people learn to work as a team?**
> • **What difficulties might they have?**

Unit 3, Speaking focus, Activity 5

Work in groups of three. Take it in turns to take the roles of examiner and candidates.

Examiner: Listen to check how well the candidates respond to and expand on each other's ideas.

Candidates: Look at the task and follow the examiner's instructions. Remember to respond to and expand on your partner's ideas.

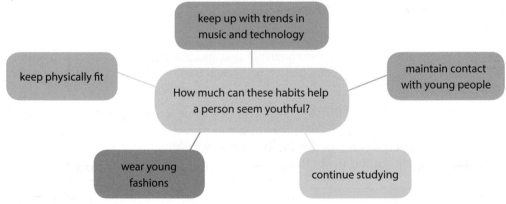

- keep up with trends in music and technology
- keep physically fit
- maintain contact with young people
- **How much can these habits help a person seem youthful?**
- wear young fashions
- continue studying

Examiner's instructions

For Part 3, say:

Now I'd like you to talk about something together for about two minutes. Here are some habits we often think make people seem youthful and a question for you to discuss. First, you have some time to look at the task. (Pause for fifteen seconds.) Now talk to each other about how much these things can help a person seem youthful.

When the candidates have spoken for two minutes, say:

Now you have about a minute to decide which habit would have the greatest long-term benefit. (Give the candidates one minute to decide.)

For Part 4, ask two of these questions:

- *How important do you think it is for older people to maintain a youthful appearance?*
- *Some people find it difficult to do enough physical activity once they grow older. Why do you think this is?*
- *Whose responsibility should it be to care for the elderly: families or the state?*
- *Which do you think is more important for an older person: spending time with their family or with other older people?*
- *Some people say that youth is wasted on the young. What do you think?*

Unit 13, Speaking focus, Activity 8

Task 1

Student A: Here are your pictures. They show people looking at things carefully. I'd like you to compare two of the pictures and say why the people might be enjoying looking at these things and what they might learn from these experiences.

Student B: Do you think it's better to look at things carefully on your own or with other people?

> • **Why might the people be enjoying looking at these things?**
> • **What might they learn from these experiences?**

Unit 14, Speaking focus, Activity 3

Task 1

Student A: Here are your pictures. They show people using recent inventions. I'd like you to compare two of the pictures and say why people might find inventions like these useful and what reactions they might get from other people when they use them.

Student B: Give your partner feedback on his/her performance using the General marking guidelines on page 207.

> • **Why might people find inventions like these useful?**
> • **What reactions might they get from other people when they use them?**

Unit 11, Speaking focus, Activity 7
Part 4

- Some people prefer to make new friends exclusively through being introduced to them by others. Why do you think this is?
- Many people keep the same friends they had at school or university throughout their lives. Why do you think this is?
- Do you think there is too much emphasis on linking up via social networking sites with people who share your interests? Why/Why not?
- It is sometimes said that fate chooses our relatives but that we choose our friends. Do you agree?

Unit 2, Speaking and Use of English focus, Activity 7
Task 2

Student B: Here are your pictures. They show people giving information. I'd like you to compare two of the pictures and say how important it is to give this information clearly and what might happen if the information is misunderstood.

Student A: Do you think it's always necessary to have important instructions written down?

> - **How important is it to give this information clearly?**
> - **What might happen if the information is misunderstood?**

Unit 5, Speaking focus, Activity 8
Task 2

Student B: Here are your pictures. They show people doing things that can be beneficial. I'd like you to compare two of the pictures and say how these activities might be beneficial to the people and what might be easy or difficult about doing them in settings like these.

Student A: Which activity do you think requires the most concentration? Why?

> - **How might these activities be beneficial to the people?**
> - **What might be easy or difficult about doing them in settings like these?**

Unit 6, Speaking focus, Activity 7

Task 2

Student B: Here are your pictures. They show people holding objects of sentimental value. I'd like you to compare two of the pictures, saying what memories the objects might bring back and how long the people might keep the objects for.

Student A: Do you think people have more sentimental objects as they get older?

> • **What memories might the objects bring back?**
> • **How long might the people keep the objects for?**

Unit 8, Speaking focus, Activity 6

Task 2

Student B: Here are your pictures. They show people packing to go away somewhere. I'd like you to compare two of the pictures, saying how difficult it might be for the people to choose what to pack and how organised they need to be.

Student A: Give your partner feedback on his/her performance using the general marking guidelines on page 207.

> • **How difficult might it be for the people to choose what to pack?**
> • **How organised do they need to be?**

Unit 13, Speaking focus, Activity 8

Task 2

Student B: Here are your pictures. They show people who have to wear a uniform doing their jobs. I'd like you to compare two of the pictures, saying why the people need to wear the uniforms and how they might feel about wearing them.

Student A: Do you think some people look more attractive wearing a uniform?

> • **Why do the people need to wear the uniforms?**
> • **How might they feel about wearing them?**

Unit 14, Speaking focus, Activity 3

Task 2

Student B: Here are your pictures. They show people working in different environments. I'd like you to compare two of the pictures and say how these environments might make people more creative and what difficulties people might have working in environments like these.

Student A: Give your partner feedback on his/her performance using the General marking guidelines on page 207.

> • **How might these environments make people more creative?**
> • **What difficulties might people have working in environments like these?**

Communication activities

Unit 1, Vocabulary focus, Activity 7

Use the verbs in Activities 4, 5 and 6 on page 9 to talk about one of the pictures. Do not describe the picture. Your partner should guess which picture you are referring to.

Student A: choose between pictures A and B.
Student B: choose between pictures C and D.

Unit 1, Listening focus, Activity 6

Work in pairs. Take it in turns to ask and answer the questions.

1   Have you ever ordered something from *room service*? What did you order?

2   Are there any drinks that you prefer at *room temperature*? Why/Why not?

3   Do you know anyone who lives in a flat or house where there is *no room to swing a cat*? How do they feel about living there?

4   Which is more important to you: living somewhere that is nice and *roomy*, having a good view or living somewhere near great entertainment facilities? Why?

5   Would you be attracted to a job that offered you free *room and board*? Why/Why not?

6   Do you ever pay for a special seat on a plane to make sure you'll have enough *leg room*? Do you think it is worth the money?

Unit 2, Speaking and Use of English focus, Activity 3

The phrases for giving opinions are in bold.

1   **I'm not saying** I'm completely addicted **but** I would feel anxious if I didn't get a text every couple of minutes. I'm just used to talking to my friends pretty much all the time. I mean, obviously, there are exceptions – I do turn my phone off when I'm in class and I don't text when I'm having dinner with my family. But **generally speaking**, I like to be in contact 24–7.

2   **That totally depends on the situation – I'm sure some people would argue that** not replying immediately shows a lack of interest or respect but **the way I see it**, there's more to life than texting. And **I don't have a problem** if my texts go unanswered for hours or even days.

3   **I think that goes without saying.** We all know people who've been dumped by text and that's a really mean and cowardly thing to do. Only the most insensitive person **would even consider** doing that.

4   **I wouldn't go that far but** yes, sometimes texting is preferable because you've got a bit more time to respond. **I think it's fair to say** that a lot of people are more outgoing and funny in their text messages than they are in a group situation.

Unit 2, Listening focus, Activity 1

? If you answered *yes* to four or more questions, you are an introvert.

? If you answered *no* to four or more questions, you are an extrovert.

? If you have a mixture of *yes* and *no* answers, you have tendencies to be both an extrovert and an introvert, depending on your mood.

Unit 4, Vocabulary focus, Activity 6

These are some possible collocations:

win/lose/gain/have/get/take (**an/the**) **advantage**
follow/lose/win/start/have **an argument**
suffer/ experience/face/overcome/have **difficulties**
follow/realise/fulfil/achieve/have **dreams**
achieve/reach/seek **perfection**
gain/find/achieve/win/lose/deserve **popularity**
reach/achieve/develop/fulfil/realise/have **potential**
receive/accept/win/deserve/give/earn **praise**
achieve/reach/fulfil/have/hit/miss **a target**
receive/accept/get/deserve/express/give **thanks**

Unit 6 Vocabulary focus, Activity 8

Student A

Play the word association game with Student B. Say an adjective from the box and ask what ideas Student B associates with the adjective. Then listen to Student B's adjective and say what ideas you associate with it.

changeable	comforting	illogical
irresponsible	unbelievable	

Unit 4, Writing focus, Activity 6

Look at the exam task and plan your introduction. Decide together what information you think should be included.

1 the actions you have chosen to discuss
2 analysis of which action is more important
3 reasons why you think the actions are important
4 why governments should promote health and fitness among young people
5 other action the government could take

Your class has attended a panel discussion on the action governments can take to promote health and fitness among young people. You have made the notes below.

Action to promote health and fitness among young people

- Improve teaching in schools.
- Improve attitudes to competitiveness.
- Improve the image of sports.

Opinions expressed during the discussion

'There need to be specialist sports teachers for children and students of all ages.'

'Some young people are put off by the pressure to compete.'

'A lot of young people don't think it's cool to take part in sports.'

Write an essay for your tutor discussing **two** of the actions in your notes. You should **explain which action is more important**, **giving reasons** to support your opinion.

You may, if you wish, make use of the opinions expressed during the discussion but you should use your own words as far as possible.

Write your **essay** in **220–260** words in an appropriate style.

Unit 6, Grammar focus, Activity 7

Which two of the buildings should be saved for posterity? With your partner, put them in order of importance and say why the two you have chosen have the greatest historical significance.

Unit 12, Use of English and Grammar focus, Activity 11

Student A

1 You promised to invite Student B to the cinema last night but you forgot. Call Student B now and make your excuses. Use *I was going to, I was planning to* and *I would have*.

2 Student B borrowed your tennis racket last week and forgot to return it. Listen to Student B explain what happened.

Unit 9, Listening focus, Activity 5

Student A

1 Take turns with Student B to match the first half of the sentences (1–6) with the second (A–F).

1 I made a *mental*

2 I'll put a bit of oil on that hinge. That should *do*

3 I meant to get some coffee from the supermarket but it completely *slipped*

A *up a mental image* of a place where you felt perfectly happy?

B *up*, which can be rather embarrassing.

C *brain* to remember which street she lived in, but I had no idea, really.

2 Work with Student B to try to explain what the phrases in italics mean.

Unit 11, Grammar focus, Activity 6

Student A

1 Decide which words you can cut to turn the relative clauses in the sentences into participle clauses. Do you need to make any other changes?

Example: I had just arrived at the party when I saw a girl ~~who was~~ wearing exactly the same outfit as me.

1 The people on the beach saw a man who was waving frantically as he was swept out by the strong current.

2 There are only fifteen places, so some people who apply to attend the course will inevitably be disappointed.

3 The bandage which was protecting the cut from infection had to be replaced every two days.

2 Check your answers with Student B. Then check that he/she has the correct answers for sentences 4–6.

4 Her prime concerns when ~~she has been~~ looking for a partner have always been status and wealth.

5 The film, ~~which was~~ released last Tuesday, has received some very damning reviews.

6 Anyone ~~who~~ wish**ing** to raise an issue for discussion during the meeting should contact the secretary at least a week beforehand.

3 Work with Student B to create a story that includes either sentence 1 or 4.

Unit 12, Use of English and Grammar focus, Activity 11

Student B

1 Student A promised to invite you to the cinema last night but didn't. Listen to Student A explain what happened.

2 You borrowed student A's tennis racket last week and forgot to return it. Call Student A now to apologise and make your excuses. Use *I was going to, I was planning to* and *I would have*.

Unit 11, Writing focus, Activity 3

Look at the exam task and decide what programme of studies you have been following.

Student A: plan the section on why you are a suitable candidate for an exchange programme.

Student B: plan the section on what benefits you expect to gain.

Look at each other's plans and write your letter.

Your school or college takes part in an exchange programme with another institution in another country. You have decided to apply to go on an exchange visit and are required to write a letter to the director of the host institution, explaining why they should accept you as a student. You should explain:

- what programme of studies you have been following at your home institution.
- why you are a suitable candidate for an exchange programme.
- what benefits you expect to gain from taking part in the programme.

Write your **letter** in **220–260** words in an appropriate style.

Unit 5, Listening focus, Activity 6

Take turns to complete the sentences. Then look at the underlined phrases in Activity 5 on page 38 and check your answers.

1 I'm not being paid much but I still think this job might give me a foot ....

2 Sometimes a carrot and .... is the only thing that gets people working.

3 I'm sorry I haven't replied to your letter but I've been .... ears in work.

4 The factory supervisor was a real .... – we only got half an hour's break at lunchtime.

5 I've been .... my nose to the grindstone trying to finish an important project.

6 I knew it would turn out to be a(n) .... job but I decided to stay in it until something better turned up.

Unit 10, Listening focus, Activity 6

Decide which of the 'nudges' (A–D) might be most effective for people who want to

1 save more money.

2 give up smoking.

3 run a marathon.

A Pay a fine for not reaching their target by a certain date.

B Have a weekly discussion about progress with an online support group for people with similar goals.

C Have text alerts sent throughout the day.

D Have reminders written on notes around the house/office.

Unit 3, Vocabulary and Grammar focus, Activity 10

Work in pairs. Identify the countable and uncountable nouns in the quotations. Then discuss whether you agree with them or not.

Advice is what we ask for when we already know the answer but wish we didn't.

(*Erica Jong*)

Chance makes our parents but choice makes our friends.

(*Jacques Delille*)

Data is not information. Information is not knowledge. Knowledge is not understanding. Understanding is not wisdom.

(*Anon*)

Unit 8, Speaking focus, Activity 7

Imagine you are travelling in Thailand. Together choose the best souvenir to buy for

1   your grandmother/grandfather.
2   your ten-year old brother/sister.
3   your boyfriend/girlfriend.
4   your boss.

Unit 11, Grammar focus, Activity 6
Student B

1   **Check that Student A has the correct answers for sentences 1–3.**

1   The people on the beach saw a man ~~who was~~ waving frantically as he was swept out by the strong current.

2   There are only fifteen, places so some people ~~who~~ apply**ing** to attend the course will inevitably be disappointed.

3   The bandage ~~which was~~ protecting the cut from infection had to be replaced every two days.

2   **Decide which words you can cut to turn the relative clauses in the sentences into participle clauses. Do you need to make any other changes? Check your answers with Student A.**

Example: I had just arrived at the party when I saw a girl ~~who was~~ wearing exactly the same outfit as me.

4   Her prime concerns when she has been looking for a partner have always been status and wealth.

5   The film, which was released last Tuesday, has received some very damning reviews.

6   Anyone who wishes to raise an issue for discussion during the meeting should contact the secretary at least a week beforehand.

3   **Work with Student A to create a story that includes either sentence 1 or 4.**

Unit 13, Vocabulary and Use of English focus, Activity 1

Answers

1 T
2 T (It takes twelve muscles to smile and eleven to frown.)
3 F (There are nineteen.)
4 T
5 T
6 T
7 F
8 F (It can make you feel better.)

Unit 13, Grammar focus, Activity 6

Decide whether you think the actions are acceptable or unacceptable. Give reasons for your answers.

1 selling a fake painting to an art collector for a lot of money when you know it's a fake
2 buying fake designer clothes and handbags and pretending they are real
3 using a fake ID to get into a nightclub when you are under age
4 faking an illness to get out of doing something you don't want to do

Unit 12, Use of English and Grammar focus, Activity 5

Top 10 most hated sounds

1 nails on a chalkboard
2 someone being sick
3 car alarm
4 a dentist's drill
5 someone spitting
6 a yapping dog
7 screaming baby/children
8 someone talking with their mouth full
9 someone grinding their teeth
10 someone's knife grinding on a plate

Unit 14, Writing focus, Activity 4

Look at the exam task.

1 Work in pairs and plan an outline for the essay.
2 Write your essay and make sure you have followed all the advice in the checklist on page 185.
3 Edit your work for any of the grammar mistakes you reviewed in the Grammar quiz on page 145.
4 Show your essay to other students and see if they can find any other mistakes or make suggestions on how your essay could be improved.

You have attended a Science Club lecture on how schools could encourage young people to train for careers in science. You have made the notes below.

Ways in which schools could encourage young people to train for careers in science

• enjoyable science lessons
• careers advice
• guest lectures from professional scientists

Some opinions expressed in the discussion

'Kids should be able to design their own experiments.'

'A lot of the careers advice given is already out of date.'

'A lot of scientists are too busy to spend time visiting schools.'

Write an essay for your tutor discussing **two** of the methods in your notes. You should **explain which method you think is more important** for governments to consider, **giving reasons** to support your opinion.

You may, if you wish, make use of the opinions expressed in the discussion but you should use your own words as far as possible.

Write your answer in **220–260** words in an appropriate style.

Unit 14, Grammar focus, Activity 1

Student B

Look at the test and follow the instructions. Then compare your answers with Student A.

Common errors quiz

Twelve of these sentences are correct and twelve contain errors. Tick (✓) the sentences that are correct. Highlight the errors and correct them. Say which grammar point is involved.

1 I have great respect and admiration for my uncle but I don't think he understands me very well.

2 No sooner had I closed the door than I realised I had left the key in the pocket of my other pair of jeans.

3 In my opinion, governments should be doing a lot more to support unemployed.

4 The person in my family with whom I have never had much rapport is my younger sister.

5 I regret informing you that all the positions have been filled and we will not be accepting any further applications.

6 Sometimes life just seems so unfair. It really shouldn't be like that.

7 I sometimes wish I stop eating so many sweets. They're really bad for your teeth.

8 Some people say that this is the beginning of a new era of greater peace and harmony. I certainly hope so.

9 She's thin as both of her sisters. Their mother was a very slim woman too.

10 It is completely impossible to find good sources of information on this topic online.

11 The university would have got in touch with you by now if you had been given the scholarship..

12 Let's ask Kim to give us a lift. Unless we'll have to get a taxi.

13 However well you think you know someone, in some ways we are all, in fact, a mystery to one another.

14 Picking up the phone, an unfamiliar voice. It said, 'Hello, dear."

15 We explained that the weather was about to improve and the man said he hoped that it would.

16 I had to visit some relatives in Melbourne. What this meant I couldn't attend the meeting.

17 She wasn't angry nor she was sad, just disappointed with their behaviour.

18 Tim has a terrible loathing of jazz. He really can't stand it.

19 That's amazing how people have got so used to using smartphones in such a short time.

20 The house is said being built in the late fifteenth century.

21 Given that she is very interested in art, she would certainly enjoy a holiday in Italy.

22 When I was born, it would be impossible to predict that I would end up living here.

23 I was told the stopover will be just over an hour but we were stranded in the airport for a whole day.

24 She warned us not to go into the water because there were jellyfish.

Unit 14, Reading focus, Activity 1

QUICK QUIZ

1 Who is normally credited with having invented the radio?
2 Who is normally credited with having invented the electric light bulb?
3 What are the two major types of electric current used today?
4 Which type is used to power cities?
5 Which type is used in most cars?
6 Who invented radar?

Unit 7, Writing focus, Activity 2

Survey results

		AGREE	DISAGREE	NEITHER
1	I like to look at most of the advertisements I am exposed to.	52%	37%	11%
2	Most advertising insults my intelligence.	48%	39%	13%
3	In general, I feel I can trust advertising.	38%	51%	11%
4	Products usually live up to the promises made in their advertisements.	50%	34%	15%
5	In general, I like advertising.	54%	35%	11%

Unit 6, Vocabulary focus, Activity 8

Student B

Play the word association game with Student A. Listen to Student A's adjective and say what ideas you associate with it. Then say an adjective from the box and ask what ideas Student A associates with it.

excitable	imaginative	incomprehensible
irresistible	unthinkable	

Unit 9, Listening focus, Activity 5

Student B

1 Take turns with Student A to match the first half of the sentences (1–6) with the second (A–F).

4 I've got two friends, one called Andy and one called Sandy, and I often get their names *muddled*
5 I was *racking my*
6 Can you *conjure*

D *the trick* and stop the noise.
E *my mind*. I'll have to go back and get some.
F *note* to call the bank the next morning.

2 Work with Student A to try to explain what the phrases in italics mean.

Grammar reference

Contents

1 Adverbs

1.1 Linking adverbials

We use linking adverbials to connect one sentence in a logical way to another. They usually appear at the beginning of a sentence and are followed by a comma. They help to make writing more cohesive.

1   Linking adverbials used to give extra information include: *additionally, as well as, besides (this), furthermore, moreover, what's more.*

    *We decided there was little to be gained by waiting any longer. **Besides**, there was a storm coming.*

2   Linking adverbials used to give a reason or result include: *for this reason, consequently, as a result, in view of, given.*

    *We decided there was little to be gained by waiting any longer. **Consequently**, we managed to catch the last train home.*

3   Linking adverbials used to make a contrast include: *on the contrary, on the other hand, in contrast, alternatively, despite this, even so.*

    *We decided there was little to be gained by waiting any longer. **Despite this**, we ended up wasting another half an hour trying to agree what to do next.*

1.2 Modifying adverbs

We can use adverbs to make adjectives, other adverbs and verbs stronger (intensifiers) or weaker (modifiers).

1   We can use these adverbs before gradable adjectives (i.e. adjectives that can be used in the comparative) and adverbs: *bitterly, barely, deeply, somewhat, seriously, really, extremely, practically, entirely, pretty, completely, quite, scarcely, totally, very.*

    *We were **bitterly** disappointed when our holiday was cancelled.*

    *He answered the question **somewhat** abruptly.*

2   Some modifying adverbs collocate with certain adjectives.

    bitterly cold/ashamed/disappointed/divided

    barely alive/legible/comprehensible

    completely serious/open/honest

    deeply serious/painful/sorry

    entirely convinced/clear/satisfactory

    pretty doubtful/hopeless

    perfectly capable/aware/reasonable/normal/ safe/straightforward

    seriously alarmed/worried/hurt

3 Extreme or absolute (non-gradable) adjectives include: *amazing, devastating, disastrous, fantastic, freezing, furious, immense, impossible, staggering.*
We can use the following adverbs with extreme adjectives: *absolutely, really, utterly, quite.*

*The building was **utterly** immense.*

> **Watch Out!** When used with non-gradable adjectives, *quite* means *absolutely*, not *fairly*.

2 Articles

2.1 The definite article: *the*

We use the definite article *the* with singular and plural nouns and with uncountable nouns

* when only one of something exists or is unique.

  *It's **the** best restaurant in the world.*

  ***The** President is running for election again.*

  ***the** New York Marathon, **the** Olympic Games*

* to talk about previously mentioned things.

  *A man and a woman walked into the waiting room. **The** man was carrying a suitcase.*

* to talk about a generic class of things.

  ***The** fax machine was invented about twenty years ago.*

  ***The** rhinoceros is under threat from poachers.*

* with national groups.

  ***The** English love football.*

* with adjectives used as nouns.

  ***The** rich can afford to pay more taxes.*

2.2 The indefinite article: *a/an*

We use the indefinite article *a/an*

* with singular countable nouns, when referring to something general or non-specific.

  *I'd like **a** coffee and **a** sandwich.*

  *I haven't got **a** pen.*

* with these numbers: 100, 1,000, 1,000,000.

  *There were over **a** thousand people at the conference.*

2.3 Zero article

We use no article (the zero article) when talking about

* uncountable, plural and abstract nouns in general.

  Time passes more slowly on holiday.

  Actors usually have nice voices.

* continents and countries.

  They are going to visit Antarctica.

  Have you been to Germany?

* mountains and lakes.

  They are going to climb Mount Kenya.

  Is Lake Victoria in South Africa?

3 Cohesion

3.1 Coherence and cohesion

We say that a text is coherent if we can see logical connections between the various parts of the text. We indicate these connections by using cohesion devices.

3.2 Cohesion devices

There are two types of cohesion: grammatical cohesion and lexical cohesion. Grammatical cohesion includes reference, substitution, ellipsis and conjunction. Lexical cohesion involves links between the vocabulary items in the text, such as collocations, repetitions or the use of synonyms, antonyms, etc.

1 Reference

Reference is the use of pronouns and proverbs to refer back or forward to full forms used earlier or later in the text.

***Ralph** spent **all morning** washing **the car**. **It** needed a clean and **he** knew **this** was the only time **he** had available.*

***Jane** saw **him** walking towards her – **Raori Johnson**, the boy **she** had met the summer before.*

2 Substitution

We use substitution to avoid repeating certain words in a sentence. Substitution can be used to replace a noun, a verb or even a phrase.

*I was making **a sandwich** for Sue, but she said she didn't want **one**.*

*We had planned **to take the scenic route** but we were advised that **to do so** would add an extra hour to our journey.*

3 Ellipsis

When we use ellipsis, we simply omit the words that we wish to avoid repeating.

A: *Are you coming to the party?*

B: *I'll try (to come to the party) but I'm not sure I can (come to the party).*

A: *Frances isn't staying with Patricia after all.*

B: *Why (is Frances) not (staying with Patricia)?*

4 Conjunction

(For more information on conjunctions, see 6 below.)

We use conjunction to link ideas in the text.

* Co-ordinating conjunctions include *and, or, but, so, nor* and *yet.*

  *I love living here **yet** I still feel homesick from time to time.*

  *I'm not keen on football, **nor** is Amy.*

* Subordinating conjunctions include: *after, although, as, as far as, as if, as long as, as soon as, as though, because, before, if, in order that, since, so, so that, than, though, unless, until, when, whenever, where, whereas, wherever* and *while*. We use them to link a subordinate clause to a main clause.

  ***As far as** I'm concerned, he can take over responsibility for the work next week.*

  *Alfonso offered to help me with the translation **so that** I could spend more time with my children.*

4 Comparing

4.1 Regular comparative and superlative forms

1 With adjectives ending in one syllable, we use *-er* and *-est* (*-ier*, *-iest* for adjectives ending in *-y*).

*His criticism was **harsher** than necessary.*

*It's the **funniest** story I've ever read.*

2 With longer adjectives, adjectives ending in *-ful/-less/-ing* and adverbs which have the same form as the adjective, we use *more/less* and *the most/least*.

*I thought the film was **more/less enjoyable** than the book.*

*The guidebook was **more/less useful** than I expected.*

*The train left early but the bus left even **earlier**.*

*The objects in the exhibition could have been displayed **more imaginatively**.*

*The **most/least impressive** building in the town is the old castle.*

3 To compare two equivalent things, we use *as … as*.

*The film is **as believable as** the book.*

4.2 Intensifying and modifying comparisons

We can use the following words to intensify and modify comparatives.

***considerably/far/much/a lot/a great deal** more/less interesting than*

***very much** bigger/better*

***more and more** difficult*

***a bit/slightly/a little** higher*

***no** worse than*

***not any** quicker*

***just/quite/easily** as interesting as*

***almost/not quite** as crowded as*

***not nearly/nowhere near** as useful as*

4.3 *like* in comparisons

1 We use *like* + noun to describe similarity.

*He's tall **like** his father.*

2 We use *nothing like as* to emphasise the difference between two things.

*Driving is **nothing like as** fast as going by train.*

> **Watch Out!** *As* is only used in comparisons in the phrases *as … as* and *not so/as … as*.

5 Conditionals

See also *Hypothetical meaning* in 10 below.

5.1 Zero conditional

FORM   *if* + present simple + present simple in the main clause

USE   to describe a general truth

*If you **heat** water, it **boils**.*

Alternatives to *if*

***Unless** they **are** cornered or startled, snakes **do not** normally **attack** people.*

***When** older people **are** dehydrated, they often **experience** a decrease in cognitive function.*

5.2 First conditional

FORM   *if*/etc. + present simple + future in the main clause

USE   to describe what is possible or likely in the present or future

*She'**ll be** absolutely thrilled **if** it **turns out** that you can go back to Australia in November.*

We can also use if/etc. + present continuous/present perfect + future or imperative in the main clause, to talk about possibility or likelihood in the present/future.

*You **won't get** the grant unless **you've managed** to get really good references.*

***If you're visiting** Santa Cruz in February, you **will be** able to enjoy the carnival.*

5.3 Second conditional

FORM   *if* + past simple/continuous + *would/could*/etc. + past participle in the main clause

USE

1 **to talk about something**
   • that is contrary to the present facts or seen as very unlikely to happen

   *If I **was/were** in your shoes, I'd seriously **consider** emigrating.*

   *If I **was/were** Prime Minister, I **wouldn't cut** education and health care spending.*

   • that is very unlikely to happen in the future

   *I **wouldn't take out** a loan **unless** I **knew** I would have no difficulty whatsoever paying it back.*

2 **to give advice**

   *I'**d try** and eat less bread **if I were you**.*

5.4 Third conditional

FORM *if* + past perfect + *would/could*/etc. + *have* + past participle in the main clause

USE to describe something in the past that could have happened but didn't or that shouldn't have happened but did

*I **wouldn't have said** anything about it **if** I'**d had** any idea he would make such a fuss.*

*She **could have had** a stopover in Dubai **if** she **had flown** with the other airline.*

5.5 Modal verbs in conditional sentences

Modal verbs (*can, could, might*, etc.) can be used in all types of conditional sentences.

*I **might pop in** to see you **if** I **can persuade** Jo to drive me.*

*If she **had** more support, she **could set up** her own business.*

*If I **hadn't been** late, we **might** never **have met**.*

5.6 Mixed conditionals

It is possible to have sentences that mix conditionals in

- an *if* clause referring to the past with a main clause referring to the present or future.

  *If I **had finished** my law degree, I **would** probably **be a** lawyer now.*

  *If we **hadn't been asked** to help, we **could go** home now.*

- an *if* clause referring to the present or future with a main clause referring to the past.

  *If you **don't like** hot weather, you **shouldn't have booked** to go to Cordoba in July.*

  *If you'**ve got to** get up so early tomorrow, you **ought to have gone** to bed by now.*

5.7 Conditional linking words and alternatives to *if*

Common conditional linking words are: *if, as/so long as, unless, even if, whether, providing, provided (that), on condition that*. When the clause with the conditional linking word is at the beginning of the sentence, there is a comma. When the main clause begins the sentence, there is no comma.

If you lay the table, I'll serve the dinner.

***As long as** you can check your email, we can stay in touch.*

*I won't stay late **unless** they need me to.*

*They're holding the carnival **even if** it is cold and wet.*

*I'll attend the meeting **provided that** I can get time off.*

In the event of cancellation, a full refund will be provided.

*I hope Val emails me today. **Otherwise,** I'll have to call her.*

> **Watch Out!** *In case* is used to describe things we do as precautions against what might happen.

*I'll book a later flight **in case** I miss the connection.*

5.8 Formal style

1 In more formal styles we can omit *if* but we have to place the auxiliary verb before the subject.

***Had I known** you were not going to be available, I would have called the meeting for another day.*

***Had I not booked** a return ticket, I would be able to stay for another month.*

***Were Tim** my son, I would not hesitate to help him.*

2 *if* + *should* is common in formal letters. For even greater formality, omit *if* and begin the sentence with *should*.

*If you **should require** any further information, please do not hesitate to contact us.*

***Should you wish** to contact me, I can be reached at the above address.*

5.9 *if* + (*should*) *happen to*

We use *if* + (*should*) *happen to* to suggest that something is more unlikely or just a chance possibility. *Should* and *happen* can be used together.

*If you **should happen to run** into my old friend Simon, do say hello to him from me.*

*If you **happen to pass** a post office, could you get me a couple of stamps?*

5.10 *suppose/what if ... ?*

Suppose means *what if ... ?* and it is used with

1 the present simple to describe something that may possibly happen or may have happened.

*Suppose someone **hears** us.*

*Suppose someone **tells** her what you said.*

2 the past simple to talk about something that is imaginary or which is unlikely to happen in the future.

*Suppose Caroline **found out** about the letter. What would you do?*

*Suppose you **got** a great job abroad. Would you emigrate?*

3 the past perfect to talk about something that could have happened in the past but didn't.

*Suppose we **had** never **met**. Do you think you would have married Silvia?*

*Suppose you **had been born** in another country. How would your life have been different?*

5.11 *if* + *will/would*

We use *if* + *will/would* to make requests more polite. In this case the auxiliary *will/would* means 'be willing to'.

*If you **will** just **bear** with me for a few moments, I'll tell the head of department that you are here.*

*If you **would be** kind enough to supply the additional documentation, we will then be able to offer sound advice on your investments.*

6 Conjunctions

We use conjunctions to join ideas within a sentence. They may come at the beginning or in the middle of a sentence. They improve the cohesion of a text.

1 Conjunctions which are used to make a contrast include *although, while, whereas, yet*.

The task wasn't difficult, **yet**
While/Although the task wasn't difficult,
} Tom found he couldn't complete it on time.

Tom found himself unable to complete the task on time, **whereas** Harry finished it quickly.

2 Conjunctions which are used to add information include *and* and *nor*.

He wasn't afraid of taking risks **and** he didn't worry
nor did he worry
} about the potential consequences.

3 Conjunctions which are used to give a condition include *as long as, provided that, if, unless* and *if only*.

As long as/Provided (that) she earned enough money to cover her bills, she didn't care about becoming rich.

Unless he improves his performance,
If he doesn't improve his performance,
} he won't be promoted.

If only he would have a bit more confidence, he would do really well.

4 Conjunctions which are used to give a reason include *as, because, since* and *so*.

As he hadn't had time to study, he didn't do as well as he'd hoped in the exam.

7 Countable and uncountable nouns

7.1 Uncountable nouns

Uncountable nouns have no plural and cannot be used with the indefinite article *a/an*. The following are common nouns that are usually uncountable: *accommodation, advice, behaviour, bread, copper* (and all other metals), *meat, sugar, English,* (and all other languages), *furniture, health, information, knowledge, luggage, maths* (and other school subjects), *news, progress, research, rice* (and all other grains and cereals), *salt,* (and all other condiments, e.g. *pepper*), *scenery, spaghetti, traffic, transport, travel, trouble, water* (and all other liquids), *weather, work*.

> **Watch Out!** Use *a slice of, a lump of* and *a piece of* with uncountable nouns for food.

Just **one lump of sugar**, please.

How many **items of luggage** are you checking in?

I'd love **another piece of** that delicious **cheese**.

7.2 Uncountable nouns for emotions and mental activity

Some uncountable nouns that refer to emotions and mental activity can be used with the indefinite article *a/an* when their meaning is limited in some way.

She has **a great passion** for opera.

He has **an extensive knowledge** of the marine industry.

7.3 Nouns which can be countable or uncountable

1 nouns we can think of as a single thing or substance, e.g. *chicken, chocolate, egg, hair, iron, paper, stone*

Do you want **a chocolate**? I think there's one left in the box.

You've got **chocolate** on your chin.

I'd like to get one of those little travel **irons**.

Australia exports **iron** to China.

Did you see that article about gluten allergies in yesterday's **paper**?

I'm trying to use **less** paper by reading things on screen rather than printing them out.

He's got a couple of grey **hairs**.

She's got short dark **hair**.

The **stone** they used to build that cathedral turned out to be very porous. (= rock)

The path slopes down to the coast and includes a steep descent over loose **stones**. (= pebbles)

2 nouns which are used to refer to particular varieties, e.g. *cheese, country*

I love **cheese** – the matured **cheeses** of Italy and Spain are my favourites.

As a city-dweller I have a great appreciation for the **country**.

Hungary is one of the few **countries** in Europe I haven't visited yet.

3 words for some drinks, e.g. *tea, beer*. The countable noun means 'a glass/cup/bottle/etc. of'.

Tea is grown in India and Sri Lanka.

I'll have **a white tea**, thanks.

4 *time, space, room*

There's no **time** like the present!

I had **a fantastic time** in Melbourne.

There's not enough storage **space** in this flat. I never know where to put anything.

Make sure you don't leave extra **spaces** between words.

There's **room** for one more. Hop in!

It really is **a lovely room** to be in.

8 Emphasis: cleft sentences with *what*

This structure is a relative clause introduced by a *wh-* word. We use it to put emphasis on key information in a sentence. It is more common in spoken English but is also used in writing.

Many people fail to understand that their actions have a major impact on the environment.

***What many people fail to understand** is that their actions have a major impact on the environment.*

I'm proposing a radical new approach to the problem of graffiti in our cities.

***What I'm proposing** is a radical new approach to the problem of graffiti in our cities.*

You should give up smoking.

***What you should do** is give up smoking.*

A sense of belonging makes people happy.

***What makes people happy** is a sense of belonging.*

9 Emphasis with inversion

9.1 Negative adverbs/adverbial expressions

We can put a negative adverb or adverbial expression at the beginning of a clause for emphasis. When we do this, there is inversion of the auxiliary and subject.

***Under no circumstances should you share** your password with others.*

***At no time did she consider** any other possibility.*

***Not until** she had failed to make contact for over twenty-four hours **did they contact** the police.*

9.2 Restrictive words and expressions

We can also put certain restrictive words or expressions at the beginning of the clause for emphasis. We are more likely to use inversion in formal or literary contexts.

***Hardly had I arrived** in Paris **when** I received a call telling me I had to return home urgently.*

***No sooner had I sat down** to have a cup of tea **than** the telephone rang.*

***Seldom have I felt** so moved by a piece of orchestral music.*

***Little did I know** that they were planning to replace me as project leader.*

***Never had his wife looked** more beautiful.*

***Only when** I saw him again **did I realise** just how good a friend he had been.*

***Not only have you missed** several classes, you have also failed to submit all the written work.*

10 Hypothetical meaning

10.1 *wish*

1 We use *wish* + past simple to express a wish that is not true in the present. We also use it to talk about wishes that might come true in the future. We use this structure when we want our own situation (or the situation of the person who is doing the wishing) to be different.

*I **wish** Kathy **lived** here.*

*Don't you **wish** you **spoke** another language?*

2 We use *wish* + *be* to say how we would change a present or future situation. We often use *were* instead of *was*, especially in more formal styles.

*I **wish** he **was/were** a little more open-minded.*

*We all **wish** the economy **wasn't/weren't** so unstable.*

3 We use *wish* + *would* to refer to general wishes for the future.

*I **wish** the weather **would improve**.*

4 We also use *wish* + *would* to talk about other people's annoying habits.

*I **wish** my brother-in-law **would sell** that old car.*

*I **wish** he **wouldn't complain** about the weather all the time.*

> **Watch Out!** This form is rarely used with *I* or *we*. To talk about wishes we have for ourselves, we use *could*.
>
> *I **wish** I **could buy** a new computer.*

5 We use *wish* + *could* to talk about an ability we would like to have.

*I **wish** I **could learn** to be a bit tidier.*

6 We use *wish* + past perfect to refer to things we are sorry about in the past or to express regret.

*I **wish** I **had started** learning Spanish when I was younger.*

*She **wishes** she **hadn't lost** her temper.*

10.2 *if only*

We use *if only* with the same verb forms as *wish* when our feelings are stronger. We often use it with an exclamation mark (!). We also use it with *would/wouldn't* to criticise someone else's behaviour.

If only I could take back the dreadful things I said!

If only the neighbours would stop making so much noise!

If only I had never left my home town!

10.3 *it's time*

We use *it's time* with the past simple to talk about the present or future. We mean that the action should have been done before. For emphasis, we can also use *it's about time* and *it's high time*.

> *It's (**about**) **time** you **went** to bed. You've got an early start tomorrow.*

> *It's (**high**) **time** we **left** for the airport. We're supposed to check in an hour and a half before the flight.*

10.4 *would rather*

1 We use *would rather* + past simple to talk about preferences for the present and future.

> *I'd **rather** you **didn't mention** this to Alex.*

> ***Would** you **rather** I **came back** a bit later?*

> *I'd **rather** we **didn't eat** out tonight. I'll cook something here.*

2 We use *would rather* + past perfect to say what we wanted to happen in the past.

> *I'd **rather** you **hadn't invited** Tim. He doesn't get on well with Eleanor.*

> *I'd **rather** you **had informed** me of your decision sooner.*

> **Watch Out!** We don't use *would rather* + past simple or past perfect when we are talking about our own preferences for ourselves or other people's preferences for themselves. In these cases we use *would rather* + infinitive without *to*.
>
> *I'd **rather fly** than catch the train.*
>
> *They'd **rather take** a taxi.*

11 Introductory *it*

11.1 *it* as introductory subject

1 We use *it* as introductory subject to avoid beginning a sentence with an infinitive or *-ing* form.

> *It would probably be unwise to visit Venice in the autumn.*

> *It's been lovely having you to stay with us.*

2 We use *it* as introductory subject when the subject of a clause is another clause.

> *It's terrible just how many young people are unemployed.*

3 We also use *it* as introductory subject in other types of sentences.

> *It's likely that his plane will be delayed.*

> *It's always a relief when the cool change arrives.*

11.2 *it* as introductory object

We use *it* as introductory object in the structure: subject + verb + it + adjective + infinitive/clause.

> *I **find it very strange** the way you never tell me where you're going.*

> *They **made it perfectly clear** that they wanted a window and an aisle seat on the plane.*

11.3 Introductory *it* in cleft sentences

We use introductory *it* to emphasise a relative clause by dividing the sentence in two parts. We also call these sentences 'cleft sentences'. For example, rather than saying *Julia gave Sally a bag for her birthday*, we can use introductory *it* to emphasise different elements in the sentence, for example:

Julia	***It was Julia who** gave Sally a bag for her birthday.*
a bag	***It was a bag that** Julia gave Sally for her birthday.*
Sally	***It was Sally who** Julia gave a bag to.*
for her birthday	***It was for her birthday** that Julia gave Sally a bag.*

12 Modal verbs

12.1 Possibility

1 We use *can* or *could* for theoretical possibility.

> ***Can/Could** there be life on other planets?*

2 We use *may/might/could* + infinitive to talk about possibility in the present or future.

> *He **may be** on holiday.* (strong possibility)

> *They **might/could be** waiting at the station.* (less possible)

3 We use *may/might/could* + *have* + past participle (perfect infinitive) to talk about the possibility of past events.

> *He **might have decided** to go home early.*

> *She **could have been** a great athlete.*

12.2 Certainty (deduction)

1 We use *must* to say that we are sure about something in the present or past.

> *That **must be** the new teacher.* (present)

> *He **must have been** asleep because he didn't hear the phone ringing.* (past)

2 We use *can't* or *couldn't* (but not *mustn't*) in negative sentences.

> *That **can't be** your mum. She looks so young!* (present)

> *They **can't/couldn't have forgotten**. I only reminded them this morning.* (past)

12.3 Obligation, prohibition and necessity

1 We use *must/mustn't* to talk about present and future obligations/prohibitions imposed by the speaker, often on him/herself.

*I **must finish** my assignment this weekend.*

*You **mustn't forget** to go to the bank. (prohibition)*

2 We use *have to/have got to* to talk about present and future obligations that are imposed by someone other than the speaker.

> **Watch Out!** *Have got to* is more common in British than American English.

*I **have (got) to see** my tutor on Monday.*

3 We use *had to* to talk about past and reported obligations of all kinds.

*They told us we **had to apply** for the course by 31 March.*

4 We can also use *need to* to talk about obligation and necessity.

*Do we **need to send in** a hard copy?*

12.4 Lack of obligation or necessity

1 We use *needn't*, *don't need to* and *don't have to* to talk about lack of obligation in the present or future.

*You **don't need to/needn't pay** me back until next month.*

2 We use *needn't + have +* past participle to say that somebody did something but that it was unnecessary.

*Sam **needn't have offered** to pay for our dinner at the restaurant.*

3 We use *didn't need to +* infinitive to say that something wasn't necessary without saying whether the person did it or not.

*You **didn't need to bring** a sleeping bag with you.*

12.5 Ability

1 We use *can/could* to express typical situations or behaviour.

*It **can be** difficult to find a summer job.*

2 We use *can/be able to* for present and future ability.

*Many children **can type** before they can write.*

3 We use *can* for the future where there is a sense of opportunity.

*They **can visit** the museum while they're here.*

4 We use *could/couldn't* and *was/were able to* to talk about general past ability.

*I **couldn't swim** until I was seven.*

5 We use *could/couldn't +* perfect infinitive to talk about unfulfilled ability in the past.

*I **could have learnt** to ski but I preferred skating.*

12.6 *should*

1 We use *should* to talk about obligations and duties in the future, present and past or to give advice. *Ought to* is sometimes used instead of *should* but is more formal.

*You **should speak** English in class.*

2 We often use *should + have +* past participle is to criticise our own or other people's actions.

*I **should have told** him myself.*

13 Participle clauses

We can use participle clauses (*-ing* and *-ed* clauses) in place of relative pronouns to make writing more concise.

13.1 *-ing* forms

An *-ing* participle has an active meaning. It can replace relative clauses which have an active verb.

*This is the letter **referring to** the loan. (= which refers to …)*

*There was a large cat **sitting** in the middle of the living room floor. (= which was sitting …)*

13.2 *-ed* forms

An *-ed* participle has a passive meaning. It can replace relative clauses which have a passive verb.

*The gallery, **designed** by a local architect, houses a collection of contemporary art. (= which was designed …)*

13.3 Other uses of participles

1 after conjunctions

***Before going** to bed, I made a list of all the things I had to do.*

2 to express reason, condition, result, etc., in place of adverbs

***Realising** that I wouldn't be able to see her before I left, I phoned and left a message on her answering machine. (= Because I realised …)*

***Having decided** to visit Rome in the spring, he enrolled in an intensive Italian course. (= After he had decided …)*

***Seen** from a distance, he looks much younger than he actually is. (If/When you see him …)*

14 Passive forms

We use the passive form in all structures. To form the passive, use the appropriate tense of the verb *be +* past participle.

*The project **will have been completed** by the end of the week. (future perfect)*

*The flowers **must have been sent** by Jim. (modal verb)*

We use passive forms to talk about actions, events and processes when the action, event or process is considered more important than the agent (the person responsible for the action, event or process). Passive forms are frequently used in academic writing and in business reports.

14.1 Impersonal passive reporting verbs

We often use reporting verbs such as *believe, claim, report, say* and *think* in impersonal passive structures in formal situations, when we don't know or don't wish to specify the subject.

- *it + be + verb + that*

  It is thought that a solution will be found. (present)

  It was claimed that the idea had been stolen. (past)

- subject + *be* + reporting verb + infinitive

  An announcement is thought to be imminent.

15 Relative clauses and pronouns

15.1 Relative pronouns and adverbs

We use the relative pronouns *who, which, whom, whose, that* and relative adverbs, *when, where* and *why* to give information about the subject or object of a sentence.

15.2 Defining relative clauses

1 The relative clause defines or identifies the person, thing, time, place or reason.

  *Chris is the man **who I met on the train**.*

  *That's the park **where we used to play football**.*

2 *That* can be used instead of *who* or *which*.

  *The person **who/that told me** asked me to keep it a secret.*

3 The relative pronoun can be left out if it is the object of the verb in the relative clause.

  *The book (which/that) **you lent me** is really good.*

4 No commas are used before and after the relative clause.

15.3 Non-defining relative clauses

1 The relative clause gives extra information which can be omitted.

2 *That* cannot be used instead of *who* or *which*.

3 Commas are used before and after the relative clause.

  *The shop, **where I worked as a student**, is closing down.*

  *The bank manager, **whose wife is a teacher at my school**, is very helpful.*

> **Watch Out!** Leaving out the commas in a non-defining relative clause can change the meaning of a sentence.

  *The doctor, **who treated me when I had flu**, is retiring.*

  *The doctor **who treated me when I had** flu is retiring.* (The other doctors are not retiring.)

15.4 Prepositions in relative clauses

Prepositions can come before or after the relative pronoun, depending on whether the sentence is formal or informal.

*The person **to whom I spoke** told me the vacuum cleaner would be delivered this morning.* (formal)

*Mrs Evans, **who I talked to just now**, sends her regards.*

16 Reported speech, reporting verbs

16.1 Changes in reported speech

1 If the report is after the time the thing was said or written, the verb form generally changes as follows.

Direct speech	Reported speech
present simple/ continuous *'I haven't got time to finish the report now,' said Jack.*	past simple/continuous *Jack said (that) **he didn't have** time to finish the report immediately.*
past simple/continuous *'I worked there for ten years,' said Kate.*	past simple/continuous or past perfect simple/ continuous *Kate said (that) she **had worked** there for ten years.*
present perfect simple/ continuous *'I've decided to apply for a new job,' Helen told me.*	past perfect simple/ continuous *Helen told me (that) she **had decided** to apply for a new job.*
will *'I'll show you where the manager's office is,' she said.*	would *She said (that) she **would show** me where the manager's office was.*
must (obligation) *'You must have a permit,' he said.*	had to *He said (that) we had to have a permit.*
can *'I can play the violin quite well,' said Ian.*	could *Ian said (that) he could play the violin quite well.*

2 The verb form does not need to change when

- the information being reported is unchanged.

  'Sea temperatures are rising,' said the lecturer.

  The lecturer told us (that) sea temperatures are rising.

- the information being reported happened recently.

  'I'll tell you about it tomorrow,' she said.

  She said (that) she'll tell me about it tomorrow. (It's still the same day.)

- the information being reported contains the modals *would, could, might, ought to* and *should* or *must* for logical deduction.

  'I think he must be late,' she said.

  She said (that) she thought he must be late.

- the information being reported contains the past perfect.

  'He had already been invited to the reception,' she said.

  She said (that) he had already been invited to the reception.

3 Other changes that occur in reported speech are shown in the table below.

Direct speech	Reported speech
tomorrow	*the next day, the day after, the following day*
now	*at that time/moment, immediately, then*
yesterday	*the day before, the previous day*
last week	*the week before, the previous week*
here	*there*
this morning	*that morning*
today	*that day*
next Friday	*the following Friday, the Friday after*
(two hours) ago	*(two hours) before/earlier*

16.2 Reported questions

1 Reported *Yes/No* questions

When there is no question word in the direct speech question, we use *if/whether*. The word order is the same as in the statement. The verb tense and other changes are the same as for other types of reported speech.

'Could I borrow your notes?' she asked.

*She asked **if/whether she could borrow** my notes.*

2 Reported *wh-* questions

The *wh-* word is followed by statement word order (subject + verb). The verb tense and other changes are the same as for other types of reported speech.

'Why did you leave that job?' she asked him.

*She asked him **why he had left** that job.*

16.3 Reporting verbs

1 verb + infinitive

agree, claim, decide, offer, promise, refuse, threaten

*We **refused to go** to the meeting.*

2 verb + object + infinitive

advise, beg, encourage, invite, order, permit, persuade, remind, tell, warn

*She **persuaded me to lend** her some money.*

3 verb (+ *that*) + clause

accept, admit, claim, doubt, explain, promise, recommend, say, suggest

*She **recommended** (**that**) **we should visit** the museum.*

4 verb + object + (*that*) + clause

promise, remind, tell, warn

*He **warned us** (**that**) **he might be** late.*

5 verb + -*ing*

admit, deny, recommend, regret, suggest

*He **suggested visiting** the museum.*

6 verb + preposition + -*ing*

apologise for, insist on, object to

*She **apologised for** forgetting my name.*

7 verb + object + preposition + -*ing*

accuse sb of, blame sb for, congratulate sb on, discourage sb from, forgive sb for

*She **discouraged him from going** to university.*

8 verb + *wh-* word + infinitive

describe, explain, know, wonder

*She **explained where to find** the library.*

9 verb + object + *wh-* word + infinitive

ask, remind, tell

*The manager **told us what to expect** in the interview.*

17 Substitution and ellipsis

We avoid repetition of words or expressions that have already been used by means of substitution and ellipsis.

17.1 Substitution

Substitution involves using other words such as *it, one, do, there, that, so, neither* and *not*.

We've been to Laos several times, but as Iain hadn't been **there** *he decided to join us on our last trip.*

Bill doesn't like Chinese food and **neither do I**.

A: *Would you like a coffee?*

B: *I'd love* **one**.

A: *Would you like to come to an exhibition opening on Thursday?*

B: **That** *sounds great.*

A: *Will we get the work finished by Sunday?*

B: *I hope* **so**.

A: *After flying all that way, she won't feel like doing much more than going to bed.*

B: *I suppose* **not**.

17.2 Ellipsis

Ellipsis involves leaving out words to avoid repetition. We do this

- after *and, but* and *or*.

  She felt hurt and angry about what they had said about her.

  They were pleased but a little embarrassed about receiving such an expensive gift.

  I'm thinking of getting her a bag for her tablet or perhaps a top.

- at the end of a verb phrase.

  She wanted to spend more than ten days in Melbourne but she couldn't.

  She said she was going to talk to an accountant and she has.

- with infinitives.

  She didn't want to give the puppies away but her mother said she had to.

  He doesn't play the piano much now. He used to, though.

18 Verb forms

18.1 Present simple

We use the present simple

1 for routine or regular repeated actions (often with adverbs and expressions of frequency like *always, usually, often, sometimes, rarely, never, every Saturday morning, twice a week*).

   We **go** *for a walk most afternoons.*

   She **doesn't go** *out on weeknights.*

   I rarely **go** *to bed before midnight.*

2 for present habits.

   I usually **get** *the tram to work.*

3 for permanent situations.

   They both **come from** *the same village in Devon.*

   They **live** *in a side street off the Rambla.*

4 for scientific facts.

   Water **boils** *at different temperatures according to the altitude.*

5 with stative verbs (verbs which are not normally used in continuous forms) like *be, have, depend, know, think, understand, disagree, like, want, hear, love, see, smell, taste.*

   He **doesn't have** *a mobile phone.*

   Do *you* **understand**?

   We disagree with the proposal and **believe** *that it should be modified.*

   These prawns **smell** *a bit strange. I* **think** *they might have gone off.*

> **Watch Out!** Some verbs have stative and dynamic meanings. We only use them in continuous forms with their dynamic meaning, but not with their stative meaning.
>
> *I'm* **feeling** *a bit rundown.* (dynamic; *feel* = experience a feeling or emotion)
>
> *I* **feel** *that the situation will improve in the near future.* (stative; *feel* = have an opinion)

6 when we are talking about the future as expressed in timetables, regulations and programmes.

   Trams **leave** *the terminus every four minutes throughout the day.*

   When **do** *the exams* **start**?

7 in time clauses with a future meaning after *as soon as, if, until, when.*

   I'll call you **when/as soon as** *I* **get** *to the airport.*

   Say hi to Lorna **if** *you* **see** *her.*

   I won't be able to confirm my travel arrangements **until** *they* **confirm** *I've been given the scholarship.*

18.2 Present continuous

We use the present continuous when we use dynamic (action) verbs to talk about

1   actions happening now.

    A: *Where's Terry?*

    B: *She's in the kitchen – she's **making** a cup of tea.*

2   changing/developing situations.

    *Inma **is losing** weight.*

3   temporary situations.

    *He's **working** as a cleaner until he can find a better job.*

4   annoying or surprising habits, with *always*.

    *I'm **always forgetting** to charge my mobile.*

    *She's **always buying** her grandchildren little presents.*

5   plans and arrangements in the future.

    *Are you **doing** anything next weekend?*

18.3 Present perfect simple

We use the present perfect simple

1   to talk about states, single or repeated actions over a long period of time up to the present (often with *ever/never, often/always*).

    *I've **always dreamed** of visiting New York.*

    *Have you **ever been** to Ireland?*

    *I've only **been** skiing once since I moved to Spain.*

    *He's **missed** at least ten of the classes this term.*

    *This is only the second time I've **travelled** by plane.*

    *It's one of the most disgusting meals I've **ever eaten**.*

2   to talk about recent single actions with a present result (often with *just, already, yet*).

    *I've **already started** making spaghetti for dinner, so I don't want to go out.*

    *Have you **finished** reading 'The Road to Riverton' yet?*

    *I've **just got back** from Australia.*

> **Watch Out!** In American English it is acceptable to use the past simple in sentences like these.
>
> *Did you eat yet?*
>
> *I already ate.*

3   to talk about an unfinished period of time up to the present (often with *for/since, this week/month/year*).

    *Irene **has lived** in Abu Dhabi for just over a year.*

    *They've **been** married since early last year.*

    *I've always **hated** long haul flights.*

    *She's **refused** to eat meat since she saw a film about animal rights.*

    *We **haven't seen** him for a couple of months.*

18.4 Present perfect continuous

We use the present perfect continuous

1   to talk about a recent activity when the effects of that activity can still be seen.

    A: *Why are you crying?*

    B: *I've **been chopping** onions.*

2   to emphasise how long an action has been going on for, or that it has been repeated many times.

    *I've **been trying** to get through to Max all morning but he doesn't have his phone switched on.*

    *I've **been working on** this essay for over two weeks.*

3   to suggest that an activity is temporary.

    *I've **been working** in advertising for the past ten years but now feel it's time for a change.*

4   to suggest that an action is not complete.

    *I've **been trying** to teach myself to play the piano but I'm still pretty terrible.*

5   We tend to prefer the present perfect simple for talking about more permanent situations.

    *She's **lived** in Rome since she was a child.*

We prefer to use the present perfect continuous for more temporary situations.

*She's **been living** out of suitcase for months, so she'll be glad to get home.*

> **Watch Out!** Sometimes there is little difference in meaning between the present perfect simple and the present perfect continuous. It is simply a difference in emphasis.
>
> *Isabel **has played/has been playing** the piano since she was five.*

18.5 Past simple

We use the past simple

1   to talk about a finished event that happened at a specific time in the past.

    *I **spoke** to my sister this morning.*

    *She **met** Bill in early 1981.*

2   to describe a sequence of finished events in chronological order.

    *She **stood up, looked** around the room and **began** to speak.*

3   to talk about habits in the past.

    *Did you **play** tennis when you were younger?*

4   to talk about states in the past.

    *When I **was** a baby, I **suffered** from persistent earaches.*

    *The museum **housed** a huge collection of artefacts from all over the Mediterranean Basin.*

5   in reported speech.

    *She claimed she **knew** nothing about the robbery.*

18.6 Past continuous

We use the past continuous

1 to describe an action in progress in the past, often to set the scene for a particular event.

*He **was lying** in a hammock with a hat over his eyes.*

2 to talk about temporary situations in the past.

*Susan **was studying** architecture in the early 1970s.*

3 to talk about an event that was in progress in the past and was interrupted.

*I **was** just **falling** asleep when the phone rang.*

4 to talk about actions in progress at the same time in the past.

*While I **was flying** back from Australia, she **was trying** to get in touch with me on my mobile.*

5 to talk about anticipated events that did not happen.

*They **were planning** to get married but then he met someone else.*

18.7 Past perfect

We use the past perfect

1 to refer to a time earlier than another past time, when this is needed to make the order of events clear.

*Everyone **had been invited** to the meeting so I don't understand why she claimed not to know about it.*

*By the time I got to Doha, I **had** already **missed** my connecting flight.*

> **Watch Out!** Be careful not to overuse the past perfect. It is not necessary with *before* or *after*, which make the sequence of events clear. Once we have established the time sequence, we can revert to the past simple.
>
> *I **dusted** the shelves before I **vacuumed** the carpet.*

2 in reported speech.

*They said they **had met** before.*

18.8 Future forms

1 We use the present simple to talk about timetables.

*The lecture **starts** in half an hour.*

2 We use *will* + infinitive

• for predicting something based on our belief or our knowledge of characteristic behaviour.

*This website **will give** you lots of useful information.*

• for promises, threats, offers and requests.

*I promise I **won't tell** anyone.*

*I'**ll book** the restaurant if you want.*

3 We use *going to* + infinitive or the present continuous to talk about plans and arrangements that have already been decided.

*She's decided she'**s going to get** another job.*

*Where **are** you **meeting** Max this evening?*

4 We use *going to* + infinitive to talk about things that are certain to happen because there is present evidence.

*I know I'**m going to enjoy** this module. It's on my favourite topic.*

5 We use *will/shall* + infinitive to talk about future actions decided at the time of speaking.

*I know! I'**ll get** her that new Kate Atkinson novel.*

6 We use the future continuous (*will/shall* + *be* + *-ing*) to say that an action will be in progress at a definite time in the future.

*I'**ll be living** in my own apartment by this time next year.*

7 We use the future perfect (*will/shall* + *have* + past participle) to describe something that will be completed before a definite time in the future.

*By the end of the month, I **will have completed** my dissertation.*

18.9 Future time expressions

1 followed by the present simple

*It won't be long **until** I start my new job.*

*It's only a matter of time **before** he hears the news.*

2 followed by *will*

***Within** the next six months she'll be a qualified doctor.*

***In twenty-five years' time** there will be less air pollution.*

3 followed by the future continuous

***Ten years from** now I'll doing the same job.*

4 followed by the future perfect

***By the time** I'm twenty-five I'll have worked in several different countries.*

5 followed by the past simple

*It's **about/high time** I left home.*

18.10 Future in the past

We often talk about the past and events or intentions which were in the future at that time.

1 We use the past continuous to talk about future events from a past perspective.

*The lecture **was starting** in fifteen minutes, so I didn't have time for lunch.*

2 We use *be going to* + infinitive to talk about unfulfilled intentions in the past.

*I **was going to call** you but my phone ran out of battery.*

3 We use *would*

- to refer to future events that did actually happen.

  *The business **would become** one of the most successful in the city.*

- to make predictions about the future from a past perspective.

  *I knew there **would be** a lot of questions to be answered.*

4 We use *was/were about to* to refer to future events that did not actually happen. In this case it is usually followed by the past participle.

*The company **was to have opened** three further shops by December.* (but something went wrong)

5 We also use *was/were to* to refer to future events that did happen. In this case it is usually followed by the infinitive.

*Adele **was to become** a best-selling artist by the age of twenty-two.*

6 Other ways we use of referring to unfulfilled intentions/events that did not happen include *was/were due to, was/were meant to, was/were supposed to.*

*The meeting **was supposed to start** at 3.30 but the client arrived over an hour late.*

7 We use *was/were about to* + infinitive and *was/were thinking of* + *-ing* to describe future actions which were interrupted.

*I **was about to call** you when you called me!*

*I **was thinking of calling** you when you called me!*

19 Verb patterns with *-ing* and infinitive

19.1 Common verbs followed by *-ing* form

These are some common verbs we use with the *-ing* form: *admit, appreciate, avoid, consider, delay, deny, detest, dislike, enjoy, escape, face, feel like, finish, forgive, give up, imagine, involve, keep, mention, mind, miss, postpone, practise, prefer, put off, recommend, regret, resent, risk, suggest, understand.*

*I **regretted telling** him what had happened.*

19.2 Common verbs followed by object + *-ing* form

These are some common verbs we use with object + *-ing* form: *discover, forbid, notice, observe, overhear, prevent (from).*

*They **discovered him sitting** by the road.*

19.3 Common verbs followed by the infinitive

These are some common verbs we use followed by infinitive: *afford, agree, appear, arrange, ask, attempt, bear, begin, care, choose, consent, decide, determine, expect, fail, forget, happen, hate, help, hesitate, hope, intend, learn, like, love, manage, mean, offer, prefer, prepare, pretend, promise, propose, refuse, remember, seem, start, swear, try, want, wish.*

*He **intended to tell** her the truth.*

19.4 Common verbs followed by object + infinitive

These are some common verbs we use followed by object + infinitive: *advise, allow, ask, cause, command, encourage, expect, forbid, force, get, hate, help, instruct, intend, invite, leave, like, mean, need, oblige, order, permit, persuade, prefer, press, recommend, remind, request, teach, tell, tempt, trouble, want, warn, wish.*

*He **persuaded me to help** him.*

*Her parents **forbade her to drive** the car.*

19.5 Common verbs followed by object + infinitive without *to*

These are some common verbs we use with object + infinitive without *to*: *let, make, hear, help.*

*He **made me tidy** my room.*

> **Watch Out!** In passive sentences *make, hear* and *help* are followed by an infinitive with *to*.
>
> *She **was made to pay** the money back.*

19.6 Verbs followed by -ing form or infinitive with a difference in meaning

Common verbs that we use with different meanings when followed by -ing form or infinitive are *remember, forget, regret, stop* and *try*.

- We use *remember/forget* + -ing when the action or event took place before the remembering or forgetting.

  *I **remember meeting** him at a party.* (I met him and I now remember that.)

- We use *remember/forget* + infinitive when the action or event took place after the remembering or forgetting.

  *I **remembered to ring** the doctor.* (I remembered and then I rang the doctor.)

- *regret* + -ing means 'be sorry about an action in the past'.

  *I **regret selling** my car.*

- *regret* + infinitive means 'be sorry about a present situation'.

  *I **regret to inform** you that your car has been stolen.*

- *stop* + -ing means 'give up doing or cease to do something'.

  *I **stopped drinking** coffee because it kept me awake at night.*

- *stop* + infinitive means 'stop doing something in order to do something else'.

  *We **stopped to have** a coffee on the way home.*

- *try* + -ing means that the action is an experiment which may or may not be successful.

  try studying at a different time of day – it might suit you better.

- *try* + infinitive means 'make an effort even though the action may be difficult or impossible'.

  Try to study for at least three hours a day.

19.7 Common verbs followed by -ing form or infinitive with little difference in meaning

Common verbs that we use with the -ing form or the infinitive with little difference in meaning are: *attempt, begin, continue, love, prefer, see* and *start*.

*I continued **working/to work** hard.*

20 *whoever, whatever, etc.*

20.1 -ever words in separate clauses

We use *however, whatever, whenever, wherever, whichever* and *whoever* to mean 'it doesn't matter/no matter how/what/when/etc.' or 'it doesn't make any difference how/what/when/etc.'.

However hard I try, it's just never good enough.

Whatever you do, don't breathe a word about the surprise party to Bea.

I wouldn't go to a place like that, whoever invited me.

Whenever we went out together, we had a great time.

Wherever I go in the world, I always take my laptop.

20.2 -ever words: additional meanings

- We use *whatever* (and the very formal *whatsoever*) as a pronoun and determiner with the meaning 'any (thing) that'.

  *I'll do **whatever** I can to persuade you not to leave.*

  Whatever he says makes her laugh.

- We also use *whatever* as a dismissive and impatient reply to a question, suggestion or explanation. It can sound rude.

  A: *Do you think I should ask Jane to marry me?*

  B: *Whatever.*

  We can make it sound less impolite by adding a clause or making a complete sentence.

  A: *Would you prefer lasagne or spaghetti bolognese for supper tonight?*

  B: *Whatever is easiest for you.*

- *Whatever* can also be used as an emphatic form of *what*. It can imply a criticism or surprise.

  Whatever were you thinking of telling Leonard I thought his experiment was stupid!

- *However, whenever, wherever* and *whoever* are all used as emphatic forms of *how, when, where* and *who*, with similar meanings to *whatever*.

  However did someone like that get the job? He's hopeless!

  Whenever did you learn Tibetan? I had no idea you spoke it.

  Wherever did you get that shirt? It looks terrible on you!

  Whoever do you think you are talking to me like that?

- *Whenever* can also mean 'at any time' or 'every time that'.

  I go to the beach whenever I can.

- *Whenever* can also mean 'I don't know exactly when'.

  Last month – or whenever it was we had the meeting, I explained that I was going away.

- The other *-ever* words can be used with similar functions and meanings.

  I'm willing to go and live wherever I can find a job.

Writing reference

Checklist

Answering the question

- Have you covered all the points in the task input?
- Have you written the right number of words?
- Have you ensured that the layout (headings, paragraphs, etc.) of your answer is appropriate for the task?

Accuracy

- Have you checked your work carefully for grammar, spelling and punctuation errors, particularly those you know you are inclined to make?
- Have you checked that your handwriting is clear and easy to read?

Range

- Have you shown that you know a wide range of grammatical structures and vocabulary in your answer?
- Have you made links between paragraphs and between sentences in paragraphs?

Style

- Have you used an appropriate level of formality for your target reader and used it consistently throughout your answer?
- If you have used the task input in your answer, have you changed the wording so that it is appropriate for your target reader?

I Model answers with hints and useful phrases

1.1 Essay

(Part 1)

For work on essays, see pages 14, 44, 66, 138 and 148.

TASK

Your class has attended a panel discussion on what methods the government should use to encourage people to buy products produced in your region or country. You have made the notes below.

Methods governments could use to encourage consumption of local products
- advertising campaigns
- education
- economic subsidies

Some opinions expressed in the discussion

'People are not aware of what is produced locally and what comes from outside.'

'Local products are often among the most expensive. They should be cheaper.'

'The producers won't use the subsidies properly.'

Write an essay for your tutor discussing **two** of the methods in your notes. You should **explain which method you think is more important** for governments to consider, **giving reasons** to support you opinion.

You may, if you wish, make use of the opinions expressed in the discussion but you should use your own words as far as possible.

Write your **essay** in **220–260** words in an appropriate style.

Useful language

Introducing the topic

- *It is often claimed that* people today read less than they did in the past.
- *Many people contend that* climate change is the most serious problem we face.
- *We often hear that* a greater effort should be made to create jobs for young people.

Linking ideas

- *While it is true that* young people make extensive use of mobile phone technology, it is not the case that this has made them less literate than their parents.
- *Not only do* people eat far more than they need to **but they also** throw away a horrifying amount of perfectly good food every day.
- *That may well be so but, surely,* people throw away food because they are simply unaware of the dreadful moral and economic cost of such a practice, both for themselves and for others.
- *In fact,* there is a growing demand for greater controls on food advertising.

Giving opinions

- *I can honestly say that* I would wholeheartedly support such a plan.
- *In my view,* the first of these approaches is likely to prove the more successful.
- *As I see it,* no one solution can be applied to such a complex issue.

Concluding

- *On balance,* I believe that the best solution is to reduce spending on new building projects.
- *Taking everything into consideration, there are many good arguments for* providing young women with grants to continue their education.

Model answer

Promoting locally produced goods

Members of the local business community often complain about the lack of support for locally produced goods. The public's indifference to local products is both the result of a lack of awareness and the huge variety of imported goods available. There is clearly scope for the government to do something about this situation. In this essay I will discuss two possible approaches that could be taken.

The first of these is a public service advertising campaign. This would alert people to the many benefits of buying local goods. The campaign could be supported by labelling products as locally made. While this would almost certainly lead to a greater level of awareness of the advantages of buying locally, more could still be done to make local goods more competitive in terms of price.

A second tactic could be to offer subsidies so that goods can be sold more cheaply. There are some drawbacks to this approach, however. Where, for example, is the guarantee that the producers would use this funding appropriately? This issue can be addressed by introducing a system of quality control. The public could thus rest assured that the local products offer good value for money.

In my view, advertising and subsidising local products must go hand in hand. Once awareness has been raised, community spirit might well lead people to choose local products. If, into the bargain, they see that they are superior in terms of quality and price, there will be far less temptation to buy products from abroad.

DO state the problem at the beginning of your essay.

DON'T express your own opinion at the beginning of your essay. Develop your essay in such a way that it guides the reader to the conclusion you draw.

DO maintain a balanced view. Don't be too categorical.

DO use rhetorical questions to involve the reader but don't overdo it.

DO use a relatively formal register and an objective tone. Don't be too emotional.

DO give your opinion in the final paragraph.

1.2 Formal letter

For work on formal letters, see pages 106 and 118.

TASK

Your town or region has applied to be included in an international database on language learning. You have been asked by the president of the local council to write a letter to the person in charge of the database, explaining why your town or region should be included. You should explain:

- what languages are spoken in your town or region and why they are important.
- what facilities there are for learning these languages.
- what opportunities there are for leisure and cultural activities to help students practise these languages.

Write your **letter** in **220–260** words in an appropriate style.

Useful language

Beginning the letter

If we know the person's title and name:

- *Dear Dr Smallwood,*
- *Dear Professor Carmichael,*
- *Dear Ms Wilkinson,* (if we know the person is a woman)
- *Dear Mr Johnson,* (if we know the person is a man)

If we are writing to a specific person (e.g. the director of a college) but we do not know the person's name, title or gender:

- *Dear Sir or Madam,*

If we do not know who will read our letter or when in the future our letter will be read (e.g. a letter of reference for a colleague):

- *To whom it may concern,*

Opening phrases

- *I am writing with regard to* …
- *I am writing in reply to* …
- *I have been asked to write to you concerning* …
- *In response to your letter of 15 January, I am writing to* …

Ending the letter

- *I very much hope you will consider* …
- *I am sure you will see* …
- *I look forward to receiving your response to* …
- *I look forward to hearing your views on* …
- *Yours sincerely,* (when we have begun the letter with the person's title and name)
- *Yours faithfully,* (when we have begun the letter with *Dear Sir or Madam* or *To whom it may concern*)

Model answer

DO use this way of opening your letter if you don't know the person's name.

DO begin by identifying the situation you are writing about.

Dear Sir or Madam,

I am writing to you on behalf of the Macquarie Valley local council. As I believe you are aware, we are keen for our region, Macquarie Valley, to be included in the International Language Learning Database.

Although English is the official language in our country, Macquarie Valley is a perfect context to study a number of other languages. As a result of immigration from Latin America and China, Macquarie Valley boasts large communities of Spanish and Mandarin speakers. As is well known, these languages are of increasing importance internationally and may even come to rival English in the future.

DO make links between paragraphs.

To satisfy the growing demand for these languages, our educational institutions provide many opportunities for formal study. The universities all offer degree courses and there are also private language schools, many of which now also teach English plus Spanish or Mandarin. In addition, home stays can be arranged with families or single people who are speakers of these languages.

DON'T use the same language as the input.

DO make links between points within the paragraph.

Aside from these more formal ways of studying, there are also many opportunities for informal contact with native speakers. One such is taking one of the walking tours of the area, which are popular with locals and tourists alike. The thriving theatre and music scenes are also excellent vehicles for extending one's knowledge of the language and culture and for meeting others.

DO say what you want the result of your letter to be in the final paragraph.

Macquarie Valley has a great deal to offer the language student. We very much hope you will consider us for inclusion in the database and look forward to hearing from you.

Yours faithfully,

Nina Strefford

Nina Strefford

If you have not used a name at the beginning of your letter, DO end it like this.

1.3 Informal letter/Email

For work on informal letters or emails, see page 96.

TASK

Read part of an email from a friend who is planning to come and visit your country.

Of course, I'd really like to see as much as I can, but with so little time (only a week) I wonder if that's feasible. Do you have any suggestions on where to go and what to do in your country?

Reply to the email message offering your friend some advice. Write your **email** in **220–260** words in an appropriate style.

Useful language

Beginning the letter/email

- ***Thanks so much for your letter/email. It was*** *so good to hear from you.*
- ***I'm really sorry not to have written/been in touch for so long/such a long time/lately. I've been*** *up to my eyes in work/preparing for my exams/out of email contact for a couple of weeks.*
- ***I thought I'd better send you a message/write/drop you a line*** *to let you know …*

Ending the letter/email

- ***I think that brings you up to date on what I've been up to. Do write soon and let me know*** *what you've been doing.*
- ***Once again, thanks so much*** *for all your help and advice.*
- ***I'm really looking forward to*** *seeing you* ***on the eighteenth/in two weeks' time in Barcelona*** *…*
- ***Please say 'hi' to*** *…* ***from me.***
- ***Give my love to*** *…*

Apologising

- ***I'm really/terribly/awfully sorry that*** *I missed your birthday.*
- ***Sorry we didn't manage to*** *get together when you were in …*

Inviting

- ***Do you fancy*** *getting together for a meal some time?*
- ***Why don't we*** *try meet up in the next couple of weeks?*
- ***I was wondering if you'd be into*** *coming along to a class reunion at the end of next month?*

Responding to an invitation

- ***Thanks very much for*** *inviting me to your farewell dinner. I can hardly wait.*
- ***I was absolutely thrilled to get your invitation*** *but unfortunately* ***it doesn't look as if I'll be able to make it.*** *As chance would have it, I'm going away that weekend*

Making a request

- ***I was wondering if you happened to*** *have time to meet a friend of mine who is planning to come to study in your country.*
- ***If you've got a spare moment, do you think you could*** *email me the information about the scholarship?*

Referring to a previous letter/email

- ***Remember*** *that course* ***you said you had*** *enrolled for?*
- ***You told me in your letter/email that*** *you were thinking of taking up yoga.*
- ***Last time you wrote, you wanted to know*** *where we were planning to go on holiday.*
- ***You know that*** *friend of mine* ***I told you about?*** *Well, …*

Model answer

DO begin by giving a reason for writing.

DO use paragraphs in which you cover each of the points mentioned in the task input.

DO think of some of your own ideas as well as the points mentioned in the task input.

DO finish your letter by arranging to see or contact the person you are writing to again soon.

Dear Samuel,

I thought I'd better reply as quickly as possible since I see you're actually leaving next Monday. I'm so excited. I can't wait to see you.

You're right that in such a short time it won't be possible to see everything. You'd need at least six months for that! What I would do is to explore one area in depth. I have to say that Victoria, where I live, would be an excellent choice.

You could start by spending a couple of days in Melbourne and then rent a car and head for the Great Ocean Road. It's a really spectacular road that follows the coastline and stretches for over 250 kilometres. If I were you, I'd plan to spend a couple of days driving along, stopping for the night in Lorne or Apollo Bay.

You asked about things to do and I have to say it's hard to know where to begin. While you're in Melbourne, I'd definitely try to visit the National Gallery of Victoria and the South Bank complex, which is nearby. There are some great bars and restaurants there. On your drive along the Ocean Road you'll see all the famous surf beaches but it's also a great area for walking. There are hundreds of tracks through the rain forest. I think you'd really enjoy that too.

Well, I'd better stop now. Give me a call as soon as you get in and we'll meet up somewhere. I might even join you on the Ocean Road trip.

All the best,
Alex

DON'T use a formal salutation like *Yours sincerely/faithfully* at the end of your letter. DO use a suitable salutation for the kind of relationship you have with the person you are writing to. If the person is a close friend or relative, you can use *With (all my) love*, *Love* or *Lots of love*; if the person is a friend, use *All the best*. For people you don't know well, use *(With) best wishes*

1.4 Report/Proposal

For work on reports, see pages 34 and 76. For work on proposals, see page 24 and 86.

> **TASK**
>
> Your local council is conducting an enquiry into the volume of visitors to the centre of your town or city with a view to encouraging more people to make greater use of shops, restaurants, cafés and entertainment facilities there. You agree to write a report describing the existing situation, including factors which discourage people from coming to the city centre and recommending ways of attracting more visitors.
>
> Write your **report** in **220–260** words in an appropriate style.

Model answer

DO use headings and bullet points. This will make it clear to your reader that your report is not an essay or review.

DO state the purpose of your report at the beginning.

DO include a sentence summarising your opinion at the beginning of the final section of your report.

DO use bullet points. DON'T overdo it, though. If you use them in more than one section, you won't be able to show the full range of structures and vocabulary you know.

DO use a relatively formal and impersonal style.

DO use the task input as a guide for how to divide your report into sections.

Visitors to our city centre

Introduction

The principal aims of this report are to provide an overview of the volume of visitors using services in our city centre and to identify factors which deter people from using them. The final section makes recommendations as to how the situation could be improved.

Current situation

I conducted interviews with a random selection of shoppers and customers in local restaurants and cafés. Fewer than half regularly visited the city centre. Among those who did make frequent use of what is on offer, most cited the pedestrianised Mitchell Mall, as their favourite area. Smaller numbers enjoyed shopping or dining around Holmes Square, though several people said they found the traffic noise disagreeable.

Factors preventing greater use of city centre services

There was a clear division between those who regularly visited the city centre and those who did so infrequently. The latter cited traffic congestion and pollution along with inflated prices for goods as factors that acted as a deterrent. For those who frequently came into town, on the other hand, the pedestrianised area and the outdoor cafés were a major attraction.

Recommendations

Clearly, more could be done to attract people to our city centre. I would make the following recommendations:

* extend the pedestrianised area to include the streets surrounding Holmes Square so as to capitalise on what is already an attractive area.
* encourage shops, cafés and restaurants to offer discounts to regular customers.
* maintain access to the pedestrianised areas for cyclists.

This final recommendation will encourage those who currently cycle into town to continue to do so, while reducing noise and pollution from motor traffic.

Although reports and proposals have a similar layout, reports are based on current circumstances or situations whereas proposals are action plans for the future. You give more space to the current situation in a report and more space to recommendations for future action in a proposal.

Useful language for a report

Stating the purpose of the report
- *The principal aim/objective/purpose of this report is to provide a description of/present results of/assess the importance of* …
- *In this report I will provide a description of/present results of/assess the importance of* …
- *This report describes/provides an assessment of / presents results of* …

Describing how you got your information
- *I conducted interviews with local council officers/a survey of* all current members of the sports club …
- Shopkeepers in the High Street **responded to an online questionnaire**.
- *I visited three of the most popular restaurants:* Oregano, the Beach on Broad Street and Frank's Fish Shack …
- *High Street shoppers were invited to attend a focus group* …

Reporting your results
- Most of those responding to the survey **stated that/ expressed the opinion that** …
- **According to** one interviewee, Mr Ross Peters, the traffic problem is …
- *A large/considerable/significant proportion of those surveyed/respondents/informants said that* …
- **Nearly three quarters of the shop keepers** (74%) had seen an improvement in the situation …

Presenting a list
- **The arguments against** banning cars in the city centre altogether **are the following:**
  1 …
  2 …
- *The following were the main reasons given for supporting* the ban: **firstly** …, **secondly** …
- **Points our informants mentioned in favour of/against** the scheme **were:**
  1 …
  2 …
- **There are several ways in which** locals and tourists alike **might be** drawn back to the city centre:
  1 …
  2 …

Making recommendations
- *Taking all the factors mentioned into account/In the light of the results of the survey/questionnaire, focus group sessions* creating a bicycle track **would appear to be the most viable solution/option/approach.**
- *I would therefore recommend* the immediate implementation of the scheme.

Useful language for a proposal

Stating the purpose of the proposal
- *The principal objectives/aims of this proposal are to* …
- *This proposal is intended to* …
- *In this proposal I describe/evaluate/present/assess* …

Background information
- *Comments made at the end of the questionnaires suggest* …
- *Following a survey among families of young children* …
- *Concerned members of the local community were invited to attend* …
- *A number of concerns with regard to the most recent street party were expressed by locals.*.

Making recommendations and suggestions
- A working group **should be set up** by …
- **There should be** an enquiry into …
- *I recommend that* a larger survey should be conducted before a final decision is reached …

Final recommendations
- **The results of the survey/questionnaire** suggest that the introduction of heavier fines **would seem to be the best option/choice/solution**.
- *If these recommendations are implemented,* the situation is bound to improve.
- *Unless these suggestions are implemented, it is unlikely that* there will be any improvement in the short term.

1.5 Review

For work on reviews, see pages 54 and 128.

TASK

The editor of your college website has asked you to write a review of two films you have seen recently, saying which one would be most suitable for an end-of-course film night at your college and saying why you would not choose the other film.

Write your **review** in **220–260** words in an appropriate style.

Useful language

Concert

types of group or musician: *hip hop/indie/rock/heavy metal artist/band/group/musician, (bass/lead/rhythm) guitarist, (backing/lead) singer, drummer, folk singer/guitarist, country and western singer, jazz band/quartet/trio/singer, orchestra, quintet/quartet/ensemble/soloist/violinist/cellist*

elements: *auditorium, cantata, concerto, hall, lyrics, piece, tune, score, song, stage, symphony, theatre*

people: *composer, conductor, songwriter*

Exhibition

types: *painting, sculpture, photography, design, handicrafts*

elements: *gallery, catalogue, displays*

Book

Fiction

types: *fantasy, historical, mystery, romance, science fiction, thriller, whodunit*

elements: *atmosphere, author, character, dialogue, novelist, plot, setting, writer*

Non-fiction

types: *coffee-table book, cook book, travel book, textbook, manual*

elements: *author, chapter, editor, illustration, index, glossary, section*

Film

types: (as for fiction +) *adaptation, animation, comedy*

elements: *animation, costume, design, photography, role, screenplay, script, set, special effects, soundtrack*

people: *actor, cinema-photographer, cast, director, producer, scriptwriter*

Play

types: (as for film +) *drama, farce, musical*

elements: *act, costume, design, lyrics, music role, scene, set, stage*

people: (as for film +) *composer, playwright*

TV programme

types: *chat shows, current affairs programme, debate, documentary, drama, series, soap opera, situation comedy*

people: *actor cast, compere, director, host, presenter producer, scriptwriter*

Background information

- *'Sisters on Holiday' is Greta Johnson's* **first novel/second film/first starring role/third individual exhibition**.
- *'Word World Three'* **opened at** *the Photographer's Space last week and* **I went along to have a look**.

A brief account of the plot

- **Set in** *late twentieth-century Honolulu,* **the film tells the story of** …/**recounts events in** *the lives of the Waikiki beach boys.*
- **In the context of the period after the Great Depression, the novel explores themes of** *alienation and intimacy.*
- **The series begins with** *the wedding of the two principal characters, Tyler Melville and Charlotte Burbrook.*

Criticism

- **The script seemed rather conventional/predictable/contrived** *to me.*
- **The plot struck me as completely bizarre/absurd/incomprehensible**.
- **The director has succeeded in creating a film that is both believable and thoroughly engaging**.
- **The characters are appealing and true to life**.
- **The dialogue is witty/stilted/natural/artificial**.
- **The dancers were quite brilliant/thoroughly amateurish**.
- **Andrea LoBianco's sets were a particular strength/weakness of the production**.

Recommendations

- **I would strongly encourage you not to miss/not to waste your money on** *'The rights of autumn'.*
- **I would definitely recommend seeing/visiting/reading/having a look at** *'Santa Cruz as it once was'.*

Model answer

DO give your reader an indication of the structure of your review at the beginning.

DO start by raising a question in your readers' minds.

DON'T give the ending away. It will ruin your readers' enjoyment of the film or book.

DON'T just tell the story. Give your assessment of what you have seen or read.

DON'T forget to cover all the points mentioned in the task input.

DO make comparisons.

DO use specific vocabulary for films, books, exhibitions or concerts.

DO include a final recommendation or evaluation at the end of your review.

End-of-course film night: my recommendations

I have seen two films that I considered as possible candidates for our end-of-term film night: 'Life before Life' and 'No More Midnight'. I enjoyed them both, but only one of them is right for our end-of-course film night, in my opinion.

'Life before Life' has many merits but is not the best film for our particular purposes It has had rave reviews partly because it stars Edwin Kamashila and the director, Sam Pickering, never fails to please the critics and audiences. The trouble is that the film is just too slow, particularly for a group of students at the end of the academic year. Over half the film involves intense discussions between Kamashila's character, Rupert, and his girlfriend, Carrie. I won't reveal whether they decide to stay together, but I fear the film would put many in our audience to sleep.

'No More Midnight', on the other hand, had me on the edge of my seat throughout. The cast are not as well known as Kamashila, but they do a great job of portraying the anxieties of a family waiting for news of a missing daughter. There's tremendous suspense but a good dose of humour, too. This makes for a film which is both utterly involving and entertaining.

I'm a fan of Pickering's films and I liked 'Life before Life' but not nearly as much as 'No More Midnight'. If we want to ensure that our audience can sit back, relax and forget about the exams, then this is definitely the film for us. Let's keep 'Life before Life' for the beginning of next semester.

2 Useful linking words and phrases

2.1 Time sequencers

Examples include *after a while, eventually, later, no sooner, hardly, at first, at last, scarcely, when.*

*We didn't see them when we arrived but, **eventually**, they got there, apologising for not having been there to meet us.*

***Scarcely** had I had time to put down my suitcase **when** my partner asked me to help him load some new software.*

2.2 Listing points

Examples include *firstly, first of all, to begin with, secondly, thirdly, then, finally, lastly.*

***Firstly**, I will discuss the attitudes to older people among my peers. I will **then** go on to explain why these attitudes need to be changed. **Finally**, I will offer some proposals as to how these changes might be achieved.*

2.3 Adding information/emphasising

Examples include *additionally, moreover, furthermore, in addition, what's more, as well as, besides, not only … but (also), on top of that, to make matters worse, in fact, as a matter of fact, seldom, rarely.*

***Not only** has the cost of the scheme proved to be prohibitive **but** no suitable site has been found.*

***Seldom** have we had to confront such important challenges as those we face today.*

2.4 Reasons, causes and results

Examples include *in view of the fact that, given the fact that, due to, owing to, for this reason, consequently, in consequence, since.*

***Due to** the increased fire danger, people are asked to avoid lighting fires in the open.*

***In view of the fact that** no suitable candidate was available here in Spain, we had to advertise the position abroad.*

*I was late for my appointment. **Consequently**, I had to wait over half an hour before the dentist could see me.*

2.5 Contrast

whereas, while

- *Whereas* and *while* are used to compare things, people or ideas and show how they are different. They are used in the same way as *but*.

  *Being self-employed means that you are entirely responsible for your own professional development, **whereas/while** if you work for a company or institution, you can expect staff training to be provided.*

- *While* is also used in the same way as *although*.

***While** there may well be arguments in favour of single-sex education, it is important to examine its limitations.*

in contrast

In contrast links two contrasting ideas in separate sentences. It is normally used at the beginning of a sentence.

*Skiing requires a lot of expensive equipment. **In contrast**, running only involves a pair of good trainers.*

even so

Even so means 'although I know that is true'. It can be used to begin a new sentence or after *but* in the second clause of a single sentence.

*I already own an e-reader and a laptop, so I don't actually need a tablet. **Even so,** I think I'll get one.*

On (the) one hand, … . On the other hand, …

These expressions are used to introduce opposite points in a discussion.

***On (the) one hand,** if you have a gap year before you start university, you will gain experience of the world. **On the other hand,** you will take longer to finish your studies and get out into the job market.*

nevertheless/however

Nevertheless and *however* are used when saying something seems different or surprising after your previous statement. *Nevertheless* is usually used at the beginning or end of the sentence. *However* can be used in the middle of a sentence if it is separated from the rest of the sentence by commas.

*Studies have demonstrated a link between stress and a shortened lifespan. **Nevertheless**, little evidence has been provided that stress in the workplace is harmful.*

*The team had considerable success earlier in the season. Since then, **however**, they have suffered a series of embarrassing defeats.*

Exam focus

Contents

See also Writing reference on pages 185–196 and General marking guidelines on pages 206–207.

See also General marking guidelines on pages 206–207.

Reading and Use of English

(1 hour 30 minutes)

Part 1 (Multiple-choice cloze)

What is being tested?

Part 1 tests your knowledge of vocabulary, including words with similar meanings, collocations and fixed phrases.

What do you have to do?

- Read a text with eight missing words.
- Choose the correct word to fill the gaps from a set of four options.
- Mark the correct letter, A, B, C or D on your answer sheet.

Strategy

1 Read the title and the text quickly to get a general understanding of what it's about, without trying to fill any of the gaps.

2 Read the text again. Stop at each gap and try to predict what the missing word might be.

3 Look at the options for each gap carefully. Try putting each of the options in the gap to see which one fits best.

4 Check the words on either side of the gap to see if the option you have chosen goes with these.

5 Read the whole text again to make sure the options you have chosen make sense. Do not leave a blank; make a guess if necessary.

6 Transfer your answers to the answer sheet.

Part 2 (Open cloze)

What is being tested?

Part 2 tests your knowledge of grammar and lexico-grammatical items such as auxiliary verbs, articles, prepositions, pronouns, phrasal verbs, etc.

What do you have to do?

- Read a text with eight missing words.
- Put one word in each of the eight gaps.
- Write the correct word on your answer sheet.

Strategy

1 Read the title and text quickly to get a general idea of what it is about, without trying to fill any of the gaps.

2 Think about what kind of word is missing (e.g. article, preposition, pronoun).

3 Write in the missing words in pencil. Only write one word in each gap.

4 When you have finished, read through the whole text again. Check it makes sense and check the spelling.

5 Transfer your answers to the answer sheet.

Part 3 (Word formation)

What is being tested?

Part 3 tests vocabulary and your knowledge of how words are formed using prefixes and suffixes. You will have to identify what part of speech is required in each gap and write the correct form (e.g. noun, adjective, adverb).

What do you have to do?

- Read a text with eight gaps.
- Use the word in capital letters at the end of each line with a gap to form a word which fits the gap. This could be a noun, an adjective, an adverb or a verb. For example, you may need to change the word at the end of a line from a noun to an adjective with a negative prefix.
- Write your answers on the answer sheet.

Strategy

1 Read the title and the text quickly to get a general idea of what it is about.

2 Read the text again. This time stop at each gap. Think about whether the missing word is positive or negative, plural or singular, a noun, verb, adjective or adverb. Use the words before and after each gap to help you decide.

3 Write the correct form of the word in the gap.

4 Read the text again to make sure your answers make sense and the words are spelt correctly.

5 Transfer your answers to the answer sheet.

Part 4 (Key word transformations)

What is being tested?

Part 4 tests your knowledge of grammatical structures as well as vocabulary and shows examiners that you can express yourself in different ways.

What do you have to do?

- Complete six sentences using three to six words (including the key word) so that they have a similar meaning to the first sentence. You will usually have to change two things.
- Write your answers on the answer sheet.

Strategy

1 Read the first sentence and the key word. Work out what it is testing (e.g. you may need a passive form in the future).
2 Identify what is missing from the second sentence.
3 Think about what kind of words need to be used with the key word.
4 Write down the missing words. Do not change the key word in any way.
5 Make sure you have not written more than six words (contractions, e.g. *don't*, count as two words) and that you have not changed the meaning at all.
6 Check your spelling and that the sentences make sense.
7 Transfer your answers to the answer sheet.

Part 5 (Multiple choice)

What is being tested?

Part 5 focuses on your ability to understand a long text in detail. The questions may test understanding of detail, the main idea and the writer's opinion, attitude or purpose. You may be asked to deduce meaning from context and to follow features of text organisation such as examples, comparisons and reference.

What do you have to do?

- Read a text and six questions. Each question has four possible answers (A, B, C or D) and follows the order of the text.
- Choose the correct option for each question, based on the information in the text.
- Mark the correct letter, A, B, C or D on your answer sheet.

Strategy

1 Read the rubric and the title and sub-heading of the text.
2 Skim the text to get a general idea of what it is about.
3 Read each question and highlight the key words. Do not worry about the four options yet.
4 Highlight the part of the text that the question relates to.
5 Read the text carefully. When you find a part of the text you have highlighted, look at the question and the four options and decide on the answer. The meaning will be the same but the language will be different.
6 Choose the best answer and then check that the other options are definitely wrong.
7 Make your decision. If you are not sure, choose the one that seems most likely.
8 When you have completed all the questions, transfer your answers to the answer sheet.

Part 6 (Cross-test multiple matching)

What is being tested?

Part 6 focuses on understanding the opinion and attitude of four different writers across four short texts. The questions test your ability to identify where the writers may have similar or different opinions to each other about a specific issue.

What do you have to do?

- Read four short texts (A–D) and four multiple matching questions. The texts are independent of each other but all talk about the same topic.
- Identify the opinion or attitude expressed in each question and decide whether the opinions in the four texts (A–D) are the same or different.
- Write the correct letter for each answer on your answer sheet.

Strategy

1 Read the four questions and underline the key words.

2 For each question, underline the section of the text (A–D) referred to (e.g. *Writer A's opinion about*) and make sure you understand the writer's point of view.

3 Read the other texts and underline the sections which talk about the same issue.

4 Find the text which has a similar or different opinion/attitude to the writer referred to in each question.

5 One question may ask you to identify the writer who has a different point of view on a specific issue to the other three writers. Check where this issue is mentioned in each text and identify the writer who expresses a differing view to the rest.

6 Check your answers again before transferring them to the answer sheet.

Part 7 (Gapped text)

What is being tested?

Part 7 tests your understanding of coherence and cohesion, text structure, as well as your global understanding.

What do you have to do?

- Read a text from which six paragraphs have been removed and placed in a jumbled order before the base text. You must decide where paragraphs (A–G) have been taken from. (There is one paragraph you do not need to use.)
- Read the seven paragraphs and decide which paragraph best fits each gap.
- Mark your answers on your answer sheet.

Strategy

1 Read the title to get an idea about the topic.

2 Read the base text carefully to make sure you understand what it is about and to get a sense of the coherence of the passage.

3 Read before and after each gap and predict what information is missing from each gap.

4 Underline any textual clues (nouns, pronouns, linking words, etc.) which will help you to identify the missing paragraph.

5 Read the seven paragraphs and look for textual clues that will connect them to the gaps. Look for topic words, synonyms and reference words.

6 If you are not sure which paragraph to choose for one gap, go on to the next gap and return to it later.

7 Read through the completed text. Check that it makes sense and that you haven't used any paragraphs more than once.

8 Try the extra paragraph in each gap again, just to check that it doesn't fit.

9 Transfer your answers to the answer sheet.

Part 8 (Multiple matching)

What is being tested?

Part 8 tests your ability to find specific information in a number of short texts, as well as an understanding of the writer's opinions and attitudes.

What do you have to do?

- Read four to six short texts around the same theme or one longer text divided into four to six paragraphs.
- Match ten questions or statements to the text or paragraph that it relates to. The text does not follow the same order as the questions.
- Write the correct letter for each answer on your answer sheet.

Strategy

1 Read the title of the text and any sub-headings.

2 Skim the text quickly to get an idea of what the text is about.

3 Read the questions carefully and highlight key words.

4 Scan each section of the text to find the information in the questions. You do not need to read in detail. Look for words or phrases which are similar in meaning to the words or phrases in the questions but don't just choose a paragraph because it contains the same words as in a question or statement.

5 Highlight possible answers in pencil. You may find similar – but not exactly the same – information in other sections.

6 Read the information carefully to check that it is an exact answer to the question.

7 Leave any questions that you are not sure about but always go back and answer them as you will not lose marks for a wrong answer. Choose the most likely answer.

8 When you have finished, transfer your answers to the answer sheet.

Writing
(1 hour 30 minutes)

Part 1 (Essay)

What is being tested?

Part 1 tests your ability to write coherently and to communicate ideas effectively in a semi-formal written style.

What do you have to do?

- Write an essay based on information and notes that you are given.
- Write between 220–260 words.

Strategy

See Writing reference on page 185.

Part 2 (Choice of task)

What is being tested?

Part 2 tests your ability to communicate your ideas effectively in an appropriate written style for the task which you have selected.

What do you have to do?

- Choose one task out of the three tasks you are given.
- Write one of them using an appropriate format and style. The task could be an email or letter, a report or proposal, or a review.
- Write between 220–260 words

Strategy

See Writing reference on page 186–187.

Listening
(approximately 40 minutes)

Part 1 (Multiple choice)
What is being tested?

In Part 1 the focus of the questions may test the main idea, the purpose, the attitude or opinion of the speakers.

What do you have to do?

- Listen twice to three short dialogues, each on a different topic, involving two speakers.
- Answer two multiple-choice questions about each of the three dialogues.
- Write the correct letter (A, B or C) on your answer sheet. (You are given five minutes at the end of the test to transfer your answers from the question paper to the answer sheet.)

Strategy

1 Read the questions and options and highlight the key words before you listen. (You are given some time to do this.)

2 The first time you listen, mark the answer you think is best.

3 Check your answers the second time you listen and make sure the options you have chosen answer the questions correctly. If you aren't sure, choose the answer you think is most likely – you may be right.

4 Transfer your answers to the answer sheet.

Part 2 (Sentence completion)
What is being tested?

In Part 2 the focus is on your understanding of detail, specific information and opinion.

What do you have to do?

1 Read eight sentences with gaps about the recording.

2 Listen twice to a monologue. It may be part of a radio report or a talk on a topic.

3 Complete eight sentences with the exact word/words from the recording.

4 Write your answers on your answer sheet.

Strategy

1 Before you listen, read the sentences carefully and highlight key words. Think about the kind of information that's missing. You have some time for this.

2 As you listen, try to complete the sentences. The sentences are in the same order as the information on the recording. Write one to three words to complete each sentence. You should only write the words you hear and you should not change these words.

3 If you can't complete a sentence the first time you listen, leave it blank.

4 The second time you listen, complete any remaining sentences and check your answers. Don't leave any of the gaps blank; guess if you aren't sure.

5 Check your spelling and grammar (e.g. singular, plural) is correct and that the sentences make sense.

6 Be careful not to make any mistakes when you copy your answers onto the answer sheet at the end of the test.

Part 3 (Multiple choice: longer text)

What is being tested?

In Part 3 the focus of the questions will be on understanding the opinions and attitudes of the speakers in a longer dialogue.

What do you have to do?

- Listen to an interview or a conversation on a topic, usually between two or three speakers.
- Answer six multiple-choice questions.
- Write the correct letter (A, B, C or D) for each answer on your answer sheet.

Strategy

1 Before you listen, read the introduction to the task to get information about who the speakers are and what they will talk about.

2 Read the questions and options and highlight the key words. Think about the kind of information you need to listen for.

3 Listen for paraphrases of the words and phrases on the recording and choose one of the options, A, B or C. If you are not sure of the answer, continue answering the other questions and come back to it in the second listening.

4 During the second listening, check the options you have chosen. Make sure you have chosen an option which answers the question correctly. The information in the other options may also be true but it may not be the right answer to the question. If you aren't sure, choose the one that seems most likely.

5 Transfer your answers to the answer sheet.

Part 4 (Multiple matching)

What is being tested?

Part 4 tests understanding of informal speech. The focus is on gist, attitude and opinion.

What do you have to do?

- Listen to five short monologues on a related topic twice.
- There are two tasks each containing eight statements. Match one statement from each task to each of the five monologues. There are three extra statements in each task which do not match any of the monologues.
- Write the correct letter (A–H) for each answer on your answer sheet.

Strategy

1 Read the rubric carefully. This tells you what topic the speakers will talk about.

2 Read the sentence. Highlight key words or phrases in each statement.

3 The first time you listen, try to identify the main idea of what the speaker is talking about and mark the statement which you think matches most closely. Listen for paraphrases or synonyms for key words in the statements. But be careful as you may hear similar words repeated in several texts because they are all on the same topic.

4 During the second listening, check that the statements match exactly what the speaker says. Don't choose a statement just because it contains a word from the monologue.

5 Transfer your answers to the answer sheet.

Speaking
(approximately 15 minutes)

Part 1 (Interview)
What is being tested?

Part 1 focuses on your general interaction and your social language skills.

What do you have to do?

- The examiner will ask you and the other candidate for some personal information.
- You will be asked different questions about things such as what you do in your spare time, your work/studies and your future plans.
- This will take around two minutes.

Strategy

1 Avoid giving one-word answers. Add detail but not too much.

2 Try to sound interesting. Don't speak in a monotone.

3 Speak clearly. Try to speak confidently and look relaxed.

4 If you don't know a word, say it in another way. Don't leave long pauses.

5 Listen carefully both to the examiner and to your partner.

6 If you don't understand the question, ask for it to be repeated.

7 Give relevant, personal answers but don't speak for too long.

Part 2 (Individual long turn)
What is being tested?

In Part 2 the focus is on your fluency and your ability to organise your ideas and express yourself clearly. You will have to make comparisons and speculate about the situations in the pictures.

What do you have to do?

- You are given three pictures on the same topic. You listen to the task, which is also printed on the page with the pictures.
- The examiner will ask you two questions about the pictures. You must answer the questions by comparing two of the pictures. You can choose which pictures you want to talk about.
- You are given one minute to do both parts of the task.
- You then listen to the other candidate speaking and look at their photos. When they have finished, you have to give a short answer to a question related to the topic.

Strategy

1 Listen carefully to the instructions. It's important that you understand exactly what you need to talk about. Ask the examiner to repeat the instructions if necessary but remember that the instructions are also written above the pictures.

2 Summarise the main similarities and any differences between two of the pictures. Talk about the general ideas and don't be tempted just to describe the pictures or go off topic. You will need to speculate and give your opinion, especially about the second part of the task.

3 Make sure you answer both questions.

4 Keep talking for the whole minute. Use paraphrases and 'fillers' if necessary. The examiner will say, 'Thank you,' when the minute is finished.

5 Listen carefully while the other candidate is speaking, and look at their pictures but don't interrupt. When the examiner asks you a question related to the pictures, give a short answer.

Part 3 (Collaborative task)

What is being tested?

Part 3 tests your ability to negotiate with the other candidate to reach a decision. You will be expected to give your opinions and evaluate ideas, as well as listen and respond to your partner's ideas.

What do you have to do?

- Work with the other candidate to discuss something together.
- The examiner gives you both the first part of the task on a task sheet with some ideas to discuss. This is also written on the page and you have some time to look at it before you speak.
- The task may involve solving a problem, negotiating, agreeing and disagreeing. Discuss the task with the other candidate for two to three minutes.
- The examiner will then give you another instruction asking you to discuss something related to the topic and to make a decision together. You have about a minute for this.

Strategy

1 Read and listen carefully to the instructions. Use the time given to look at the task on the sheet. Ask for clarification if you do not understand.

2 You should discuss each of the prompts in some detail but don't spend too long on any one idea.

3 One of you should start the discussion. Then take turns to give your opinions, agree, disagree, etc.

4 Turn-taking skills are important. Avoid dominating the discussion or interrupting rudely. It is important to involve and encourage your partner, and follow up on what they say.

5 Explain things in a different way if you can't think of a word or phrase and don't leave long pauses. Use words such as *right* or *OK* to 'fill the gaps'.

6 Try to use a range of functional language, such as asking for and reacting to opinions, agreeing and disagreeing, suggesting, speculating, opening and summarising the discussion.

7 You should be prepared to compromise in the second part of the task in order to reach a decision.

Part 4 (Discussion)

What is being tested?

Part 4 gives you the opportunity to show the examiner that you can discuss a topic in more depth, develop and expand your ideas and justify your opinions.

What do you have to do?

- In this part of the test, the examiner asks you both questions which develop the topic in Part 3 and may lead to a more general discussion.
- You may add to what the other candidate has said or disagree with their ideas.
- The discussion will last for around four minutes.

Strategy

1 If you don't understand the question, ask the examiner to repeat it.

2 Give opinions and express your feelings about issues. Give reasons or examples to justify your opinions.

3 Listen to what the other candidate says and ask questions or give follow-up comments.

4 Take the opportunity to use a range of language but don't dominate the discussion.

Marking guidelines

Writing

Band	Content	Communicative Achievement	Organisation	Language
5	All the necessary information is included. Has a very positive effect on the reader.	Communicates complex ideas in a consistently effective way.	Organises ideas skilfully. Text is easy to follow. Uses a range of linking words effectively to make text coherent.	Uses a range of complex vocabulary accurately and appropriately. Able to produce both advanced and more basic grammatical forms confidently with minimal errors.
4	A mix of bands 3 and 5			
3	Most of the necessary information and/or some irrelevant information is included. Has a satisfactory effect on the reader.	Generally communicates complex ideas effectively.	Organises ideas clearly and generally uses a variety of linking words effectively.	Generally uses complex vocabulary appropriately. Uses a satisfactory range of grammatical structures. Occasionally makes errors in the use of more complex forms but these do not cause difficulty for the reader.
2	A mix of bands 1 and 3			
1	May not provide all the necessary information or gives irrelevant information. Target reader is adequately informed.	Able to communicate simple ideas clearly.	Text is basically well-organised but may occasionally be difficult to follow.	Uses a limited range of vocabulary appropriately. May use more complex vocabulary inaccurately. Simple grammatical forms are used appropriately with minimal errors. More complex forms are attempted with some success.
0	No relevant information provided.			

Speaking

Band	Grammatical Resource	Lexical Resource	Discourse Management	Pronunciation	Interactive Communication
5	Has good control of complex grammatical forms.	Uses a varied range of vocabulary effectively.	Able to speak fluently and confidently with very little hesitation Expresses ideas effectively using a varied range of linking words and discourse markers*.	Is easy to understand. Uses intonation and sentence and word stress to convey meaning effectively Pronunciation of individual sounds is clear.	Able to initiate, negotiate and respond effectively.
4	A mix of bands 3 and 5				
3	Uses a range of simple and grammatical forms mainly accurately.	Uses a varied range of vocabulary mainly appropriately.	Able to produce extended speech with very little hesitation. Expresses ideas clearly using an appropriate range of linking words and discourse markers*.	Is easy to understand. Uses intonation and sentence and word stress appropriately Pronunciation of individual sounds is clear.	Able to initiate, negotiate and respond appropriately.
2	A mix of bands 1 and 3				
1	Uses simple grammatical forms and a limited range of more complex forms mainly accurately.	Uses vocabulary appropriately when discussing familiar topics.	Able to produce extended speech with some hesitation. Uses a range of linking words and discourse markers*.	Is easy to understand. Intonation and sentence and word stress are generally appropriate Pronunciation of individual sounds is generally clear.	Able to initate, negotiate and respond appropriately with very little help.
0	Below band 1				

*Discourse markers are spoken words or phrases which help to make the meaning clear (e.g., *actually*, *basically*, *what I mean is*).

Pearson Education Limited
Edinburgh Gate
Harlow
Essex CM20 2JE
England
and Associated Companies throughout the world.

www.pearsonELT.com/examsplace

© Pearson Education Limited 2014

First published 2014
Fourth impression 2015

ISBN: 978-1-4479-0704-6 (Gold Advanced Coursebook)
ISBN: 978-1-4479-5544-3 (Gold Advanced Coursebook with
        MyEnglishLab: Cambridge Advanced)

Set in Myriad Pro
Printed in Italy by L.E.G.O. S.p.A.

Acknowledgements
The publishers and author(s) would like to thank the following people and institutions for their feedback and comments during the development of the material: Henrick Oprea, Atlantic Idiomas (Brazil), Daniela Donati (Italy), Diana Pena (Mexico), Melenia Misztal (Poland), Kamal K Sirra, Michael Smith (Spain), Pauline Bokhari, Tom O'Brien (UK); Jacky Newbrook (exam consultant)

Author Acknowledgements
The authors would like to thank Nick Kenny and Jacky Newbrook for their helpful suggestions, our families for their support and all the team at Pearson for their hard work.

We are grateful to the following for permission to reproduce copyright material:

Text
Extract in unit 1 adapted from "How acquiring The Knowledge changes the brains of London cab drivers" by Ed Yong, *Discover Magazine*, 08/12/2011, http://blogs.discovermagazine.com, copyright © Ed Yong. Reproduced with kind permission; Extract in unit 2 from "How fast R U? Girl wins $50,000 in texting competition after racking up 14,000 texts-per-month habit", *The Daily Mail*, 24/06/2009, copyright © Daily Mail 2009; Extracts in unit 2 and 3 adapted from "How to have a conversation", *The Financial Times*, 09/03/2012 (John McDermott); and "Recipe for success", *The Financial Times*, 25/05/2012 (Natalie Grahame), copyright © The Financial Times Limited. All Rights Reserved; Extract in unit 3 from The Antidote: Happiness for People Who Can't Stand Positive Thinking by Oliver Burkeman, copyright © 2012 by Oliver Burkeman. Reproduced with permission of Canongate Books, Text Publishing, Faber and Faber, Inc. an affiliate of Farrar, Straus and Giroux, LLC, and Penguin Canada Books Inc.; Extract in unit 3 adapted from "Roger Black: My greatest mistake", *The Guardian*, 21/05/2011 (Graham Snowdon), copyright © Guardian News & Media, 2011; Extract in unit 4 adapted from "Spending money on others promotes happiness", *Science*, Vol 319, 1687 (Elizabeth W. Dunn, Lara B. Aknin, Michael I. Norton), copyright © 2008, American Association for the Advancement of Science; Extract in unit 5 adapted from "The Museum Time Bomb: Overbuilt, Overtraded, Overdrawn" by James M Bradburne, http://www.informallearning.com/archive/Bradburne-65.htm. Reproduced by permission of Informal Learning Experiences, Inc. and James Bradburne; Extract in unit 5 adapted from "Dead Interesting", *The Financial Times*, 02/12/2011 (Lucy Kellaway), copyright © The Financial Times Limited. All Rights Reserved; Extract in unit 6 adapted from "I Like You: How Joe Girard Sold Cars", 7 February 2012 by Ryan Healy, www.ryanhealy.com, copyright © Ryan Healy. Reproduced with kind permission; Extract in unit 7 adapted from "Why you're always matched with douchebags online" by Christopher Scanlon, 27 July 2012, http://www.dailylife.com.au, copyright © Dr Christopher Scanlon. Reproduced with kind permission; Extract in unit 7 from "What friends are for ...", *The Guardian*, 28/01/2009 (Hannah Pool), copyright © Guardian News & Media, 2009; Extract in unit 8 adapted from "My favourite travel souvenir", *The Guardian*, 09/12/2011 (Michael Hughes), copyright © Guardian News & Media, 2011; Extract in unit 9 from "How Barbara Arrowsmith-Young rebuilt her own brain", *The Guardian*, 12/06/2012 (John Henley), copyright © Guardian News & Media, 2012; Extract in unit 9 adapted from "Your brain really is forgetting… a LOT" by Brett McLauchlin, 27 April 2009, http://radar.oreilly.com/2009/04/your-brain-is-forgetting.html, copyright © O'Reilly Media, Inc.; Extract in unit 10 adapted from "The future of food", *The Guardian*, 22/01/2012 (John Vidal), copyright © Guardian News & Media, 2012; Extract in unit 13 from 'Silence' 6 December 2009 by Michael Joseph lmsw, http://psychoutblog.com/2009/12/06/silence, copyright © Michael Joseph Therapy; Extract in unit 13 adapted from "Museum of Endangered Sounds: Phil Hadad, Marybeth Ledesma, and Greg Elwood Explain Their Project (interview)", *The Huffington Post*, 06/08/2012, http://www.huffingtonpost.com. Reproduced with permission; Extract in unit 13 adapted from "Irving Penn: Your reviews", *The Daily Telegraph*, 22/04/2010, copyright © Telegraph Media Group Limited; Extract in Progress Test 2 adapted from "Investing in young people 2013", *The Financial Times*, 24/01/2013 (Charles Batchelor), copyright © The Financial Times Limited. All Rights Reserved.

In some instances we have been unable to trace the owners of copyright material, and we would appreciate any information that would enable us to do so.

The publisher would like to tahnk the following for their kind permission to reproduce their photographs:

(Key: b-bottom; c-centre; l-left; r-right; t-top)

Alamy Images: ajith achuthan 53, Agencja FREE 95, ajs / Wildscape 61c, Walter G. Allgöwer / imagebroker 166tr, Dan Atkin 160bc, Mark Edward Atkinson / Blend Images 159bc, blickwinkel / Koenig 161tc, BuildPix / Construction Photography 163cl, Peter Cavanagh 155tr, David Coleman 157tr, Roger Cracknell 01 / classic 61b, Randy Duchaine 137c, Igor E. / Image Source 155tl, Paul John Fearn 147t, ffotowales 156c, Stuart Forster 155bl, Paul Francis 46, BRETT GARDNER 59, Chris Gascoigne 160br, Terry Gibbins 166bc, matt griggs 8, GYRO PHOTOGRAPHY / a.collectionRF / amana images inc. 103, IE109 / Image Source 48, IE203 / Image Source Plus 104, IE379 / Image Source 139t, 139b, itanistock 28, JLImages 12, Mike Kemp / Tetra Images 153bc, Eileen Langsley Sport 42, Barry Lewis 166tl, Neil McAllister 61t, Patti McConville 15, Paddy McGuinness 141, Megapress 81t, 81b, David L. Moore - WA 41, keith morris 156l, B. O'Kane 160bl, Maxim Pavlov 126, Clément Philippe / Arterra Picture Library 163tr, Photo Researchers 147b, Dundee Photographics 152c, Pictorial Press Ltd 27, Jason Politte 161bc, Tosporn Preede 166br, Q74 153br, Radius Images 43, 121, Robert Read 17r, redsnapper 114, Frances Roberts 150, Mike Robinson 105t, 105b, Alex Segre 160tc, Paul Seheult / Eye Ubiquitous 87, SHOUT 163br, Friedrich Stark 51tr, David Sutherland 32, Peter Titmuss 81c, Vibrant Pictures 158tr, stock_wales 156r, John Warburton-Lee Photography 157tl, Wavebreakmedia Ltd PH14 158tc, Chris Whitehead / Cultura Creative (RF) 47r, Janine Wiedel Photolibrary 160tl, David Wootton 159bl; **Barcroft Media:** YikeBike / Barcroft Media 157bc; **Corbis:** Artiga Photo / Crush 134t, Frank and Helena / cultura 90, Rune Hellestad / Corbis Entertainment 137t, Jutta Klee / Solus 155br, Wayne Lynch / All Canada Photos 120, Hans-Peter Merten / Robert Harding World Imagery 6c, Marc Oeder / Ivy 134b, Louie Psihoyos / Eureka Premium 58; **DK Images:** Pat Aithe 66, Steve Gorton 70; **Fotolia.com:** bjonesphotography 99, Gail Johnson 161t; **Getty Images:** A.B. / The Image Bank 91t, Luis Alvarez / E+ 138, Bain News Service / Interim Archives 84, Thomas Barwick / Iconica 116, Dean Belcher / Stone 16, Cultura / Luc Beziat / StockImage 159tr, Michael Blann / Stone 140, John Burke / Brand X Pictures 152r, Mark D Callanan / Iconica 68, VisitBritain / Alan Chandler 60, Tom Cockrem / Photolibrary 166bl, Iain Crockart / Digital Vision 157tc, Peter Dazeley / Photographer's Choice 152l, The Detroit Free Press / MCT via Getty Images 93, PhotoAlto / Odilon Dimier 17l, 52, DreamPictures / Shannon Faulk 100l, 100r, Emmanuel Faure / Stone 91c, Fuse 56, Jonathan Gelber 159tc, Izabela Habur / E+ 19, Johnny Haglund / Lonely Planet Images 21, Mike Harrington / Riser 158bl, Noel Hendrickson / Blend Images 144t, Hill Creek Pictures / UpperCut Images 159br, DimaChe / iStock Vectors 13t, 13b, Jupiterimages / Workbook Stock 80, Riser / Bernhard Lang 113, Frans Lemmens / The Image Bank 130, John Lund / Blend Images 137b, Catherine MacBride / Flickr 34, Kevin Mackintosh / Stone 149, Ronald Martinez 36, Moment / Cultura 142, Michael Ochs Archives 123b, Sarah Palmer / Flickr 124, PETER PARKS / AFP 157br, Javier Pierini / Taxi 157bl, ERIC PIERMONT / AFP 55, Purestock 119, Rayes / Digital Vision 91b, Joel Sartore / National Geographic 144b, Donald Iain Smith / Flickr 30, Tempura / E+ 131, YOSHIKATSU TSUNO / AFP 160tr, Westend61 47l; **Google UK:** 11; **Masterfile UK Ltd:** Minden Pictures 98; **Nature Picture Library:** Georgette Douwma 106; **Pearson Education Ltd / Jules Selmes:** 35; **PhotoDisc:** 128; **Rex Features:** Patrick Frilet 153tr, Garo / Phanie 155bc, KeystoneUSA-ZUMA 132, Andy Lauwers 38b, Sinopix 133t, 133b, Solent News 97, South West News Service 153tc; **Francesco Romoli:** 26; **Science Photo Library Ltd:** 108; **Shutterstock.com:** 06photo 9, Africa Studio 129, Subbotina Anna 123t, Mark Bridger 110, Alexander Chaikin 94, Songquan Deng 83, Elena Elisseeva 39, Adam Gregor 155tc, Brian A Jackson 37, Robert Kneschke 158bc, Rajat Kohli 78, mangostock 153tl, margouillat photo 73, Skrynnik Mariia 18, Cheryl A. Meyer 163bl, Monkey Business Images 158tl, Robert Neumann 57, Ph0neutria 163tl, PhotoStock10 77, Real Deal Photo 151, salajean 161b, TalyaPhoto 125, Kemal Taner 115, TDway 158br, Mirco Vacca 51bl, wavebreakmedia 64, WitthayaP 166tc, Arman Zhenikeyev 75; **SuperStock:** Corbis 86, Image Source 153bl; **Taste # 5 Umami Paste :** 71; **Tudor Photography:** 25; **Veer/Corbis:** Olly 159tl; www.imagesource.com: 136; www.leviroots.com: 38tr; **Helen Wyllie :** 88

All other images © Pearson Education

Every effort has been made to trace the copyright holders and we apologise in advance for any unintentional omissions. We would be pleased to insert the appropriate acknowledgement in any subsequent edition of this publication.

Illustrations:
Helen Wyllie : 74; All other illustrations: Oxford Designers and Illustrators